On Art, Religion, Philosophy

*the text of this book is printed
on 100% recycled paper*

G.W. F. Hegel

On Art, Religion, Philosophy

*Introductory Lectures
to the Realm of
Absolute Spirit*

Edited and with an Introduction by

J. GLENN GRAY

HARPER TORCHBOOKS
Harper & Row, Publishers
New York and Evanston

HARPER TORCHBOOKS/Advisory Editor in the
Humanities and Social Sciences: BENJAMIN NELSON

ON ART, RELIGION, PHILOSOPHY

On Art is a translation of *Vorlesungen über die Aesthetik, Erster Band;* the
version reprinted here is from the translation by Bernard Bosanquet in *The
Introduction to Hegel's Philosophy of Fine Art,* published in 1905 by Routledge
& Kegan Paul, Ltd., London. Reprinted by permission.

On Religion is a translation of *Vorlesungen über die Philosophie der Religion,
Erster Band;* the Introduction reprinted here is from the translation by E. B.
Speirs and J. Burdon Sanderson in *Lectures on the Philosophy of Religion,* published in 1895 by Routledge & Kegan Paul, Ltd., London. Reprinted by permission.

On Philosophy is a translation of *Vorlesungen über die Geschichte der Philosophie,
Erster Band;* the version reprinted here is by E. S. Haldane, published in 1892 by
Routledge & Kegan Paul, Ltd., London, under the title *Introduction from Hegel's
Lectures on the History of Philosophy.* Reprinted by permission.

All the translations have been emended slightly or otherwise edited by the Editor
for the Torchbook edition.

First Edition: HARPER TORCHBOOKS, 1970,
Harper & Row, Publishers, Incorporated,
10 East 53rd Street, New York, N.Y. 10022.

Contents

On Art, Religion, Philosophy

Introduction:

Hegel's Understanding of Absolute Spirit
J. Glenn Gray

I

Revival of interest in Hegel's philosophy, evident in Europe over the last fifteen years, has begun to affect—or infect, if one disapproves—our own intellectual circles and academic intelligentsia. Explanations for this revival are various, and indeed there is probably no single cause. In the century and a half since it was promulgated, Hegel's thought has alternately fascinated and repelled Germans and foreigners alike. Hegelian revivals seem to be a cyclical phenomenon, occasioned by political catastrophes and consequent cultural shifts of perspective.

In Europe the two movements most often cited as causes of the current renaissance are existentialism and neo-Marxism. From its inception existentialism was not simply a reaction against the leading tenets of the Hegelian synthesis, but also an incorporation of many of Hegel's insights as well as his dialectical method. Without Hegel, Kierkegaard would never have been the twentieth-century influence he has become. Unaware as Kierkegaard may have been of how much he was borrowing from the arsenal of his great opponent, twentieth-century existentialists such as Merleau-Ponty and Sartre are no longer innocent in this respect. They use quite frankly those insights of Hegel that suit their purpose and have done much to "existentialize" Hegel and his best-known follower and opponent, Karl Marx. In recent years Sartre has even tried to incorporate existentialism into Marxism by exploiting the writings of the young Marx, now often seen as precursors of existentialist themes.

1

The neo-Marxists of Germany on both sides of the Iron Curtain and now extending well beyond Germany's shifting boundaries have not had to "return" to Hegel, for in many respects they never left him. What can be said is that they have rediscovered the common bonds between Hegel and Marx and are no longer content with the sort of piety that led Marx on occasion to defend "that dead dog, Hegel." In their minds, Hegel was from the beginning linked indissolubly with the intellectual foundations of that new way of experiencing the world during the last century which we know variously as dialectical materialism, Marxism, or Communism.

It is, then, not at all surprising that these currently vital philosophical movements on the European continent should have brought about the renewed study and exploitation of the Hegelian writings we are now witnessing.

There is perhaps a third cause, less palpable and unconfined by movements, either political or philosophical, which is at work in this revival. Hegel's deepest longing—amounting to a passion—was for a reconciliation of all the conflicting forces which in his age the Enlightenment and subsequent Romanticism had set in motion. His passion for a synoptic view that would reconcile reason and reality, the real and the ideal, or mind and nature could be satisfied only by a comprehensive system in which every legitimate source of conflict and division was incorporated as an organic part of the whole. All his life he struggled against alienation—giving first currency to this term and its psychological and philosophical origins. Though profoundly aware of the divisive aspects of politics, economics, art, religion, and philosophy in his day, he never tired of seeking to heal these divisions intellectually through his principle of the concrete universal, seeing everything in terms of the larger whole. For him, estrangement could never have the final word.

Today we are convinced, rightly or wrongly, that division, fragmentation, and alienation are at an entirely new level of virulence. Like Hegel, some of our young intellectuals, who are not necessarily either existentialists or Marxists, are once more becoming concerned with systematic thinking in philosophy. This is not an interest in Hegel's system, it should be emphasized, but in his systematic approach to the large intellectual problems of his age in order to get what help we can in coping with our own.

I believe that the drive toward reconciliation and synthesis is a durable component of the human psyche. If so, these can only be achieved by a systematic search for underlying principles and their interrelations. Serious students in any age are hence likely to be drawn to Hegel, not because of his system, but to learn from him how to bring order and historical perspective to the tangled problems of their time. It is quite possible that the current concern with Hegel would have arisen even in the absence of existentialist and neo-Marxist thought.

II

One can make a good case for considering the Introductions assembled in this book as the proper starting point for the college student desiring acquaintance with Hegel. For they are the distillation of his mature views on the three most important activities of the human spirit in its career through time. Art, religion, and philosophy are for Hegel the content of absolute spirit or mind. (The German word *Geist* is rendered both as "spirit" and "mind," depending on the context; often both English terms are required.) Hegel contrasted the sphere of absolute spirit with objective spirit, the sphere of politics, economics, and the institutions of any society. There is also for him subjective spirit, the sphere of the private and individual interests and concerns of life. In a people's history these spheres are, of course, organically related and mutually dependent on each other. They are separable only in philosophical analysis, for the purpose of knowledge and understanding. Nevertheless, the realm of absolute spirit became most important for Hegel, because individuals, institutions, states, all things that belong to the other two realms, pass away and perish. Only the inner content of a people's strivings and more or less conscious ideals outlive them, to be passed to posterity in the creations of art, religion, and philosophy. In these three spheres, as Hegel puts it, a people gives to itself what it regards as the true, and these truths alone escape the slaughterbench of history.

Hence it is no accident that at the peak of his career—during the 1820s at the University of Berlin—Hegel lectured most often on these three subjects. The lectures on aesthetics, philosophy of religion, and the history of philosophy are the fruit of a lifetime of devoted study and reflection on these three subject matters. His life had been passed in obscurity and with more than usual hardship and insecurity, both financial and psychological. Born in 1770 in Stuttgart to a family of modest means, Hegel was educated to be a pastor and received in 1788 a scholarship to the Tübingen Seminary. Though he showed considerable academic promise in his university studies and was able to attain the doctorate in philosophy by 1793, he was hardly the equal, either in personality or accomplishments, of his good friends there, Schelling and Hölderlin. It was the precocious Schelling who rescued Hegel in 1801 from a long tenure as private tutor to wealthy families in Bern and Frankfurt, helping him to qualify for a university teaching career. This was at the University of Jena, where Schelling at age twenty-three already held a teaching post.

Jena, however, was soon to be the scene of the famous victory of Napoleon, and Hegel lost his instructorship in 1807 and was forced to become editor of an insignificant local newspaper in Bamberg. Publication of his first book, *The Phenomenology of Spirit,* now widely regarded as a great classic of philosophy, did not in those chaotic times help to advance his career—at least until much later. It required again the aid of friends to secure him the principalship of a secondary school in Nuremberg, where he remained as a teacher and chief administrative officer for eight years. Here for the first time he was financially able to marry—at age forty-one he wed a twenty-year-old girl. The marriage was a successful and harmonious one and marked an improvement in Hegel's fortunes and happiness. In 1812 he published the *Science of Logic* in three volumes. Yet he served four years longer as a school principal before he received at age forty-six a call to a professorship at the University of Heidelberg, his first secure and financially adequate post. Now his name was gradually becoming known, and two years later he accepted an invitation to take over Fichte's chair in philosophy at the University of Berlin. From 1818 to 1831, when he died unexpectedly after a sudden illness, Hegel's fame grew from year to year until he was nationally and internationally recognized as Germany's greatest living philosopher, his reputation as a thinker equalled only by his friend Goethe's reputation as a poet.

That reputation, after a lifetime of obscurity, was due in large part to these lectures in aesthetics, religion, and history of philosophy, which he repeated at intervals in the semesters between 1818 and 1831, constantly reworking and improving them for his students. Upon his death, circles of his devoted students decided to collate their notes from different semesters and with the aid of Hegel's own lecture notes, made available to them by his widow and son Karl, published the lectures under the titles of *Aesthetics, Philosophy of Religion,* and *History of Philosophy.* This task was naturally difficult, since Hegel constantly revised his notes and changed his emphases and examples from year to year. The editors had constantly to exercise judgment on what to include and what to exclude in order to avoid repetition; also to determine whether to use what Hegel had written down in his lecture notes or what student lecture notes claimed he had said. Apparently, Hegel did not follow his own notes very closely while lecturing to students.

Though today's student should not forget in reading these Introductions that they were never intended for publication in their present form, there are definite advantages to their informal lecture style. As spoken words they are more easily comprehensible than are Hegel's published books. Goethe was one of the first to remark, after a long visit from Hegel, the great difference between reading Hegel's books and talking to him: "That which seems unclear and abstruse in the writings of such a man—because we cannot apply it directly to our needs—becomes in vital conversation with him very soon our own property." In his lectures Hegel did not assume that his audience was familiar with his *Phenomenology* or *Logic* or *Encyclopedia* and sought to be intelligible to the beginning student. Like his predecessor Kant in this respect and also like the whole subsequent tradition of German philosophy, Hegel seems to have drawn a large distinction between the informality of lecturing and the formal requirements of the printed communication.

There is also a deeper reason for the greater clarity and comprehensibility of these late lectures. In 1816 Hegel confessed in a letter in which he applied for a university position that the abstruseness of his lecturing at Jena in the early days lay in the fact that "I had not yet worked my way to clarity" and that eight years as a *gymnasium* teacher had taught him the necessity of being clear in communicating his ideas! This is a significant admission and applies as truly to his *Phenomenology* and *Logic* as to his early lecturing. A great deal of the subject matter of these earlier works is absorbed in these later lectures, whose Introductions are here reprinted. The incomparably greater intelligibility of these latter works can be attributed, I am convinced, to the fact that Hegel had matured greatly over the years.

Hitherto, American students have been introduced to Hegel chiefly through his *Philosophy of History* and *Philosophy of Right,* materials which constitute the realm of objective spirit. Hegel scholars are likely to prefer the *Phenomenology* and *Logic*, because they contain his metaphysics in purest form. But there is no reason for studying Hegel's works in the order of their development or even in the order of logic. It is an academic prejudice to believe that the logical and chronological order of a thinker's writings should take precedence over the psychological order in teaching. Just as students of Aristotle should begin with his *Politics* and *Ethics*, believed by many scholars to be the last composed by the man Hegel regarded as the supreme philosopher, so it is appropriate with Hegel to study his last productions first. For they are in as many respects the summit of his achievement as are Aristotle's *Politics* and *Ethics*.

Nevertheless, the student should not for a moment forget that this book contains only the Introductions to much larger works. To succeed in its purpose this book must stimulate the reader—according to his special interests—to read the whole of the *Philosophy of Fine Art* or the *Philosophy of Religion* or the *History of Philosophy*. All three lecture series are eminently worthwhile; it is painful to omit Hegel's famous treatment of tragedy from the first of these, his discussion of the transition from Greek religion to Christianity from the second, and his startlingly novel characterization of the meaning of Socrates' ideas and martyrdom from the third. And these are only three favorite sections of the larger works.

Hegel is so often at his best in illuminating historical details, as for example his penetration of the Stoic outlook or the significance of Sophocles' *Antigone* or Shakespeare's *Hamlet*. Though he did much to separate the specialized subject matters of philosophy we have now grown accustomed to, his greater worth seems to lie in specific insights within one or the other of these specialties. Hence, much is lost to the student who stops with this book alone. For, as Hegel remarks, an introduction to one of these subject matters can only be "a sort of overture to the exposition of the subject itself" and must aim "at being a general concatenation and direction of our reflection on the real subject matter before us."

Still a Hegelian introduction is much more than the term usually implies in the English-speaking world. For Hegel tries to give us in these introductory pages an overview, which is a kind of summary of what he is later to take up in detail.

Furthermore, these Introductions contain his major principles of interpretation as well as the method of approach to the three realms of mind. Possibly even more important, Hegel discusses in all three Introductions the interrelations of art, religion, and philosophy and why they form an organic unity as manifestations of absolute mind or spirit. If the student studies this volume with care, he can learn much of Hegel's essential position in the history of thought. He will be in an incomparably better position to read with understanding not only the lectures they introduce, but also the earlier published books of Hegel. For it is no exaggeration to say that Hegel's synoptic grasp of the wide realm of mind—which was for him the history of culture generally—is displayed masterfully in these introductory lectures. They contain in compressed, lucid form many, perhaps most, of the large concepts Hegel struggled with throughout his whole life. For this reason, too, they are well fitted to serve as a general introduction to his total philosophy.

III

Nevertheless, the road to understanding can be greatly smoothed by brief clarifications of a half-dozen Hegelian concepts which he presupposes in these *Einleitungen*. Let me now give a rapid exposition of the most important of these presuppositions.

In *The Phenomenology of Spirit* Hegel asserted that "the true is the whole." This basic principle, to which he held firmly throughout his subsequent career, meant several things to him, all of them momentous. Using this simple five-word sentence as a guide, one can interpret nearly all of Hegel's philosophy.

"The true is the whole" implies most obviously that anything short of the whole—a subject matter viewed from all its aspects—is necessarily one-sided, incomplete, hence partially false. The negative proposition implicit in the statement "the true is the whole" is that the partial is the false. Hegel is not dealing here with formal logic, however, but is referring to the materials of human history and culture. Though he is profoundly convinced—in contrast to Kant—that reality is knowable, the thing in itself as well as the phenomenal world, his conviction is just as deep that few persons, if any, ever reach to this knowledge of reality. They get hold of a single perspective on any subject matter, like the romanticists' glorifying of feeling or the Enlightenment's absolutizing of ratiocinative reason or the early Christians' grasp of faith, and become convinced that their time-bound and perspective-bound interpretation is the whole story. Indeed, according to Hegel, the part is always and everywhere masquerading as the whole. Every past era has been persuaded that its view of truth was *the* truth. The power of the spirit of any age—what Hegel termed the *Zeitgeist*—is such that it holds nearly everyone in its spell. The overwhelming majority of men are always prisoners of the prevailing perspectives of their period, their particular situations, and their national cultures.

Hegel's attempt to think what is true within his own limitations involved him in an immersion in the history of Western civilization that is hardly comparable to any philosopher's before him and few since. The true is the whole meant for him that the apprehension of truth lies in history. Anyone who seeks to avoid being merely a creature of his particular *Zeitgeist* must learn not only the results and conclusions of any past epoch or process but its beginnings and long development as well. For, as he liked to put it, a thing is not exhausted in its contents or its results but in working the matter out. The true is a process, not a conclusion; spirit is not a substance but an activity. This deep-rooted conviction led Hegel to conceive philosophy—and to an almost equal extent, art and religion—as the *history* of thought. The active being of anything can be known only by knowing what it has been.

But this is emphatically not historicism, an interest in the past for its own sake. As he writes at the beginning of our third Introduction:

The acts of thought appear at first to be a matter of history, and, therefore, things of the past, and outside our real existence. But in reality we are what we are through history: or, more accurately, as in the history of thought, what has passed away is only one side, so in the present, what we have as a permanent possession is essentially bound up with our place in history. The possession of self-conscious reason, which belongs to us of the present world, did not arise suddenly, nor did it grow only from the soil of the present. This possession must be regarded as previously present, as an inheritance, and as the result of labour—the labour of all past generations of men.

It is difficult to overemphasize the importance of this central Hegelian persuasion that we are what we are by virtue of that vital, ever-changing, all-pervasive tradition called Western civilization. As he was accustomed to say in lectures not contained in this book: "The life of the ever-present spirit is a circle of progressive embodiments, which looked at in one aspect still exist beside each other, and only as looked at from another point of view appear as past. The grades which spirit seems to have left behind it, it still possesses in the depths of its present."

Today's student, influenced deeply by technology and science and consequently by the conception that contemporary times are unprecedented, is likely to brush aside impatiently this Hegelian doctrine. Though the student can accept easily in this era of mass communication the notion of the *Zeitgeist* and its pervasive influence on all of us, he finds it difficult indeed to realize that the same thinker insisted that the only way we could know intimately the spirit of our own epoch is to enter truly into the spirit of past ages. For Hegel the two doctrines depended on each other. Only he who comprehended the past by diligent study and by repeated efforts of the creative imagination could lay claim to understanding the dominant forces of the present. This emphasis, I am convinced, is one of the best reasons for close study of Hegel in our time.

Hegel is one of the most historically minded philosophers the West has produced. No one else, so far as I know, ever lectured on the history of art, religion, philosophy, politics and law, and even the philosophy of history, at the same time. He did this not in the interest of scholarship or encyclopedism, but because he conceived history metaphysically and metaphysics historically. A recent British scholar, J. N. Findlay, has called Hegel the most teleological thinker after Aristotle. One should add that he is much more historically minded than the great Stagirite. For Aristotle the idea of *telos* is biologically based; for Hegel on the contrary it is human history in which we observe myriad processes attaining their fulfillments and goals.

This teleological and historical path to understanding led him to adopt and adapt the Aristotelian distinction between the potential and the actual, that is, between any process at its inception and in its fully developed state. For this distinction in Greek Hegel used the rather inelegant German terms *an sich* (in-itself) and *für sich* (for-itself) and then combined them in the barbarous expression *Anundfürsichsein*. (It may be noted that the existentialist Sartre has made a career of further adapting these terms into *en soi* and *pour soi* as categories of his metaphysics.) For Hegel when something is "in itself" it is merely implicit and has not yet achieved any awareness of its relations and connections in a spiritual sense with that of which it is an organic part. In the course of development it becomes for-itself, that is, explicit, self-aware, actualized. Yet this self-awareness also signifies alienation and separation from its origin and inherent dependencies. It is the stage of antithesis when the particular or the individual considers itself the whole. Only when a final process of development has been reached—for example, in a person or a community of persons, in an art form or a religion, etc.—has its *telos* been attained and the process is in-and-for-itself. Even this stage is for Hegel ever relative; there are still higher stages in the unending tide of history. There are still greater possibilities of comprehending how the true is the whole and how the goal is implicit in the beginning and in the intervening process.

Another germinal idea of Hegel's, intimately related to the foregoing—indeed only another way of putting it—is that the true is the concrete. In the realm of sense objects and our representing them the concrete is, of course, what is particular, tangible, visible. But in the realm of concepts Hegel teaches that concreteness means something quite different. It is the interrelated, the many-sided, the entire context of any subject matter in contrast to the abstract, which signifies etymologically "that which is drawn out from" its living context and viewed in isolation. Hegel always uses the word "abstract" pejoratively. The abstract is the in-itself before any person or historical process has come to itself, entered into its development, gained self-awareness.

Only when a student of philosophy learns to approach a subject in terms of its manifold relations, both internal and to other subject matters, does he begin to see it concretely in its wholeness and truth. A study of a nation's art, for example, can be abstract if pursued in isolation from its laws, religion, economics, social ethics, etc., for the fine arts embody a people's vision of reality. Though specialization on a specific aspect of a rich culture is unavoidable and desirable, the investigator should not for a moment forget that he is abstracting from the total context, in which alone the true resides.

Furthermore, that which is true in thinking and in reality is discoverable only in the union of the particular and the general (in the sense of genus or universal). Hegel never confuses the general with the abstract, as we so frequently do. The true is the concrete universal, that is, a grasping conceptually of the organic togetherness of particular and universal—the universal being the principle or underlying source of the various particulars which flow from this source. The truly concrete universal would be the totality of everything that is and has ever been. But since such a level of concreteness is in fact, if not in theory, impossible for mortals, it is necessary to content oneself with striving for a conceptual grasp of ever-larger unities of particulars and universals.

Hegel teaches that the meaning of progress in history lies in this slow, often regressive, but sure advance in man's grasp of these concrete universals. We are ever approaching toward but never attaining such final unities. Meanwhile, creative and comprehensive thinkers are increasingly able to see interrelations that were hidden from their predecessors. Within our human limitations, certain principles as well as the processes which these principles comprehend are absolute and infinite after their own kind. That is, they are self-complete and do not refer beyond themselves for explanation or justification; hence they are truly concrete universals, if not the most inclusive conceivable.

It is important for the student today to realize that terms like absolute and infinite, which sound extravagant and speculative to us, had a degree of precision and exact signification to Hegel's students. Unless we choose to believe that we are more enlightened and advanced than those students of a century and a half ago, we should take care to investigate and seek to understand such terms and concepts as Hegel used them.

The true is the Idea (*Idee*). Hegel uses this crucial term in a fashion inherited from Plato, with characteristic additions. The *Idee* is not something simply in men's heads (in the way either mental images or concepts are) but a form or structure of reality, plus our more or less adequate awareness of it. The Idea is the ideal union of objective reality in its essential features with the human world of thought. To become truly actual or realized, the external world must be assimilated to a kind of thinking that eschews all accidental properties of a subject and penetrates to the essential and enduring substance in process. Hegel calls this kind of thinking absolute knowing or science. It is far removed from sense perception or mental representation or imagining, though all these activities are lower stages of the act of conception, by which the true union of subjective and objective realities, thinking and being, is brought about.

The Idea is only truly grasped in a concept (*Begriff*). For Hegel the concept is that act of thinking which is most general and concrete, hence most philosophical; conceiving builds upon and stands at the apex of the activities of sensing, imagining, opining, and calculating; they are stages (or moments, in Hegel's terminology) of this supreme intellectual effort. The concept, to be sure, does not exhaust the reality of the Idea, since the latter is the structure of reality itself, but it does at times succeed in understanding this reality. In traditional terminology, Hegel is called an idealist, even an absolute idealist, because he believes that reality is in principle knowable and that nothing can resist the awesome power of *Geist* to penetrate to the truth. If from a narrow perspective the multifarious events of the world and nature seem chaotic and patternless, the mind that ranges over world history is able to discern interconnections and directions that are concealed from the chronicler of one nation or one epoch. Though Hegel as a student of history experienced with great poignancy how destruction and death befall all nations, striking down the best as impartially as the worst, he held firmly to the philosophical faith that man's career on earth exhibited, in the wider perspective, order and purpose. History is certainly tragic, but it is not absurd.

This brings us to the last and in some ways most important sense of Hegel's doctrine that the true is the whole. In line with his historical consciousness and trust in the teleological character of history in the large, Hegel teaches that the true is in an incessant whirl of sublimation, of being *aufgehoben*. The German verb *aufheben* means literally "to lift something up"—e.g. an apple from the ground. But figuratively and intellectually it has two other, seemingly contradictory connotations. For one thing, it means "to preserve or save or store up"; for another, it means "to cancel out or annul." This double meaning of a single, ordinary German word Hegel seizes upon as the core of his dialectical method of interpreting the past, a method which has played a momentous role down to the present. The historical past of individuals, peoples, even epochs is, according to him, a continuous process of canceling out or annulling that past and yet at the same time preserving its essentials in a higher synthesis, which is a blend of the old and the new, the past and the present. In the things of nature there is a simple unfolding from bud to flower to fruit, but in the life of mind there is incessant conflict, division, and strife, the goal of which is a fuller, more concrete, and freer grasp of the true as the whole. We are the products of the past of human culture, yet mind is of such a nature that it forever presses forward toward transforming, sublimating what we have been by means of new insights, new forms, and new institutions. The spirit of any age is an inexhaustible blend of the spirit of past epochs, only richer and more self-aware than any of the preceding.

This dialectical method of understanding the past enabled Hegel to cope with the negative and disruptive powers of history—to affirm even wars as means to new principles of insight and understanding. For estrangement and alienation are an unavoidable part of the spirit's struggle to become actually what it is potentially. Without heartbreak and countless tragedies, the riches of present culture could not have been achieved, nor could individuals have become what they are. Hegel may be an idealist in metaphysics, but this signifies no lack of realism regarding history's course. Indeed, he is an anti-idealist in the popular sense of that term, for Hegel was convinced that the world as it is, not as it ought to be, must be the focus of our concern. For the romanticists' yearning for a purer, higher sphere of existence, Hegel has considerable scorn, even when some of them could be counted as former friends.

Were he alive today, Hegel would be passionately interested in the contest for world supremacy of democratic and Communist forms of social organization. But he would scarcely tire of pointing out how much democracy has absorbed of the original program of Marx and Engels, and correspondingly, how much current Communist programs are adopting our ideas. Eventually, according to his vision of dialectical advance, these forms will synthesize and find themselves opposed by another form of political and social organization which we cannot even envision today. Yet the dialectical conflict in politics is but a derivation of other conflicts in the realms of art, religion, and philosophy, where the process of canceling out and preserving goes on in a quieter and less noticed but more determinative fashion than it does on the noisy, brutal stage of world history. For Hegel the dialectical process is all-pervasive; it can take transient and trivial forms. But its chief products are found in that highest realm of absolute spirit or mind, whose outlines he follows in the Introductions of the present volume.

IV

Finally we must consider briefly the interrelations of these activities of absolute spirit. Since Hegel deals at some length in the pages to follow with the way in which art, religion, and philosophy are integral stages or moments of the advance of *Geist*, I shall limit myself to cautions against common misinterpretations. The relations among art, religion, and philosophy are exceedingly complex and perhaps not altogether clear to Hegel himself. Had he himself published these Introductions, it is probable that he would have worked out more carefully the continuities and disconnections among these ideal creations of absolute spirit.

Hegel's passion for system and hierarchy led him to organize these self-contained activities of spirit into the order of first art, then religion, then philosophy. At once the question arises whether this is an order of merit, for example, whether religion is not more revealing of truth as the whole than art is, and philosophy than religion. Some interpreters have held this to be the case and find their support in certain remarks in these Introductions, notably the famous one where Hegel asserts that "art is, and remains for us, on the side of its highest destiny, a thing of the past." Similarly, it is possible to gain the impression from these lectures that Hegel conceived religion as a kind of poor man's philosophy. Only those few who possess sufficient intellectual power to rise to the level of the pure concept are capable of grasping truth today in its fullness and consummation. Thus even within the realm of absolute spirit, supposedly not subject to the ravages of time, Hegel introduced distinctions which place art and religion on a lower level of reality than is philosophy. So such critics hold.

On this controverted matter the student who reads this book with care will be in a position to form his own conclusions. In my opinion, however, Hegel's distinctions among these creative activities concern their form or mode of expression, not their content. All three are equally directed toward the truth of man and his world—art using the most sensuous medium, philosophy the most conceptual. "It is in works of art," writes Hegel, "that nations have deposited the profoundest intuitions and ideas of their hearts, and fine art is frequently the key—with many nations there is no other— to the understanding of their wisdom and of their religion." And he was wont to close his introduction to the lectures on aesthetics with a reference to the wide pantheon of art, "whose architect and builder is the spirit of beauty as it awakens to self-knowledge, and to complete which the history of the world will need its evolution of ages."

The apparent contradiction here between the fine arts as enduring revelations of the eternal Idea in its truth and at the same time as having already passed their zenith can be explained—though hardly explained away—by a certain ambivalence in Hegel's own attitudes. On the one hand, he believed like so many Germans of his time that the art of classical Greece had never been surpassed. Romantic artists, his blanket term for all the artists of "modern" times, were seeking to reveal a content for which their sensuous and perceptual form was inadequate. Yet the requirements of his system constrained him to discover some advance in the Romantic over the classical, despite his reverence for the latter. Furthermore, his esteem for his great contemporaries, Goethe and Schiller, and his even higher regard for Shakespeare caused him to realize that works of art shared with religion and philosophy an equal role in the unfolding of truth about man and his world. What he is trying to say, I believe, is that art is no longer *the* way but one way—for most people still the most convincing and accessible—to the true.

Perhaps Hegel was also convinced that in his own particular epoch philosophy had gained a certain pre-eminence over art and religion. By virtue of the conceptual system that had been worked out in contemporary philosophy from Descartes through Leibniz, Kant, Schelling, and himself, philosophers were currently able to attain a greater degree of concrete universality and establish the long process of spirit's development more adequately than were the other two activities of absolute spirit. He may have felt this way. But his historical sense did not permit him to believe that the spirit of his own age would continue to prevail. Hegel was supremely uninterested in prophecy, in what the future would bring. Instead, his concern was to understand the past in the present. If art is "for us a thing of the past," the emphasis is on the "for us." "In the evolution of ages" yet to be, art will continue to awaken man to self-knowledge and play a supreme role in the history of truth.

The interrelations of religion, specifically Christianity, and philosophy in Hegel's system are even more controversial. In the nineteenth century Hegel's *Lectures on the Philosophy of Religion* were often used, particularly in Britain and America, as the best possible defense of orthodox Christianity. Yet on the Continent of Europe they led more frequently to a radically modernist criticism of religion, often to the point of atheism. This is clearly not the place even to hint at this long—and still continuing—dispute. In all events there is an enormous literature concerned with it. But the reader of the pages to follow should note carefully a few salient points that are hardly disputable. First, Hegel considers himself to be a sound and orthodox Lutheran. Second, he can write at the beginning of the lectures on religion: "All that has worth and dignity for man, all wherein he seeks his happiness, his glory, and his pride, finds its ultimate centre in religion, in the thought, the consciousness, and the feeling of God. Thus God is the beginning of all things, and the end of all things."

Moreover, he can and does speak of the unity of philosophy and religion.

Thus philosophy and religion come to be one. Philosophy is itself, in fact, worship; it is religion, for in the same way it renounces subjective notions and opinions in order to occupy itself with God. Philosophy is thus identical with religion, but the distinction is that it is so in a peculiar manner, distinct from the manner of looking at things which is commonly called religion as such. What they have in common is, that they are religion; what distinguishes them from each other is merely the kind and manner of religion we find in each.

If one takes these statements in isolation, it is easy to conclude that, far from relegating religion to a lower rank than philosophy, Hegel is doing precisely the opposite. Philosophy is religion, is worship, and not the other way round.

Nevertheless, a close study of Hegel's lectures will convince the student that the distinction between philosophy and religion can hardly be dismissed by remarking that it is merely "the kind and manner of religion we find in each." For Hegel's identification of God with absolute spirit is hardly what theologians, not to mention lay Christians, understand by God. The idea of God as a transcendent and personal being finds little or no place in Hegel's mature philosophy of religion. His God is the god of the philosophers, more Greek than Judaic. Hegel insists that God can be fully known, not only through direct revelation, but with equal sureness through conceptual thought. The former may teach us that God *is,* only the latter what He is. Though religion may be awakened in the heart without philosophical knowledge, according to Hegel, unless we make progress toward systematic knowledge of the Divine as absolute spirit our religion remains abstract, fanatical, unfruitful. In other words, the truth to be discovered in religion is subject to historical change and development no less than poetic and philosophic truth. It is by no means a unique intrusion of God into the historical process at a unique time. Rather religious truth is a progressive revelation of God *in* history, secular as much as sacred, political as much as priestly.

Accordingly, for Hegel faith and reason are not opposed as is usual in Lutheran Christianity. Nor is "science"—what we today would call organized knowledge—in any sense an enemy of genuine religious faith. These are customary opposites and opponents which Hegel is earnestly intent on sublimating and integrating in his system. He retained a genuine piety toward the simple religion of the heart, which without much reflection seeks to know God and worship him in spirit and in truth. But the worship that is peculiar to philosophy is of an altogether different order, resting on knowledge and the conviction that God is everywhere manifest, in the state and its institutions as truly as in the church and its sacraments.

In his insistence that God is completely knowable through mind as it develops in history, Hegel reveals his preference for theology as the highest manifestation of religion. In a philosophical theology or a theological philosophy we discover the identity of the three consummate activities of *Geist.* Perhaps Hegel's most characteristic doctrine of the interrelations of these activities is found in the closing words of the inaugural address he gave at Heidelberg on October 28, 1816.

Man, because he is mind, should and must deem himself worthy of the highest; he cannot think too highly of the greatness and power of his mind, and, with this belief, nothing will be so difficult and hard that it will not reveal itself to him. The being of the universe, at first hidden and concealed, has no power which can offer resistance to the search for knowledge; it has to lay itself open before the seeker—to set before his eyes and give for his enjoyment, its riches and its depths.

Hence art, religion, and philosophy are for Hegel different paths to the same goal: the understanding of the concrete universal or the true as the whole. In terms of this goal all three do each other's work, each in its own fashion. In different epochs and for peoples of different mentalities—or for any one of us in different periods of our lives—one or the other may seem more concrete and fruitful in aiding us to grasp the meaning of experience. Unlike most of us, Hegel was much at home in all three spheres. Though he was predominantly a philosopher, he was capable of entering into and enjoying the fine arts in ways that any critic might envy. And his knowledge of theology was astonishing.

The student, therefore, should study these Introductions not in terms of a hierarchy but as distinctive perspectives on the highest activities of the spirit of man, a spirit that is not for Hegel a substance but *is* its activity. Needless to say, he need not agree with Hegel's analyses and conclusions in order to learn much from them. By now we should be safely past the compulsion to be either Hegelians or anti-Hegelians. Perhaps the best one can learn is to become more reflective about the interconnections and unities this nineteenth-century thinker saw in what have since become separate and warring disciplines. The capacity "to see life steadily and to see it whole" may be impossible in an age like our own. But Hegel had in his day the courage—or boldness and arrogance, if you will—to make the attempt.

On Art

The work that follows is a translation of Georg Wilhelm Friedrich Hegel's *Vorlesungen über die Aesthetik,* Erster Band. The version reprinted here is from the translation by Bernard Bosanquet in *The Introduction to Hegel's Philosophy of Fine Art* (London: Routledge & Kegan Paul, Ltd., 1905), pp. 37-211. The translation has been emended slightly for the Torchbook edition by J. Glenn Gray.

The present course of lectures deals with aesthetics. Their subject is the wide *realm of the beautiful*, and, more particularly, their province is *art*—we may restrict it, indeed, *to fine art.*

The name "aesthetics" in its natural sense is not quite appropriate to this subject. "Aesthetics" means more precisely the science of sensation or feeling. Thus understood, it arose as a new science, or rather as something that was to become a branch of philosophy for the first time, in the school of Wolff, at the epoch when works of art were being considered in Germany in the light of the feelings which they were supposed to evoke—feelings of pleasure, admiration, fear, pity, etc. The name was so inappropriate, or, strictly speaking, so superficial, that for this reason it was attempted to form other names, e.g. "Kallistic." But this name, again, is unsatisfactory, for the science to be designated does not treat of beauty in general, but merely of *artistic* beauty. We shall, therefore, permit the name Aesthetics to stand, because it is nothing but a name, and so is indifferent to us, and, moreover, has up to a certain point passed into common language.

As a name, therefore, it may be retained. The proper expression, however, for our science is the "Philosophy of Art," or, more definitely, the "Philosophy of Fine Art."

By the above expression we at once exclude the *beauty of nature*. Such a limitation of our subject may appear to be an arbitrary demarcation resting on the principle that every science has the prerogative of marking out its boundaries at pleasure. But this is not the sense in which we are to understand the limitation of Aesthetics to *the beauty of art*. It is true that in common life we are in the habit of speaking of beautiful colour, a beautiful sky, a beautiful river, and, moreover, of beautiful flowers, beautiful animals, and, above all, of beautiful human beings. We will not just now enter into the controversy of how far such objects can justly have the attribute of beauty ascribed to them, or how far, speaking generally, natural beauty ought to be recognized as existing besides artistic beauty. We may, however, begin at once by asserting that artistic beauty stands *higher* than nature. For the beauty of art is the beauty that is born—born again, that is—of the mind; and by as much as the mind and its products are higher than nature and its appearances, by so much is the beauty of art higher than the beauty of nature. Indeed, if we look at it *formally*—i.e. only considering in what way it exists, not what there is in it—even a silly fancy such as may pass through a man's head is *higher* than any product of nature; for such a fancy must at least be characterized by intellectual being and by freedom. In respect of its content, on the other hand, the sun, for instance, appears to us to be an absolutely necessary factor in the universe, while a blundering notion passes away as accidental and transient; but yet, in its own being, a natural existence such as the sun is indifferent, is not free or self-conscious, while if we consider it in its necessary connection with other things we are not regarding it by itself or for its own sake, and, therefore, not as beautiful.

To say, as we have said in general terms, that mind and its artistic beauty stand *higher* than natural beauty is no doubt

to determine almost nothing. For "higher" is an utterly indefinite expression, which designates the beauty of nature and
that of art as if merely standing side by side in the space of
the imagination and states the difference between them as
purely quantitative and, therefore, purely external. But the
mind and its artistic beauty, in being *"higher"* as compared
with nature, have a distinction which is not simply relative.
Mind, and mind only, is capable of truth, and comprehends
in itself all that is, so that whatever is beautiful can only be
really and truly beautiful as it partakes in this higher element
and as it is created thereby. In this sense the beauty of nature
reveals itself as but a reflection of the beauty that belongs to
the mind, as an imperfect, incomplete mode of being, as a
mode whose really substantial element is contained in the
mind itself.

Moreover, we shall find the restriction to fine art very
natural, for, however much has been and is said—though less
by the ancients than by ourselves—of the beauties of nature,
yet no one has taken it into his head to emphasize the point
of view of the *beauty* of natural objects, and to attempt to
make a science, a systematic account of these beauties. The
aspect of *utility*, indeed, has been accentuated, and a science,
e.g. of natural things useful against diseases, a materia medi-
ca, has been compiled, consisting in a description of minerals,
chemical products, plants, and animals that are of use for
curative purposes. But the realm of nature has not been ar-
rayed and estimated under the aspect of beauty. In dealing
with natural beauty we find ourselves too open to vagueness
and too destitute of a criterion, for which reason such a
review would have little interest.

The above prefatory remarks upon beauty in nature and in
art, upon the relation between the two, and the exclusion of
the former from the region of the subject proper, are meant
to remove any idea that the limitation of our science is owing
merely to choice and to caprice. But this is not the place to
demonstrate the above relation, for the consideration of it

falls within our science itself, and therefore it cannot be discussed and demonstrated till later.

Supposing that for the present we have limited ourselves to the beauty of art, this first step brings us at once into contact with fresh difficulties.

The first thing that may suggest itself to us is the question of whether fine art shows itself to *deserve* a scientific treatment. Beauty and art, no doubt, pervade all the business of life like a kindly genius, and form the bright adornment of all our surroundings, both mental and material, soothing the sadness of our condition and the embarrassments of real life, killing time in entertaining fashion, and where there is nothing good to be achieved, occupying the place of what is vicious, better, at any rate, than vice. Yet although art presses in with its pleasing shapes on every possible occasion, from the rude adornments of the savage to the splendour of the temple with its untold wealth of decoration, still these shapes themselves appear to fall outside the real purposes of life. And even if the creations of art do not prove detrimental to our graver purposes, if they appear at times actually to further them by keeping evil at a distance, still it is so far true that art belongs rather to the relaxation and leisure of the mind, while the substantive interests of life demand its exertion. Hence it may seem unsuitable and pedantic to treat with scientific seriousness what is not in itself of a serious nature. In any case, upon such a view art appears as a superfluity, even if the softening of the mental temper which preoccupation with beauty has power to produce does not turn out a detrimental, because effeminating, influence. In this aspect of the matter, the fine arts being granted to be a *luxury*, it has been thought necessary in various ways to take up their defence with reference to their relation towards *practical* necessities, and more especially towards morality and piety, and, as it is impossible to demonstrate their harmlessness, at least to make it credible that the mental luxury in question afforded a larger sum of advantages than of disadvantages. With this view very serious aims have been ascribed

to art, and it has been recommended in various ways as a
mediator between reason and sensuousness, between inclination and duty, as the reconciler of these elements in the
obstinate conflict and repulsion which their collision generates. But the opinion may be maintained that, assuming such
aims of art, more serious though they are, nothing is gained
for reason and duty by the attempt at mediation, because
these principles, as essentially incapable of intermixture, can
be parties to no such compromise but demand in their manifestation the same purity which they have in themselves.
And it might be said that art itself is not made any more
worthy of scientific discussion by such treatment, seeing that
it is still doubly a servant—to higher aims, no doubt, on the
one hand, but none the less to vacuity and frivolity on the
other; and in such service can at best only display itself as a
means, instead of being an end pursued for its own sake.

Finally, art, considered as a means, seems to labour under
this defect of form: that, supposing it to be subordinated to
serious ends and to produce results of importance, still the
means employed by art for such purposes is *deception*. For
beauty has its being in appearance. Now, it will readily be
admitted that an aim which is real and true in itself ought not
to be attained by deception, and if it does here and there
achieve some success in this way, that can only be the case to
a limited extent, and even then deception cannot approve
itself as the right means. For the means should correspond to
the dignity of the end, and only what is real and true, not
semblance or deception, has power to create what is real and
true; just as science, for instance, has to consider the true
interests of the mind in accordance with the truth of reality
and the true way of conceiving it.

In all these respects it may appear as if fine art were *unworthy* of scientific consideration, because, as is alleged, it is
at best a pleasing amusement, and even if it pursues more
serious aims is in contradiction with their nature, but is at
best the mere servant alike of amusement and of serious aims,
and yet has at command, whether as the element of its being

or as the vehicle of its action, nothing beyond deception and semblance.

But, in the second place, it is a still more probable aspect of the question that, even if fine art were to form a subject of philosophical reflections in a general way, it would be no *appropriate* matter for strictly scientific treatment. The beauty of art presents itself to sense, to feeling, to perception, to imagination; its sphere is not that of thought, and the apprehension of its activity and its production demand another organ than that of the scientific intelligence. Moreover, what we enjoy in the beauty of art is precisely the *freedom* of its productive and plastic energy. In the origination, as in the contemplation, of its creations we appear to escape wholly from the fetters of rule and regularity. In the forms of art we seek repose and animation in place of the austerity of the reign of law and the sombre self-concentration of thought; we would exchange the shadowland of the Idea for cheerful vigorous reality. And lastly, the source of artistic creations is the free activity of fancy, which in her imagination is more free than nature's self. Not only has art at command the whole wealth of natural forms in the brilliant variety of their appearance, but also the creative imagination has power to expatiate inexhaustibly beyond their limit in products of *its own*. It may be supposed that, in presence of this immeasurable abundance of inspiration and its free creations, thought will necessarily lose the courage to bring them *completely* before it, to criticize them, and to array them under its universal formulas.

Science, on the contrary, everyone admits, is compelled by its form to busy itself with thought, which abstracts from the mass of particulars. For this reason, on the one hand, imagination with its contingency and caprice—that is, the organ of artistic activity and enjoyment—is of necessity excluded from science. And on the other hand, seeing that art is what cheers and animates the dull and withered dryness of the notion, reconciles with reality its abstraction and its dissociation therefrom, and supplies out of the real world what is lacking to the notion, it follows, we may think, that a *purely* intellectual treatment of art destroys this very means of supplementation, annihilates it, and reduces the notion once more to its simplicity, devoid of reality, and to its shadowy abstractness. And further, it is objected that science, as a matter of *content,* occupies itself with what is *necessary.* Now, if Aesthetics puts aside the beauty of nature, we not only gain nothing in respect of necessity but to all appearance have got further away from it. For the expression *nature* at once gives us the idea of necessity and uniformity—that is to say, of a behaviour which may be hoped to be akin to science and capable of submitting thereto. But in the mind generally, and more particularly in the imagination, compared with nature, caprice and lawlessness are supposed to be peculiarly at home; and these withdraw themselves as a matter of course from all scientific explanation.

Thus in all these aspects—in origin, in effect, and in range—fine art, instead of showing itself fitted for scientific study, seems rather in its own right to resist the regulating activity of thought and to be unsuitable for strict scientific discussion.

These and similar objections against a genuinely scientific treatment of fine art are drawn from common ideas, points of view, and considerations, which may be read *ad nauseam* in full elaboration in the older writers on beauty and the fine arts, especially in the works of French authors. And in part they contain facts which have a certain truth; in part, too, the argumentation[1] based upon these facts appears plausible at first sight. Thus, for example, there is the fact that the forms of beauty are as manifold as the phenomenon of beauty is omnipresent; and from this, if we choose, we may proceed to conclude to a universal *impulse of beauty* in human nature, and then go on to the further inference: that because ideas of beauty are so endlessly various, and therefore, as

---

1. "Raisonnement"—a disparaging term in Hegel.

seems obvious, are something *particular*, it follows that there can be no universal laws of beauty and of taste.

Before it is possible for us to turn from such considerations to our subject proper, it is our business to devote a brief introductory discussion to the objections and doubts which have been raised. In the first place, as regards the *worthiness* of art to be scientifically considered, it is no doubt the case that art can be employed as a fleeting pastime, to serve the ends of pleasure and entertainment, to decorate our surroundings, to impart pleasantness to the external conditions of our life, and to emphasize other objects by means of ornament. In this mode of employment art is indeed not independent, not free, but servile. But what *we* mean to consider, is the art which is *free* in its end as in its means.

That art is in the abstract capable of serving other aims, and of being a mere pastime, is moreover a relation which it shares with thought. For, on the one hand, science, in the shape of the subservient understanding, submits to be used for finite purposes, and as an accidental means, and in that case is not self-determined but determined by alien objects and relations; but, on the other hand, science liberates itself from this service to rise in free independence to the attainment of truth, in which medium, free from all interference, it fulfils itself in conformity with its proper aims.

Fine art is not real art till it is in this sense free, and only achieves its highest task when it has taken its place in the same sphere with religion and philosophy and has become simply a mode of revealing to consciousness and bringing to utterance the divine nature, the deepest interests of humanity, and the most comprehensive truths of the mind. It is in works of art that nations have deposited the profoundest intuitions and ideas of their hearts; and fine art is frequently the key—with many nations there is no other—to the understanding of their wisdom and of their religion.

This is an attribute which art shares with religion and philosophy, only in this peculiar mode, that it represents even the highest ideas *in sensuous forms*, thereby bringing them nearer to the character of natural phenomena, to the senses, and to feeling. The world, into whose depths *thought* penetrates, is a suprasensuous world, which is thus, to begin with, erected as a *beyond* over against immediate consciousness and present sensation; the power which thus rescues itself from the *here*, that consists in the actuality and finiteness of sense, is the freedom of thought in cognition. But the mind is able to heal this schism which its advance creates; it generates out of itself the works of fine art as the first middle term of reconciliation between pure thought and what is external, sensuous, and transitory, between nature with its finite actuality and the infinite freedom of the reason that comprehends.

The *element* of art was said to be in its general nature an *unworthy* element, as consisting in appearance and deception. The censure would be not devoid of justice if it were possible to class appearance as something that ought not to exist. An appearance or show, however, is essential to existence. Truth could not be if it did not appear and reveal itself, were it not truth *for* someone or something, *for* itself as also *for* mind. Therefore, there can be objection not against appearance in general, but, if at all, against the particular mode of appearance in which art gives actuality to what is in itself real and true. If, in this aspect, the *appearance* with which art gives its conceptions life as determinate existences is to be termed a *deception*, this is a criticism which primarily receives its meaning by comparison with the external world of phenomena and its immediate contact with us as *matter*, and in like manner by the standard of our own world of feeling, that is, the inner world of *sense*. These are the two worlds to which, in the life of daily experience, in our own phenomenal life, we are accustomed to attribute the value and the title of actuality, reality, and truth, in contrast to art, which we set down as lacking such reality and truth. Now, this whole sphere of the empirical inner and outer world is just what is not the world of genuine reality, but is to be entitled a mere appearance more strictly than is true of art, and a crueller deception. Genuine reality is only to be found beyond the immediacy of feeling and of external objects. Nothing is genuinely real but that which is actual in its own right,[2] that which is the substance of nature and of mind, fixing itself indeed in present and definite existence, but in this existence still obtaining its essential and self-centered being, and thus and no otherwise attaining genuine reality. The dominion of these universal powers is exactly what art accentuates and reveals. The common outer and inner worlds also no doubt present to us this essence of reality, but in the shape of a chaos of accidental matters, encumbered by the immediateness of sensuous presentation, and by arbitrary states, events, characters, etc. Art liberates the real import of appearances from the semblance and deception of this bad and fleeting world and imparts to phenomenal semblances a higher reality, born of mind. The appearances of art, therefore, far from being mere semblances, have the higher reality and the more genuine existence in comparison with the realities of common life.

Just as little can the representations of art be called a deceptive semblance in comparison with the representations of historical narrative, as if that had the more genuine truth. For history has not even immediate existence, but only the intellectual presentation of it, for the element of its portrayals, and its content remains burdened with the whole mass of contingent matter formed by common reality with its occurrences, complications, and individualities. But the work of art brings before us the eternal powers that hold dominion in history, without any such superfluity in the way of immediate sensuous presentation and its unstable semblances.

Again, the mode of appearance of the shapes produced by art may be called a deception in comparison with philosophic thought, with religious or moral principles. Beyond a doubt the mode of revelation which a content attains in the realm of thought is the truest reality; but in comparison with the

2. "Das An—und Fürsichseyende."

show or semblance of immediate sensuous existence or of historical narrative, the artistic semblance has the advantage that in itself it points beyond itself and refers us away from itself to something spiritual that it is meant to bring before the mind's eye. Whereas immediate appearance does not give itself out to be deceptive, but rather to be real and true, though all the time its truth is contaminated and infected by the immediate sensuous element. The hard rind of nature and the common world give the mind more trouble in breaking through to the idea than do the products of art.

But if, on the one side, we assign this high position to art, we must no less bear in mind, on the other hand, that art is not, either in content or in form, the supreme and absolute mode of bringing the mind's genuine interests into consciousness. The form of art is enough to limit it to a restricted content. Only a certain circle and grade of truth is capable of being represented in the medium of art. Such truth must have in its own nature the capacity to go forth into sensuous form and be adequate to itself therein if it is to be a genuinely artistic content, as is the case with the gods of Greece. There is, however, a deeper form of truth, in which it is no longer so closely akin and so friendly to sense as to be adequately embraced and expressed by that medium.

Of such a kind is the Christian conception of truth; and more especially the spirit of our modern world, or, to come closer, of our religion and our intellectual culture, reveals itself as beyond the stage at which art is the highest mode assumed by man's consciousness of the absolute. The peculiar mode to which artistic production and works of art belong no longer satisfies our supreme need. We are above the level at which works of art can be venerated as divine, and actually worshipped; the impression which they make is of a more considerate kind, and the feelings which they stir within us require a higher test and a further confirmation. Thought and reflection have taken their flight above fine art. Those who delight in grumbling and censure may set down this phenomenon for a corruption and ascribe it to the predominance of passion and selfish interests, which scare away at once the seriousness and the cheerfulness of art. Or we may accuse the troubles of the present time and the complicated condition of civil and political life as hindering the feelings, entangled in minute preoccupations, from freeing themselves and rising to the higher aims of art, the intelligence itself being subordinate to petty needs and interests, in sciences which only subserve such purposes and are seduced into making this barren region their home.

However all this may be, it certainly is the case that art no longer affords that satisfaction of spiritual wants which earlier epochs and peoples have sought therein, and have found therein only; a satisfaction which, at all events on the religious side, was most intimately and profoundly connected with art. The beautiful days of Greek art and the golden time of the later Middle Ages are gone by. The reflective culture of our life of today makes it a necessity for us, in respect of our will no less than of our judgment, to adhere to general points of view and to regulate particular matters according to them, so that general forms, laws, duties, rights, maxims are what have validity as grounds of determination and are the chief regulative force. But what is required for artistic interest as for artistic production is, speaking generally, a living creation, in which the universal is not present as law and maxim, but acts as if at one with the mood and the feelings, just as, in the imagination, the universal and rational is contained only as brought into unity with a concrete sensuous phenomenon. Therefore, our present in its universal condition is not favourable to art. As regards the artist himself, it is not merely that the reflection which finds utterance all round him and the universal habit of having an opinion and passing judgment about art infect him and mislead him into putting more abstract thought into his works themselves, but also the whole spiritual culture of the age is of such a kind that he himself stands within this reflective world and its conditions, and it is impossible for him to abstract from it by will and resolve, or to contrive for himself and bring to pass, by means of

peculiar education or removal from the relations of life, a
peculiar solitude that would replace all that is lost.

In all these respects art is, and remains for us, on the side
of its highest destiny, a thing of the past. Herein it has further lost for us its genuine truth and life, and is transferred
into our *ideas* more than it asserts its former necessity, or
assumes its former place, in reality. What is now aroused in us
by works of art is our immediate enjoyment, and together
with it, our judgment; in that we subject the content and the
means of representation of the work of art and the suitability
or unsuitability of the two to our intellectual consideration.
Therefore, the *science* of art is a much more pressing need in
our day than it was in times in which art, simply as art, was
enough to furnish a full satisfaction. Art invites us to consideration of it by means of thought, not to the end of stimulat-
ing art production, but in order to ascertain scientifically
what art is.

As soon as we propose to accept this invitation we are met
by the difficulty which has already been touched upon in the
suggestion that, though art is a suitable subject for philosophical reflection in the general sense, yet it is not so for systematic and scientific discussion. In this objection there lies the
false idea that a philosophical consideration may, nevertheless, be unscientific. On this point it can only be remarked
here with brevity that, whatever ideas others may have of
philosophy and philosophizing, I regard the pursuit of philosophy as utterly incapable of existing apart from a scientific
procedure. Philosophy has to consider its object in its necessity, not, indeed, in its subjective necessity or external arrangement, classification, etc., but it has to unfold and demonstrate the object out of the necessity of its own inner nature.
Until this explication is brought to pass the scientific element
is lacking to the treatment. Insofar, however, as the objective
necessity of an object lies essentially in its logical and metaphysical nature, the isolated treatment of art must be con-
ducted with a certain relaxation of scientific stringency. For
art involves the most complex presuppositions, partly in ref-

erence to its content, partly in respect of its medium and element, in which art is constantly on the borders of the arbitrary or accidental. Thus it is only as regards the essential innermost progress of its content and of its media of expression that we must call to mind the outline prescribed by its necessity.

The objection that works of fine art elude the treatment of scientific thought because they originate out of the unregulated fancy and out of the feelings, are of a number and variety that defy the attempt to gain a conspectus, and therefore take effect only on feeling and imagination, raises a problem which appears still to have importance. For the beauty of art does in fact appear in a form which is expressly contrasted with abstract thought, and which the latter is forced to destroy in exerting the activity which is its nature. This idea coheres with the opinion that reality as such, the life of nature and of mind, is disfigured and slain by comprehension; that, so far from being brought close to us by the thought which comprehends, it is by it that such life is absolutely dissociated from us, so that, by the use of thought as the *means* of grasping what has life, man rather cuts himself off from this his purpose. We cannot speak fully on this subject in the present passage, but only indicate the point of view from which the removal of this difficulty, or impossibility depending on maladaptation, might be effected.

It will be admitted, to begin with, that the mind is capable of contemplating itself and of possessing a consciousness, and a *thinking* consciousness, of itself and all that is generated by itself. Thought—to think—is precisely that in which the mind has its innermost and essential nature. In gaining this thinking consciousness concerning itself and its products, the mind is behaving according to its essential nature, however much freedom and caprice those products may display, supposing only that in real truth they have mind in them.

Now art and its works as generated and created by the mind (spirit) are themselves of a spiritual nature, even if their mode of representation admits into itself the semblance of sensuous being and pervades what is sensuous with mind. In this respect art is, to begin with, nearer to mind and its thinking activity than is mere external unintelligent nature; in works of art, mind has to do but with its own. And even if artistic works are not abstract thought and notion, but are an evolution of the notion *out of* itself, an alienation from itself towards the sensuous, still the power of the thinking spirit (mind) lies herein, *not merely* to grasp *itself only* in its peculiar form of the self-conscious spirit (mind), but just as much to recognise itself in its alienation in the shape of feeling and the sensuous, in its other form, by transmuting the metamorphosed thought back into definite thoughts, and so restoring it to itself. And in this preoccupation with the other of itself the thinking spirit is not to be held untrue to itself as if forgetting or surrendering itself therein, nor is it so weak as to lack strength to comprehend what is different from itself, but it comprehends both itself and its opposite. For the notion is the universal, which preserves itself in its particularizations, dominates alike itself and its "other," and so becomes the power and activity that consists in undoing the alienation which it had evolved.

And thus the work of art in which thought alienates itself belongs, like thought itself, to the realm of comprehending thought, and the mind, in subjecting it to scientific consideration, is thereby but satisfying the need of its own inmost nature. For because thought is its essence and notion, it can in the last resort only be satisfied when it has succeeded in imbuing all the products of its activity with thought, and has thus for the first time made them genuinely its own. But, as we shall see more definitely below, art is far from being the highest form of mind and receives its true ratification only from science.

Just as little does art elude philosophical consideration by unbridled caprice. As has already been indicated, it is its true task to bring to consciousness the highest interests of the mind. Hence it follows at once with respect to the *content* that fine art cannot rove in the wildness of unfettered fancy, for these spiritual interests determine definite bases for its content, however manifold and inexhaustible its forms and shapes may be. The same holds true for the forms themselves. They, again, are not at the mercy of mere chance. Not every plastic shape is capable of being the expression and representation of those spiritual interests, of absorbing and of reproducing them; every definite content determines a form suitable to it.

In this aspect too, then, we are in a position to find our bearings according to the needs of thought in the apparently unmanageable mass of works and types of art.

Thus, I hope, we have begun by defining the content of our science, to which we propose to confine ourselves, and have seen that neither is fine art unworthy of a philosophical consideration, nor is a philosophical consideration incompetent to arrive at a knowledge of the essence of fine art.

II

If we now investigate *the required mode of scientific consideration*, we here again meet with two opposite ways of treating the subject, each of which appears to exclude the other, and so to hinder us from arriving at *any true result*.

On one side we see the science of art merely, so to speak, busying itself about the actual productions of art from the outside, arranging them in series as a history of art, initiating discussions about extant works, or sketching out theories intended to provide the general points of view that are to govern both criticism and artistic production.

On the other side we see science abandoning itself independently to reflection upon the beautiful and producing mere generalities which do not touch the work of art in its peculiarity, creating, in short, an abstract philosophy of the beautiful.

1. As regards the former mode of treatment, which starts from the empirical side, it is the indispensable road for anyone who means to become a student of art. And just as in the

present day every one, even though he is not busied with natural science, yet pretends to be equipped with the essentials of physical knowledge, so it has become more or less obligatory for a cultivated man to possess some acquaintance with art, and the pretension to display oneself as a dilettante and connoisseur is pretty universal.

If such information is really to be recognised as art scholarship, it must be of various kinds and of wide range. The first necessity is an exact acquaintance with the immeasurable region of individual works of art of ancient and modern times, works which in part have actually perished, in part belong to distant countries or portions of the world, or which adverse fortune has withdrawn from one's own observation. Moreover, every work belongs to its *age*, to its *nation*, and to its environment, and depends upon particular historical and other ideas and aims. For this reason art scholarship further requires a vast wealth of historical information of a very special kind, seeing that the individualized nature of the work of art is related to individual detail and demands special matter to aid in its comprehension and elucidation. And lastly, this kind of scholarship needs, like every other, not only a memory for information, but a vivid imagination in order to retain distinctly the images of artistic forms in all their different features, and especially in order to have them present to the mind for purposes of comparison with other works.

Within this kind of consideration, which is primarily historical, there soon emerge various points of view which cannot be lost sight of in contemplating a work of art, inasmuch as our judgments must be derived from them. Now these points of view, as in other sciences which have an empirical starting point, when extracted and put together form universal criteria and rules, and, in a still further stage of formal, generalization, *theories of the arts*. This is not the place to go into detail about literature of this kind, and it may, therefore, suffice to mention a few writings in the most general way. For instance, there is Aristotle's "Poetics," the theory of tragedy contained in which is still of interest; and to speak more particularly, among the ancients, Horace's "Ars Poetica" and Longinus's "Treatise on the Sublime" suffice to give a general idea of the way in which this kind of theorizing has been carried on. The general formulas that were abstracted by such writers were meant to stand especially as precepts and rules, according to which, particularly in times of degeneration of poetry and art, works of art were meant to be produced. The prescriptions, however, compiled by these physicians of art had even less assured success than those of physicians whose aim was the restoration of health.

Respecting theories of this kind, I propose merely to mention that, though *in detail* they contain much that is instructive, yet their remarks were abstracted from a very limited circle of artistic productions, which passed for *the* genuinely beautiful ones, but yet always belonged to a but narrow range of art. And again, such formulas are in part very trivial reflections which in their generality proceed to no establishment of particulars, although this is the matter of chief concern.

The above-mentioned Horatian epistle is full of these reflections, and, therefore, is a book for all men, but one which for this very reason contains much that amounts to nothing, e.g.:

> Omne tulit punctum qui miscuit utile dulci
> Lectorem delectando pariterque monendo—

"He carries all votes, who has mingled the pleasant and the useful, by at once charming and instructing his reader." This is just like so many copybook headings, e.g. "Stay at home and earn an honest livelihood," which are right enough as generalities but lack the concrete determinations on which action depends.

Another kind of interest was found, not in the express aim of directly causing the production of genuine works of art, but in the purpose which emerged of influencing men's judgment upon works of art by such theories, in short of *forming taste*. In this aspect, Hume's "Elements of Criticism," the writings of Batteux, and Ramler's "Introduction to the Fine Arts," were works much read in their day. Taste in this sense has to do with arrangement and treatment, the harmony and finish of what belongs to the external aspect of a work of art. Besides, they brought in among the principles of taste views that belonged to the psychology that was then in vogue, and that had been drawn from empirical observation of capacities and activities of the soul, of the passions and their probable heightening, succession, etc. But it remains invariably the case that every man judges works of art, or characters, actions, and incidents according to the measure of his insight and his feelings; and as that formation of taste only touched what was meagre and external, and moreover drew its precepts only from a narrow range of works of art and from a *borné* culture of intellect and feelings, its whole sphere was inadequate, and incapable of seizing the inmost and the true, and of sharpening the eye for the apprehension thereof.

Such theories proceed in general outline, as do the remaining nonphilosophic sciences. The content that they subject to consideration is borrowed from our ordinary idea of it, as something found there; then further questions are asked about the nature of this idea, inasmuch as a need reveals itself for closer determinations, which are also found in our idea of the matter, and drawn from it to be fixed in definitions. But in so doing, we find ourselves at once on uncertain and debatable ground. It might indeed appear at first as if the beautiful were a perfectly simple idea. But it soon becomes evident that manifold sides may be found in it, one of which is emphasized by one writer and another by another, or, even if the same points of view are adopted, a dispute arises on the question which side after all is to be regarded as the essential one.

With a view to such questions it is held a point of scientific completeness to adduce and to criticize the various definitions of the beautiful. We will do this neither with historical *exhaustiveness,* so as to learn all the subtleties which have emerged in the defining process, nor for the sake of the *historical* interest, but we will simply produce by way of illustration, some of the more interesting modern views which come pretty close in their purport to what in fact the Idea of the beautiful does involve. For such purpose we have chiefly to mention Goethe's account of the beautiful, which Meyer embodied in his "History of the Fine Arts in Greece," on which occasion he also brings forward Hirt's view, though without mentioning him.

Hirt, one of the greatest of genuine connoisseurs in the present day, in his brochure about artistic beauty (*Horen,*[3] 1797, seventh number), after speaking of the beautiful in the several arts, sums up his ideas in the result that the basis of a just criticism of beauty in art and of the formation of taste is the conception of the *characteristic.* That is to say, he defines the beautiful as the "perfect, which is or can be an object of eye, ear, or imagination." Then he goes on to define the perfect as "that which is adequate to its aim, that which nature or art aimed at producing within the given genus and species in the formation of the object." For which reason, in order to form our judgment on a question of beauty, we ought to direct our observation as far as possible to the individual marks which constitute a definite essence. For it is just these marks that form its characteristics. And so by *character* as the law of art he means "that determinate individual modification whereby forms, movement and gesture, bearing and expression, local colour, light and shade, chiaroscuro and attitude distinguish themselves, in conformity, of course, with the requirements of an object previously selected."

This formula gives us at once something more significant than the other definitions. If we go on to ask what "the characteristic" is, we see that it involves in the first place *a content,* as, for instance, a particular feeling, situation, inci-

---

3. *Die Horen*—the monthly magazine whose establishment by Schiller, in 1795, first brought Schiller and Goethe into contact. It only existed for three years. See Scherer, Eng. Trans., ii. 173.

dent, action, individual; and secondly, the *mode* and *fashion* in which this content is embodied in a representation. It is to this, the mode of representation, that the artistic law of the "characteristic" refers, inasmuch as it requires that every particular element in the mode of expression shall subserve the definite indication of its content and be a member in the expression of that content. The abstract formula of the characteristic thus has reference to the degree of appropriateness with which the particular detail of the artistic form sets in relief the content that it is intended to represent. If we desire to illustrate this conception in a quite popular way, we may explain the limitation which it involves as follows: In a dramatic work, for instance, an action forms the content; the drama is to represent how this action takes place. Now, men and women do all sorts of things; they speak to each other from time to time, at intervals they eat, sleep, put on their clothes, say one thing and another, and so forth. But in all this, whatever does not stand in immediate connection with that particular action considered as the content proper is to be excluded, so that in reference to it nothing may be without import. So, too, a picture, that only represented a single phase of that action might yet include in it—so wide are the ramifications of the external world—a multitude of circumstances, persons, positions, and other matters which at that moment have no reference to the action in question and are not subservient to its distinctive character.

But according to the rule of the characteristic, only so much ought to enter into the work of art as belongs to the display and, essentially, to the expression of that content and no other; for nothing must appear as otiose and superfluous.

This is a very important rule, which may be justified in a certain aspect. Meyer, however, in his above-mentioned work, gives it as his opinion that this view has vanished and left no trace, and, in his judgment, to the benefit of art. For he thinks that the conception in question would probably have *led* to caricature. This judgment at once contains the perversity of implying that such a determination of the beautiful had to do with *leading*. The philosophy of art does not trouble itself about precepts for artists, but it has to ascertain what beauty in general is, and how it has displayed itself in actual productions, in works of art, without meaning to give rules for guidance. Apart from this, if we examine the criticism, we find it to be true, no doubt, that Hirt's definition includes caricature, for even a caricature may be characteristic; but, on the other hand, it must be answered at once that in caricature the definite character is intensified to exaggeration, and is, so to speak, a superfluity of the characteristic. But a superfluity ceases to be what is properly required in order to be characteristic, and becomes an offensive iteration, whereby the characteristic itself may be made unnatural. Moreover, what is of the nature of caricature shows itself in the light of the characteristic representation of what is ugly, which ugliness is, of course, a distortion.

Ugliness, for its part, is closely connected with the content, so that it may be said that the principle of the characteristic involves as a fundamental property both ugliness and the representation of what is ugly. Hirt's definition, of course, gives no more precise information as to what is to be characterized and what is not, in the artistically beautiful, or about the content of the beautiful, but it furnishes in this respect a mere formal rule, which nevertheless contains some truth, although stated in abstract shape.

Then follows the further question—what Meyer opposes to Hirt's artistic principle, i.e. what he himself prefers. He is treating, in the first place, exclusively the principle shown in the artistic works of the ancients, which principle, however, must include the essential attribute of beauty. In dealing with this subject he is led to speak of Mengs and Winckelmann's principle of the Ideal, and pronounces himself to the effect that he desires neither to reject nor wholly to accept this law of beauty, but, on the other hand, has no hesitation in attaching himself to the opinion of an enlightened judge of art (Goethe), as it is definite, and seems to solve the enigma more precisely.

Goethe says: "The highest principle of the ancients was the *significant*, but the highest result of successful *treatment*, the *beautiful*."

If we look closer at what this opinion implies, we find in it again two elements: the content or matter in hand and the mode and fashion of representation. In looking at a work of art we begin with what presents itself immediately to us, and after that go on to consider what is its significance or content.

The former, the external element, has no value for us simply as it stands; we assume something further behind it, something inward, a significance, by which the external semblance has a soul breathed into it. It is this, its soul, that the external appearance indicates. For an appearance which means something does not present to the mind's eye itself and that which it is qua external, but something else; as does the *symbol*, for instance, and still more obviously the *fable*, whose moral and precept constitutes its meaning. Indeed every *word* points to a meaning and has no value in itself. Just so the human eye, a man's face, flesh, skin, his whole figure, are a revelation of mind and soul, and in this case the meaning is always something other than what shows itself within the immediate appearance. This is the way in which a work of art should have its meaning, and not appear as exhausted in these mere particular lines, curves, surfaces, borings, reliefs in the stone, in these colours, tones, sounds, of words, or whatever other medium is employed; but it should reveal life, feeling, soul, import, and mind, which is just what we mean by the significance of a work of art.

Thus this requirement of *significance* in a work of art amounts to hardly anything beyond or different from Hirt's principle of the *characteristic*.

According to this notion, then, we find distinguished as the elements of the beautiful something inward, a content, and something outer which has that content as its significance; the inner shows itself in the outer and gives itself to be known by its means, inasmuch as the outer points away from itself to the inner.

We cannot go into detail on this matter.

But the earlier fashion alike of rules and of theories has already been violently thrown aside in Germany—especially owing to the appearance of genuine living poetry—and the rights of genius, its works and their effects, have had their value asserted against the encroachment of such legalities and against the wide, watery streams of theory. From this foundation both of an art which is itself genuinely spiritual and of a general sympathy and communion with it, have arisen the receptivity and freedom which enabled us to enjoy and to recognise the great works of art which have long been in existence, whether those of the modern world, of the Middle Ages, or even of peoples of antiquity quite alien to us (e.g. the Indian productions); works which by reason of their antiquity or of their alien nationality have, no doubt, a foreign element in them, yet in view of their content—common to all humanity and dominating their foreign character—could not have been branded as products of bad and barbarous taste except by the prejudices of theory. This recognition, so to speak generally, of works of art which depart from the sphere and form of those upon which more especially the abstractions of theory were based led, in the first instance, to the recognition of a peculiar kind of art—that is, of romantic art—and it therefore became necessary to apprehend the idea and the nature of the beautiful in a deeper way than was possible for those theories. With this influence there cooperated another, viz. that the idea in its self-conscious form, the thinking mind, attained at this time, on its side, a deeper self-knowledge in philosophy, and was thereby directly impelled to understand the essence of art, too, in a profounder fashion.

Thus, then, even judging by the phases of this more general evolution of ideas, the theoretical mode of reflection upon art which we were considering has become antiquated alike in its principles and in its particulars. Only the *scholarship* of the history of art has retained its permanent value, and cannot but retain it, all the more that the advance of intellectual receptivity, of which we spoke, has extended its range of vision on every side. Its business and vocation consists in the aesthetic appreciation of individual works of art and in acquaintance with the historical circumstances that externally condition such works; an appreciation which, if made with sense and mind, supported by the requisite historical information, is the only power that can penetrate the entire individuality of a work of art. Thus Goethe, for instance, wrote much about art and particular works of art. Theorizing proper is not the purpose of this mode of consideration, although no doubt it frequently busies itself with abstract principles and categories and may give way to this tendency without being aware of it. But for a reader who does not let this hinder him, but keeps before him the concrete accounts of works of art, which we spoke of just now, it at all events furnishes the philosophy of art with the perceptible illustrations and instances, into the particular historical details of which philosophy cannot enter.

This, then, may be taken to be the first mode of the study of art, starting from particular and extant works.

2. There is an essential distinction between this and the opposite aspect, the wholly theoretical reflection, which made an effort to understand beauty as such out of itself alone and to get to the bottom of its idea.

It is well known that Plato was the first to require of philosophical study, in a really profound sense, that its objects should be apprehended not in their *particularity* but in their *universality*, in their genus, in their own nature and its realization: inasmuch as he affirmed that the truth of things did not consist in individual good actions, true opinions, beautiful human beings, or works of art, but in *goodness, beauty, truth* themselves. Now, if the beautiful is in fact to be known according to its essence and conception, this is only possible with the help of the thinking idea, by means of which the logico-metaphysical nature of the *Idea as such,* as also that of the *particular Idea of the beautiful,* enters into the thinking consciousness. But the study of the beautiful in its separate nature and in its own Idea may itself turn into an abstract Metaphysic, and even though Plato is accepted in such an inquiry as foundation and as guide, still the Platonic abstraction must not satisfy us, even for the logical Idea of beauty. We must understand this Idea more profoundly and more in the concrete, for the emptiness of content which characterizes the Platonic Idea is no longer satisfactory to the fuller philosophical wants of the mind of today. Thus it is, no doubt, the case that we, too, in modern times, must in our philosophy of art start from the Idea of the beautiful, but we ought not to abide by the fashion of Platonic Ideas, which was purely abstract and the mere beginning of the philosophic study of beauty.

3. The philosophic conception of the beautiful, to indicate its true nature at least by anticipation, must contain, reconciled within it, the two extremes which have been mentioned, by combining metaphysical universality with the determinateness of real particularity. Only thus is it apprehended in its truth, in its real and explicit nature. It is then fertile out of its own resources, in contrast to the barrenness of one-sided reflection. For it has in accordance with its own conception to develop into a totality of attributes, while the conception itself as well as its detailed exposition contains the necessity of its particulars, as also of their progress and transition one into another. On the other hand, again, these particulars, to which the transition is made, carry in themselves the universality and essentiality of the conception as the particulars of which they appear. The modes of consideration of which we have so far been treating lack both these qualities,[4] and for this reason it is only the complete

---

4. The exhibition of particulars as contained in the principle, and of the principle as contained in particulars.

conception of which we have just spoken that can lead to substantive, necessary, and self-complete determinations.

III

After the above prefatory remarks, we approach closer to our subject, the philosophy of artistic beauty. Inasmuch as we are undertaking to treat it scientifically we must begin with its *conception* or notion. Not till we have established this conception can we map out the division, and with it the plan of the entirety of the science; for a division, if it is not, as is the case with unphilosophical inquiries, taken in hand in a purely external manner, must find its principle in the conception of the object itself.

In presence of such a demand we are at once met by the question, "Whence do we get this conception?" If we begin with the given conception of artistic beauty itself, that is enough to make it a *presupposition* and mere assumption; now, mere assumptions are not admitted by the philosophical method, but whatever it allows to pass must have its truth demonstrated, i.e. displayed as necessary.

We will devote a few words to coming to an understanding upon this difficulty, which concerns the introduction to every philosophical branch of study when taken in hand by itself.

The object of every science presents prima facie two aspects: in the first place, that such an object *is*; in the second place, *what* it is.

In ordinary science little difficulty attaches to the first of these points. It might even, at first sight, look ridiculous if the requirement were presented that in astronomy and physics it should be demonstrated that there was a sun, heavenly bodies, magnetic phenomena, etc. In these sciences, which have to do with what is given to sense, the objects are taken from external experience, and instead of demonstrating them (*beweisen*) it is thought sufficient to show them (*weisen*). Yet even within the nonphilosophical sciences, doubts may arise about the existence of their objects, as, for example, in psychology, the science of mind, it may be doubted if there *is* a soul, a mind, i.e. something subjective, separate, and independent, distinct from what is material; or in theology, whether a God *is*. If, moreover, the objects are of subjective kind, i.e. are given only in the mind, and not as external sensuous objects, we are confronted by our conviction that there is nothing in the mind but what its own activity has produced. This brings up the accidental question whether men have produced this inner idea or perception in their minds or not, and even if the former is actually the case, whether they have not made the idea in question vanish again, or at any rate degraded it to a merely *subjective idea*, whose content has no natural and independent being. So, for instance, the beautiful has often been regarded not as naturally and independently necessary in our ideas but as a mere subjective pleasure or accidental sense. Our external intuitions, observations, and perceptions are often deceptive and erroneous, but still more is this the case with the inner ideas, even if they have in themselves the greatest vividness and are forcible enough to transport us irresistibly into passion.

This doubt whether an object of inward ideas and inward perception as such is or is not, as also the accidental question whether the subjective consciousness has produced it in itself, and whether the act or mode in which it brought it before itself was in its turn adequate to the object in its essential and independent nature—all this is just what arouses in men the higher scientific need, which demands that, even if we have an idea that an object is, or that there is such an object, the object must yet be displayed or demonstrated in terms of its necessity.

This proof, if it is developed in a really scientific way, must also satisfy the further question of *what* an object is. But to expound this relation would carry us too far in this place, and we can only make the following remarks on the point.

If we are to display the necessity of our object, the beautiful in art, we should have to prove that art or beauty was a result of antecedents such as, when considered in their true conception, to lead us on with scientific necessity to the conception of fine art. But in as far as we begin with *art*, and propose to treat of the essence of *its* conception and of the realization of that conception, not of antecedents which go before it *as demanded by* its nature, so far art, as a peculiar scientific object, has, for us, a presupposition which lies beyond our consideration, and which, being a different content, belongs in scientific treatment to a different branch of philosophical study. We have thus no other alternative than to presuppose the conception of art, something that is the case with all philosophical sciences when considered individually and in isolation. For it is nothing short of the whole of philosophy that is the knowledge of the universe as in itself *one single* organic totality which develops itself out of its own conception and which, returning into itself so as to form a whole in virtue of the necessity in which it is placed towards itself, binds itself together with itself into *one single* world of truth. In the coronal of this scientific necessity, each individual part is just as much a circle that returns into itself, as it has, at the same time, a necessary connection with other parts. This connection is a backward out of which it derives itself, as well as a forward, to which in its own nature it impels itself on and on, in as far as it is fertile by creating fresh matter out of itself, and issuing it into the further range of scientific knowledge.

Therefore, it is not our present aim to demonstrate the Idea of beauty from which we set out—that is, to derive it according to its necessity from the presuppositions which are its antecedents in science. This task belongs to an encyclopedic development of philosophy as a whole and of its particular branches. For us, the conception of beauty and of art is a presupposition given in the system of philosophy. But as we cannot in this place discuss this system, and the connection of art with it, we have not yet the conception of the beautiful before us *in a scientific form*. What we have at command are merely the elements and aspects of it, as they are or have at former periods been presented, in the diverse ideas of the beautiful and of art in the mere common consciousness.

Having started from this point, we shall subsequently pass to the more profound consideration of the views in question, in order thereby to gain the advantage of, in the first place, obtaining a general idea of our object, and further, by a brief criticism effecting a preliminary acquaintance with its higher principles, with which we shall have to do in the sequel. By this mode of treatment our final introduction will act, so to speak, as the overture to the account of the subject itself, and will serve the purpose of a general collection and direction of our thoughts towards the proper subject matter of our discussion.

What we know, to begin with, as a current idea of the work of art, comes under the three following general predicates:

1. We suppose the work of art to be no natural product, but brought to pass by means of human activity.

2. To be essentially made *for* man, and, indeed, to be more or less borrowed from the sensuous and addressed to man's sense.

3. To contain an *end*.

1. As regards the first point, that a work of art is taken to be a product of human activity, this view has given rise to the view that this activity, being the *conscious* production of an external object, can also be *known*, and *expounded*, and learnt, and prosecuted by others. For, what one can do, it might seem, another can do, or imitate, as soon as he is acquainted with the mode of procedure; so that, supposing universal familiarity with the rules of artistic production, it would only be a matter of any one's will and pleasure to carry out the process in a uniform way, and so to produce works of art. It is thus that the above-mentioned rule-providing theories and their precepts, calculated for practical observance, have arisen. But that which can be executed accord-

ing to such instruction can only be something formally regular and mechanical. For only what is mechanical is of such an external kind that no more than a purely empty exercise of will and dexterity is required to receive it among our ideas and put it in act, such an exercise not needing to be supplemented by anything concrete or anything that goes beyond the precepts conveyed in general rules. This is most vividly displayed when precepts of the kind in question do not limit themselves to what is purely external and mechanical, but extend to the meaning-laden spiritual activity of true art. In this region the rules contain nothing but indefinite generalities; e.g. "The theme ought to be interesting, and each individual ought to be made to speak according to his rank, age, sex, and position." But if rules are meant to be adequate on this subject, their precepts ought to have been drawn up with such determinateness that they could be carried out just as they are expressed, without further and original activity of mind. Being abstract, however, in their content, such rules reveal themselves, in respect of their pretension of being adequate to fill the consciousness of the artist, as wholly inadequate, inasmuch as artistic production is not formal activity in accordance with given determinations. For it is bound as spiritual activity to work by drawing on its own resources, and to bring before the mind's eye a quite other and richer content and ampler individual creations than any abstract formulas can dictate. Such rules may furnish guidance in case of need, if they contain anything really definite, and therefore of practical utility, but their directions can apply only to purely external circumstances.

The tendency that we have just indicated has therefore been abandoned, and, in place of it, the opposite principle has been pursued to no less lengths. For the work of art came to be regarded no longer as the product of a *general activity* in mankind, but as the work of a mind endowed with wholly peculiar gifts. This mind, it is thought, has then nothing to do but *simply* to give free play to its particular gift, as though it were a specific force of nature, and is to be entirely released from attention to laws of universal validity, as also from the interference of reflection in its instinctively creative operation. And, indeed, it is to be guarded therefrom, inasmuch as its productions could only be infected and tainted by such a consciousness. In this aspect the work of art was pronounced to be the product of *talent* and *genius*, and stress was laid on the natural element which talent and genius contain. The view was partly right. Talent is specific, and genius universal capability, with which a man has not the power to endow himself simply by his own self-conscious activity. We shall treat this point more fully in the sequel.

In this place we have only to mention the aspect of falsity in the view before us, in that all consciousness respecting the man's own activity was held, in the case of artistic production, not merely superfluous, but even injurious. Production on the part of talent and genius then appears, in general terms, as a *state*, and, in particular, as a state of *inspiration*. To such a state, it is said, genius is in part excited by a given object, and in part it has the power of its own free will to place itself therein, in which process, moreover, the good service of the champagne bottle is not forgotten. This notion became prominent in Germany in the so-called epoch of genius, which was introduced by the early poetical production of Goethe, and subsequently sustained by those of Schiller. In their earliest works these poets began everything anew, in scorn of all the rules which had then been fabricated, transgressed these rules of set purpose, and, while doing so, distanced all rivals by a long interval.

I will not enter more closely into the confusions which have prevailed respecting the conception of inspiration and genius, and which prevail even at the present day respecting the omnipotence of inspiration as such. We need only lay down as essential the view that, though the artist's talent and genius contains a natural element, yet it is essentially in need of cultivation by thought, and of reflection on the mode in which it produces, as well as of practice and skill in producing. A main feature of such production is unquestionably external workmanship, inasmuch as the work of art has a purely technical side, which extends into the region of handicraft, especially in architecture and sculpture, less so in painting and music, least of all in poetry. Skill in this comes not by inspiration, but solely by reflection, industry, and practice. And such skill is indispensable to the artist, in order that he may master his external material and not be thwarted by its stubbornness.

Moreover, the higher an artist ranks, the more profoundly ought he to represent the depths of heart and mind; and these are not known without learning them, but are only to be fathomed by the direction of a man's own mind to the inner and outer world. So here, too, *study* is the means whereby the artist brings this content into his consciousness, and wins the material and substance of his conceptions.

In this respect one art may need the consciousness and cognition of such substance more than others. Music, for instance, which concerns itself only with the undefined movement of the inward spiritual nature, and deals with musical sounds as, so to speak, feeling without thought, needs little or no spiritual content to be present in consciousness. It is for this reason that musical talent generally announces itself in very early youth, while the head is still empty and the heart has been but little moved, and is capable of attaining to a very considerable height in early years, before mind and life have experience of themselves. And again, as a matter of fact, we often enough see very great expertness in musical composition, as also in execution, subsist along with remarkable barrenness of mind and character.

The reverse is the case with poetry. In poetry all depends on the representation—which must be full of matter and thought—of man, of his profounder interests, and of the powers that move him; and therefore mind and heart themselves must be richly and profoundly educated by life, experience, and reflection before genius can bring to pass anything mature, substantial, and self-complete. Goethe's and Schiller's first productions are of an immaturity, and even of a rudeness and barbarism, that are really shocking. This phenomenon, that the greater part of those attempts display a predominant mass of thoroughly prosaic and in part of frigid and commonplace elements, furnishes the chief objection to the common opinion, that inspiration is inseparable from youth and youthful fire. Those two men of genius, it may be said, were the first to give our nation works of true poetry, and yet it was only their mature manhood that presented us with creations profound, substantial, and the outcome of genuine inspiration, while no less thoroughly perfect in form. Thus, too, it was not till his old age that Homer devised and uttered his immortal songs.

A third view, which concerns the idea of the work of art as a product of human activity, refers to the position of such a work in relation to the external appearances of nature. It was an obvious opinion for the common consciousness to adopt on this matter that the work of art made by man ranked *below* the product of nature. The work of art has no feeling in itself, and is not through and through a living thing, but, regarded as an external object, is dead. But we are wont to prize the living more than the dead. We must admit, of course, that the work of art has not in itself movement and life. An animated being in nature is within and without an organization appropriately elaborated down to all its minutest parts, while the work of art attains the semblance of animation on its surface only, but within is common stone, or wood and canvas, or, as in the case of poetry, is idea, uttering itself in speech and letters. But this aspect, viz. its external existence, is not what makes a work into a production of fine art; it is a work of art only insofar as, being the offspring of mind, it continues to belong to the realm of mind, has received the baptism of the spiritual, and only represents that which has been moulded in harmony with mind. A human interest, the spiritual value which attaches to an incident, to an individual character, to an action in its plot and in its denouement, is apprehended in the work of art, and exhibited more purely and transparently than is possible on the soil of common unartistic reality. This gives the work of art a higher rank than anything produced by nature, which has not sustained this passage through the mind. So, for instance, by reason of the feeling and insight of which a landscape as depicted by an artist is a manifestation, such a work of mind assumes a higher rank than the mere natural landscape. For everything spiritual is better than anything natural. At any rate, no existence in nature is able, like art, to represent divine ideals.

Upon that which, in works of art, the mind borrows from its own inner life it is able, even on the side of external existence, to confer *permanence*; whereas the individual living thing of nature is transient, vanishing, and mutable in its aspect, while the work of art persists. Though, indeed, it is not mere permanence, but the accentuation of the character which animation by mind confers, that constitutes its genuine pre-eminence as compared with natural reality.

Nevertheless, this higher rank assigned to the work of art is in turn disputed by another idea of the common consciousness. It is said that nature and its products are a work of God, created by his goodness and wisdom, whereas the work of art is *merely* a human production, made after man's devising by man's hands. In this antithesis between natural production as a divine creation and human activity as a merely finite creation, we at once come upon the misconception that God does *not* work in man and through man, but limits the range of his activity to nature alone. This false opinion is to be entirely abandoned if we mean to penetrate the true conception of art. Indeed, in opposition to such an idea, we must adhere to the very reverse, believing that God is more honoured by what mind does or makes than by the productions or formations of nature. For not only is there a divinity in man, but in him it is operative under a form that is appropriate to the essence of God, in a mode quite other and higher than in nature. God is a Spirit, and it is only in man that the medium through which the divine element passes has the form of conscious spirit and actively realizes itself. In nature the corresponding medium is the unconscious, sensible, and external, which is far below consciousness in value. In the products of art God is operative neither more nor less than in the phenomena of nature; but the divine element, as it makes itself known in the work of art, has attained, as being generated out of the mind, an adequate thoroughfare for its existence; while existence in the unconscious sensuousness of nature is not a mode of appearance adequate to the Divine Being.

Granting, then, that the work of art is made by man as a creation of mind, we come to the last question, which will enable us to draw a deeper result from what has been said. What is man's need to produce works of art? On the one hand the production may be regarded as a mere toy of chance and of man's fancies, which might just as well be let alone as pursued. For, it may be said, there are other and better means for effecting that which is the aim of art, and man bears in him interests that are yet higher and of more import than art has power to satisfy. But, on the other hand, art appears to arise from the higher impulse and to satisfy the higher needs, at times, indeed, even the highest, the absolute need of man, being wedded to the religious interests of whole epochs and peoples and to their most universal intuitions respecting the world. This inquiry concerning the not contingent but absolute need of art we cannot as yet answer completely, seeing that it is more concrete than any shape which could here be given to the answer. We must, therefore, content ourselves for the present with merely establishing the following points.

The universal and absolute need out of which art, on its formal side, arises has its source in the fact that man is a *thinking* consciousness, i.e. that he draws out of himself, and makes explicit *for himself*, that which he is, and, generally, whatever is. The things of nature are only *immediate and single*, but man as mind *reduplicates* himself, inasmuch as prima facie he *is* like the things of nature, but in the second place just as really is *for* himself, perceives himself, has ideas of himself, thinks himself, and only thus is active self-real-izedness. This consciousness of himself man obtains in a two-fold way: *in the first place theoretically*, insofar as he has inwardly to bring himself into his own consciousness, with all that moves in the human breast, all that stirs and works therein, and, generally, to observe and form an idea of himself, to fix before himself what thought ascertains to be his real being, and, in what is summoned out of his inner self as in what is received from without, to recognise only himself.

Secondly, man is realised for himself by *practical* activity, inasmuch as he has the impulse, in the medium which is directly given to him, to produce himself, and therein at the same time to recognise himself. This purpose he achieves by the modification of external things upon which he impresses the seal of his inner being, and then finds repeated in them his own characteristics. Man does this in order as a free sub-ject to strip the outer world of its stubborn foreignness, and to enjoy in the shape and fashion of things a mere external reality of himself. Even the child's first impulse involves this practical modification of external things. A boy throws stones into the river, and then stands admiring the circles that trace themselves on the water, as an effect in which he attains the sight of something that is his own doing. This need trav-erses the most manifold phenomena, up to the mode of self-production in the medium of external things as it is known to us in the work of art. And it is not only external things that man treats in this way, but himself no less, i.e. his own natural form, which he does not leave as he finds it but alters of set purpose. This is the cause of all ornament and decora-tion, though it may be as barbarous, as tasteless, as utterly disfiguring, or even as destructive as crushing Chinese ladies' feet, or as slitting the ears and lips. It is only among cultivat-ed men that change of the figure, of behaviour, and of every kind and mode of self-utterance emanates from spiritual edu-cation.

The universal need for expression in art lies, therefore, in man's rational impulse to exalt the inner and outer world into a spiritual consciousness for himself, as an object in which he recognises his own self. He satisfies the need of this spiritual freedom when he makes all that exists explicit for himself *within*, and in a corresponding way realises this his explicit self *without*, evoking thereby, in this reduplication of himself, what is in him into vision and into knowledge for his own mind and for that of others. This is the free rationality of man, in which, as all action and knowledge, so also art has its ground and necessary origin. The specific need of art, however, in contradistinction to other action, political or moral, to religious imagination and to scientific cognition, we shall consider later.

2. We have so far been considering that aspect of the work of art in which it is made by man. We have now to pass on to its second characteristic, that it is made for man's *sense* and for this reason is more or less borrowed from the sensuous.

This reflection has furnished occasion for the consideration to be advanced that fine art is intended to arouse feeling, and indeed more particularly the feeling which we find suits us—that is, pleasant feeling. Looking at the question thus, men have treated the investigation of fine art as an investigation of the feelings and have asked what feelings it must be held that art ought to evoke—fear, for example, and compassion; and then, how these could be pleasant—how, for example, the contemplation of misfortune could produce satisfaction. This tendency of reflection is traceable particularly to Moses Mendelssohn's times, and many such discussions are to be found in his writings. Yet such an investigation did not lead men far, for feeling is the indefinite dull region of the mind; what is felt remains wrapped in the form of the most abstract individual subjectivity, and therefore the distinctions of the actual subject matter itself. For instance, fear, anxiety, alarm, terror, are no doubt of one and the same sort of feeling variously modified, but in part are mere quantitative heightenings, in part are forms which in themselves have nothing to do with their content itself, but are indifferent to it. In the case of fear, for instance, an existence is given in which the subject (i.e. a person) has an interest but at the same time sees approaching the negative that threatens to annihilate this existence, and so finds immediately in himself, as a contradictory affection of his subjectivity, the two at once, this interest and that negative.

Now, such fear considered in itself is not enough to condition any content but is capable of receiving into itself the most diverse and opposite matters. Feeling, as such, is a thoroughly empty form of subjective affection. No doubt this form may in some cases be manifold in itself, as are hope, grief, joy, or pleasure; and, again, may in such diversity comprehend varied contents, as there is a feeling of justice, moral feeling, sublime religious feeling, and so forth. But the fact that such content is forthcoming in different forms of feeling is not enough to bring to light its essential and definite nature; they remain purely subjective affections of myself, in which the concrete matter vanishes, as though narrowed into a circle of the utmost abstraction. Therefore, the inquiry into the feelings which art arouses, or ought to arouse, comes utterly to a standstill in the indefinite and is a mode of study which precisely abstracts from the content proper and from its concrete essence and notion. For reflection upon feeling contents itself with the observation of the subjective affection in its isolation, instead of diving into and fathoming the matter in question itself, the work of art, and, while engaged with it, simply letting go the mere subjectivity and its states. In feeling it is just this empty subjectivity that is not merely retained, but given the first place, and that is why men are so fond of having emotions. And for the same reason such a study becomes tedious from its indefiniteness and emptiness, and repulsive from its attentiveness to little subjective peculiarities.

Now, as a work of art does not merely do in general something of the nature of arousing emotion—for this is a purpose which it would have in common, without specific difference, with eloquence, historical composition, religious edification, and so forth—but is beautiful, reflection hit upon the idea, seeing that beauty was the object, of searching out a *peculiar feeling of beauty* to correspond to it and of discovering a particular *sense of beauty*. In this search it soon appeared that such a sense is no blind instinct made rigidly definite by nature, and capable from the beginning in its own independent essence of discerning beauty. Hence it followed that education came to be demanded for this sense, and the educated sense of beauty came to be called *taste*, which, although an educated appreciation and apprehension of the beautiful, was yet supposed to retain the nature of immediate feeling. We have already mentioned how abstract theories undertook to educate such a sense of taste, and how external and one-sided that sense remained. The criticism of the time when those views prevailed was not only defective in *universal* principles but also, in its particular references to individual works of art, was less directed to justifying a *definite* judgment—the power to make one not having at that time been acquired—than to advancing the general education of taste.

For this reason such education in its turn came to a standstill in the indefinite, and merely endeavoured so to equip feeling with a sense of beauty by help of reflection, that there might thenceforth be capacity to find out beauty whenever and wherever it should exist. Yet the depths of the matter remained a sealed book to mere taste, for these depths demand not only sensibility and abstract reflection, but the undivided reason and the mind in its solid vigour, while taste was only directed to the external surface about which the feelings play and on which one-sided maxims may pass for valid. But for this very reason what is called good taste takes fright at all more profound effects of art and is silent where the reality comes in question and where externalities and trivialities vanish. For when great passions and the movements of a profound soul are unveiled, we are no longer concerned with the finer distinctions of taste and its pettifog-

ging particularities. Taste feels that genius strides contemptu-
ously over such ground as this, and, shrinking before its power, becomes uneasy, and knows not which way to turn.

And thus, as we should expect, men have abandoned the
tendency to consider works of art solely with an eye to the
education of taste and with the purpose of merely displaying
taste. The connoisseur, or scholar of art, has replaced the art
judge, or man of taste. The positive side of art scholarship, so
far as it concerns a thorough acquaintance with the entire
circumference of the individual character in a given work of
art, we have already pronounced to be essential to the study
of art. For a work of art, owing to its nature as at once
material and individual, is essentially originated by particular
conditions of the most various kinds, to which belong especially the time and place of its production, then the peculiar
individuality of the artist, and in particular the grade of technical development attained by his art. Attention to all these
aspects is indispensable to distinct and thorough insight and
cognition, and even to the enjoyment of a work of art; it is
with them that connoisseurship, or art scholarship, is chiefly
occupied, and all that it can do for us in its own way is to be
accepted with gratitude. Yet, though such scholarship is entitled to rank as something essential, still it ought not to be
taken for the sole or supreme element in the relation which
the mind adopts towards a work of art, and towards art in
general. For art scholarship (and this is its defective side) is
capable of resting in an acquaintance with purely external
aspects, such as technical or historical details, etc., and of
guessing but little, or even knowing absolutely nothing, of
the true and real nature of a work of art. It may even form a
disparaging estimate of the value of more profound considerations in comparison with purely positive, technical, and historical information. Still, even so, art scholarship, if only it is
of a genuine kind, at least strives after definite grounds and
information, and an intelligent judgment, with which is closely conjoined the more precise distinction of the different,

even if partly external, aspects in a work of art, and the estimation of their importance.

After these remarks upon the modes of study which have arisen out of that aspect of a work of art in which, being a sensuous object, it is invested with a relation to man as a sensuous being, we will now consider this aspect in its more essential relations to art as such, and so partly as regards the work of art as object, partly with respect to the subjectivity of the artist, his genius, talent, and so on, but without entering into matter relative to these points that can only proceed from the knowledge of art in its universal concept. For we are not yet on genuinely scientific ground, but have only reached the province of external reflection.

The work of art then, of course, presents itself to sensuous apprehension. It is addressed to sensuous feeling, outer or inner, to sensuous perception and imagination, just as is the nature that surrounds us without, or our own sensitive nature within. Even a speech, for instance, may be addressed to sensuous imagination and feeling. Notwithstanding, the work of art is not only for the *sensuous* apprehension as sensuous object, but its position is of such a kind that as sensuous it is at the same time essentially addressed to the *mind*, that the mind is meant to be affected by it, and to find some sort of satisfaction in it.

This intention of the work of art explains how it is in no way meant to be a natural product and to possess natural life, whether a natural product is to be ranked higher or lower than a *mere* work of art, as it is often called in a depreciatory sense.

For the sensuous aspect of the work of art has a right to existence only in as far as it exists for man's mind, but not in as far as qua sensuous thing it has separate existence by itself. If we examine more closely in what way the sensuous is presented to man, we find that what is sensuous may bear various relations to the mind.

The lowest mode of apprehension, and that least appropriate to the mind, is purely sensuous apprehension. It consists

naturally in mere looking, listening, feeling, just as in seasons
of mental fatigue it may often be entertaining to go about
without thought and just to hear and look around us. The
mind, however, does not rest in the mere apprehension of
external things by sight and hearing; it makes them objects
for its own inner nature, which then is itself impelled in a
correspondingly sensuous form to realize itself in the things
and relates itself to them as *desire*. In this appetitive relation
to the outer world, the man stands as a sensuous particular
over against the things as likewise particulars. He does not
open his mind to them with general ideas as a thinking being
but has relations dictated by particular impulses and interests
to the objects as themselves particulars, and preserves himself
in them, inasmuch as he uses them, consumes them, and puts
in act his self-satisfaction by sacrificing them to it. In this
negative relation desire requires for itself not merely the superficial appearance of external things, but themselves in
their concrete sensuous existence. Mere pictures of the wood
that it wants to use, or of the animals that it wants to eat,
would be of no service to desire, Just as little is it possible for
desire to let the object subsist in its freedom. For its impulse
urges it just precisely to destroy this independence and freedom of external things and to show that they are only there
to be destroyed and consumed. But at the same time the
subject himself, as entangled in the particular limited and
valueless interests of his desires, is neither free in himself, for
he does not determine himself out of the essential universality and rationality of his will, nor free in relation to the outer
world, for his desire remains essentially determined by things
and related to them.

This relation of desire is not that in which man stands to
the work of art. He allows it to subsist as an object, free and
independent, and enters into relation with it apart from desire, as with an object which only appeals to the theoretic
side of the mind. For this reason the work of art, although it
has sensuous existence, yet, in this point of view, does not
require concrete sensuous existence and natural life; indeed,

it even *ought* not to remain on such a level, seeing that it has to satisfy only the interests of mind, and is bound to exclude from itself all desire. Hence it is, indeed, that practical desire rates individual things in nature, organic and inorganic, which are serviceable to it, higher than works of art, which reveal themselves to be useless for its purpose and enjoyable only for other modes of mind.

A second mode in which the externally present may be related to the mind is, in contrast with singular sensuous perception and desire, the purely theoretical relation to the intelligence. The theoretic contemplation of things has no interest in consuming them as particulars, in satisfying itself sensuously, and in preserving itself by their means, but rather in becoming acquainted with them in their universality, in finding their inner being and law, and in conceiving them in terms of their notion. Therefore the theoretical interest lets the single things be and holds aloof from them as sensuous particulars, because this sensuous particularity is not what the contemplation exercised by the intelligence looks for. For the rational intelligence does not belong, as do the desires, to the individual subject as such, but only to the individual as at the same time in his nature universal. Insofar as man has relation to things in respect of this universality, it is his universal reason which attempts to find itself in nature, and thereby to reproduce the inner essence of things, which sensuous existence, though having its ground therein, cannot immediately display. But again, this theoretic interest, the satisfaction of which is the work of science, is in the scientific form no more shared by art than the latter makes common cause with the impulse of the purely practical desires. Science may, no doubt, start from the sensuous thing in its individuality, and may possess a sensuous idea of the way in which such an individual presents itself in its individual colour, shape, size, etc. Still, this isolated sensuous thing, as such, has no further relation to the mind, inasmuch as the intelligence aims at the universal, the law, the thought and notion of the object. Not only, therefore, does it abandon all intercourse with the thing as a given individual, but it transforms the thing within the mind, making a concrete object of sense into an abstract matter of thought, and so into something quite other than the same object qua sensuous phenomenon. The artistic interest, as distinguished from science, does not act thus. Artistic contemplation accepts the work of art just as it displays itself qua external object, in immediate determinateness and sensuous individuality clothed in colour, figure, and sound, or as a single isolated perception, etc., and does not go so far beyond the immediate appearance of objectivity which is presented before it, as to aim, like science, at apprehending the notion of such an objective appearance as a universal notion.

Thus, the interest of art distinguishes itself from the practical interest of *desire* by the fact that it permits its object to subsist freely and in independence, while desire utilizes it in its own service by its destruction. On the other hand, artistic contemplation differs from theoretical consideration by the scientific intelligence, in cherishing interest for the object as an individual existence, and not setting to work to transmute it into its universal thought and notion.

It follows, then, from the above, that though the sensuous must be present in a work of art, yet it must only appear as surface and *semblance* of the sensuous. For, in the sensuous aspect of a work of art, the mind seeks neither the concrete framework of matter, that empirically thorough completeness and development of the organism which desire demands, nor the universal and merely ideal thought. What it requires is sensuous presence, which, while not ceasing to be sensuous, is to be liberated from the apparatus of its merely material nature. And thus the sensuous in works of art is exalted to the rank of a mere *semblance* in comparison with the immediate existence of things in nature, and the work of art occupies the mean between what is immediately sensuous and ideal thought. It is not as yet pure thought, but despite the sensuousness it is also no longer simple material existence, like stones, plants, and organic life. Rather the sensuous in the work of art is itself something ideal, not, however, the ideal of thought but as thing still in an external way. This semblance of the sensuous presents itself to the mind externally as the shape, the visible look, and the sonorous vibration of things—supposing that the mind leaves the objects uninterfered with (physically), but yet does not descend into their inner essence (by abstract thought), for if it did so, it would entirely destroy their external existence as separate individuals *for it*. For this reason the sensuous aspect of art only refers to the two *theoretical* senses of *sight* and *hearing*, while smell, taste, and feeling remain excluded from being sources of artistic enjoyment. For smell, taste, and feeling have to do with matter as such, and with its immediate sensuous qualities; smell with material volatilization in air, taste with the material dissolution of substance, and feeling with warmth, coldness, smoothness, etc. On this account these senses cannot have to do with the objects of art, which are destined to maintain themselves in their actual independent existence, and admit of no purely sensuous relation. The pleasant for these latter senses is not the beautiful in art.

Thus art on its sensuous side purposely produces no more than a shadow world of shapes, sounds, and imaginable ideas; and it is absolutely out of the question to maintain that it is owing to simple powerlessness and to the limitations on his actions that man, when evoking worlds of art into existence, fails to present more than the mere surface of the sensuous, than mere *schemata*. In art, these sensuous shapes and sounds present themselves, not simply for their own sake and for that of their immediate structure, but with the purpose of affording in that shape satisfaction to higher spiritual interests, seeing that they are powerful to call forth a response and echo in the mind from all the depths of consciousness. It is thus that, in art, the sensuous is *spiritualized*, i.e. the *spiritual* appears in sensuous shape.

But for this very reason we have a product of art only in so far as it has found a passage through the mind and has been generated by spiritually productive activity. This leads us to

the other question which we have to answer—how, that is,
the sensuous side, which is indispensable to art, is operative
in the artist as a productive state of the subject or person.

This, the method and fashion of production, contains in
itself as a subjective activity just the same properties which
we found objectively present in the work of art; it must be a
spiritual activity which, nevertheless, at the same time has in
itself the element of sensuousness and immediateness. It is
neither, on the one hand, purely mechanical work, as mere
unconscious skill in sensuous sleight of hand, or a formal
activity according to fixed rules learnt by rote. Nor is it, on
the other hand, a scientific productive process, which passes
from sense to abstract ideas and thoughts, or exercises itself
exclusively in the element of pure thinking. Rather the spiritual and the sensuous side must in artistic production be as
one. For instance, it would be possible in poetical creation to
try and proceed by first apprehending the theme to be treated as a prosaic thought, and by then putting it into pictorial
ideas, and into rhyme, and so forth; so that the pictorial
element would simply be hung upon the abstract reflections
as an ornament or decoration. Such a process could only
produce bad poetry, for in it there would be operative as two
separate activities that which in artistic production has its
right place only as undivided unity.

This genuine mode of production constitutes the activity
of artistic *imagination*. It is the rational element which, qua
spirit, only exists in as far as it actively extrudes itself into
consciousness, but yet does not array before it what it bears
within itself till it does so in sensuous form. This activity has,
therefore, a spiritual import, which, however, it embodies in
sensuous shape. Such a process may be compared with the
habit even of a man with great experience of the world, or,
again, with that of a man of *esprit* or wit, who, although he
has complete knowledge of the main stakes of life, of the
substantive interests that hold men together, of what moves
them, and of what is the power that they recognize, yet
neither has himself apprehended this content in the form of

general rules, nor is able to explain it to others in general reflections, but makes plain to himself and to others what occupies his consciousness always in particular cases, whether real or invented, in adequate instances, and the like. For in his ideas, everything shapes itself into concrete images, determinate in time and place, to which, therefore, names and other external circumstances of all kinds must not be wanting. Yet such a kind of imagination rather rests on the recollection of states that he has gone through, and of experiences that have befallen him, than is creative in its own strength. His recollection preserves and reproduces the individuality and external fashion of occurrences that had such and such results with all their external circumstances, and prevents the universal from emerging in its own shape. But the productive imagination of the *artist* is the imagination of a great mind and heart, the apprehension and creation of ideas and of shapes, and, indeed, the exhibition of the profoundest and most universal human interests in the definite sensuous mould of pictorial representation.

From this it follows at once, that in one aspect imagination unquestionably rests on natural gifts—speaking generally, on talent—because its mode of production requires a sensuous medium. It is true that we speak in the same way of scientific "talent," but the sciences only presuppose the universal capacity of thought, which has not, like imagination, a natural mode (as well as an intellectual one), but abstracts just precisely from all that is natural (or native) in an activity; and thus it would be more correct to say that there is no specifically scientific talent in the sense of a *mere* natural endowment. Now, imagination *has* in it a mode of instinct-like productiveness, inasmuch as the essential plasticity and sensuousness of the work of art must be subjectively present in the artist as natural disposition and natural impulse, and, considering that it is unconscious operation, must belong to the natural element in man, as well as to the rational. Of course, natural capacity leaves room for other elements in talent and genius, for artistic production is just as much of a spiritual and self-conscious nature; we can but say that its spirituality must, somehow, have an element of natural, plastic, and formative tendency. For this reason, though nearly everyone can reach a certain point in an art, yet, in order to go beyond this point, with which the art in the strict sense begins, it is impossible to dispense with native artistic talent of the highest order.

Considered as a natural endowment, moreover, such talent reveals itself for the most part in early youth, and is manifested in the impelling restlessness that busies itself, with vivacity and industry, in creating shapes in some particular sensuous medium and in seizing on this species of utterance and communication as the only one, or as the chief and the most suitable one. And thus, too, a precocious technical facility, that up to a certain grade of attainment is without effort, is a sign of natural talent. A sculptor finds everything transmute itself into shapes, and he soon begins to take up the clay and model it. And, speaking generally, whatever men of such talents have in their imagination, whatever rouses and moves their inner nature, turns at once into shape, drawing, melody, or poem.

Thirdly, and to conclude: the *content* of art is also in some respects borrowed from the sensuous, from nature; or, in any case, even if the content is of a spiritual kind, it can only be seized and fixed by representing the spiritual fact, such as human relations, in the shape of phenomena with external reality.

3. The question then arises, what the interest or the *end* is which man proposes to himself when he reproduces such a content in the form of works of art. This was the third point of view which we set before us with reference to the work of art, and the closer discussion of which will finally make the transition to the actual and true conception of art.

If in this aspect we glance at the common consciousness, a current idea which may occur to us is:

(*a*) The principle of the *imitation of nature*. According to this view the essential purpose of art consists in imitation, in the sense of a facility in copying natural forms as they exist in a way that corresponds precisely to them; and the success of such a representation, exactly corresponding to nature, is supposed to be what affords complete satisfaction.

This definition contains, prima facie, nothing beyond the purely formal aim that whatever already exists in the external world, just *as* it is therein, is now to be made a second time by man as a copy of the former, as well as he can do it with the means at his command. But we may at once regard this repetition as a *superfluous* labour, seeing that the things which pictures, theatrical representations, etc., imitate and represent—animals, natural scenes, incidents in human life —are before us in other cases already, in our own gardens or our own houses, or in cases within our closer or more remote circle of acquaintance. And, looking more closely, we may regard this superfluous labour as a presumptuous sport which comes far short of nature. For art is restricted in its means of representation; and can produce only *one-sided* deceptions— for instance, a semblance of reality addressed to one sense only; and, in fact, it invariably gives rise, if it rests in the formal purpose of *mere imitation*, to a mere parody of life instead of a genuine vitality. Just so the Turks, being Moham-medans, tolerate, as is well known, no pictures copied from men or the like; and when James Bruce, on his journey to Abyssinia, showed paintings of fish to a Turk, the man was amazed at first, but soon enough made answer: "If this fish shall rise up against you on the last day, and say, 'You have created for me a body, but no living soul,' how will you defend yourself against such an accusation?" The prophet, moreover, it is recorded in the Sunna, said to the two wom-en, Ommi Habiba and Ommi Selma, who told him of pictures in Ethiopian churches, "These pictures will accuse their au-thors on the day of judgment!"

There are, no doubt, as well, examples of completely de-ceptive imitation. Zeuxis' painted grapes have from antiquity downward been taken to be the triumph of this principle of the imitation of nature, because the story is that living doves pecked at them. We might add to this ancient example the modern one of Büttner's monkey, which bit in pieces a painted cockchafer in Rösel's "Diversions of the Insect World" and was pardoned by his master, in spite of his having thereby spoilt a beautiful copy of this valuable work, because of this proof of the excellence of the pictures. But when we reflect on these and similar instances, it must at once occur to us that, in place of commending works of art because they have *actually* deceived *even* pigeons and monkeys, we ought simply to censure the people who mean to exalt a work of art by predicating, as its highest and ultimate quality, so poor an effect as this. In general, we may sum up by saying that, as a matter of mere imitation, art cannot maintain a rivalry with nature, and, if it tries, must look like a worm trying to crawl after an elephant.

Considering the unvarying failure—comparative failure, at least—of imitation when contrasted with the original in nature, there remains as end nothing beyond our pleasure in the sleight of hand which can produce something so like nature. And it is doubtless open to man to be pleased at producing over again what is already present in its own right, by his labour, skill, and industry. But enjoyment and admiration, even of this kind, naturally grow frigid or chilled precisely in proportion to the resemblance of the copy to the natural type, or are even converted into tedium and repugnance. There are portraits which, as has been wittily said, are sickeningly like; and Kant adduces another instance relative to this pleasure in imitation as such, viz. that we soon grow tired of a man—and there are such men—who is able to mimic the nightingale's strain quite perfectly; and as soon as it is discovered that a man is producing the notes, we are at once weary of the song. We then recognize in it nothing but a conjuring trick, neither the free production of nature nor a work of art; for we expect from the free productive capacity of human beings something quite other than such music as this, which only interests us when, as is the case with the nightingale's note, it gushes forth from the creature's own vitality without special purpose, and yet recalls the utterance of human feeling. In general, such delight at our skill in mimicking can be but limited, and it becomes man better to take delight in what he produces out of himself. In this sense the invention of any unimportant and technical product has the higher value, and man may be prouder of having invented the hammer, the nail, and so forth, than of achieving feats of mimicry. For this fervour of abstract copying is to be compared to the feat of the man who had taught himself to throw lentils through a small opening without missing. He displayed this skill of his before Alexander, and Alexander presented him with a bushel of lentils as a reward for his frivolous and meaningless art.

Moreover, seeing that the principle of imitation is purely formal, to make it the end has the result that *objective beauty* itself disappears. For the question is in that case no longer *of what nature* that is which is to be copied, but only whether it is *correctly* copied. The object and content of the beautiful comes then to be regarded as a matter of entire indifference. That is to say, if we go outside the principle and speak of a difference of beauty and ugliness in considering beasts, men, landscapes, actions, or characters, this must nevertheless, in presence of the maxim in question, be set down as a distinction that does not belong particularly to art, for which nothing is left but abstract imitation. In this case the above-mentioned lack of criterion in dealing with the endless forms of nature reduces us, as regards the selection of objects and their distinction in beauty and ugliness, to subjective *taste* as an ultimate fact, which accepts no rule and admits of no discussion. And, in fact, if in selecting objects for representation we start from what *men* think beautiful or ugly, and therefore deserving artistic imitation—that is, from their taste—then all circles of natural objects open to us, and not one of them will be likely to fail of a patron.

Among men, for instance, it is the case that at any rate every bridegroom thinks his bride beautiful, and indeed, perhaps, he alone; though not, it may be, every husband his

wife; and that subjective taste for such beauty has no fixed
rule one may hold to be the good fortune of both parties. If
we, moreover, look quite beyond individuals and their accidental taste, to the taste of nations, this again is full of extreme diversity and contrast. How often we hear it said that a
European beauty would not please a Chinese or even a Hot-
tentot, insofar as the Chinaman has quite a different conception of beauty from the Negro, and the Negro in turn from
the European, and so forth. Indeed, if we look at the works
of art of those extra-European peoples—their images of the
gods, for instance—which their fancy has originated as vener-
able and sublime, they may appear to us as the most grue-
some idols, and their music may sound to our ears as the
most horrible noise; while they, on their side, will regard our
sculptures, paintings, and musical productions as trivial or
ugly.

But even if we abstract from an objective principle of art,
and if beauty is to be based on subjective and individual
taste, we shall still soon find on the side of art itself that the
imitation of nature, which certainly appeared to be a universal principle and one guaranteed by high authority, is at any
rate not to be accepted in this universal and merely abstract
form. For if we look at the different arts it will at once be
admitted that even if painting and sculpture represent objects
which appear like those of nature, or the type of which is
essentially borrowed from nature, yet works of architecture
on the other hand—and architecture belongs to the fine arts—
and the productions of poetry, in as far as they do not confine themselves to mere description, are by no means to be
called imitations of nature. At least, if we desired to maintain
the principle as valid in the case of these latter arts, we
should have to make a long circuit by conditioning the proposition in various ways, and reducing the so-called truth at
any rate to probability. But if we admitted probability we
should again be met by a great difficulty in determining what
is probable and what is not; and still, moreover, one would

neither consent nor find it possible to exclude from poetry all wholly arbitrary and completely original imaginations.

The end of art must, therefore, lie in something different from the purely formal imitation of what we find given, which in any case can bring to the birth only *tricks* and not *works* of art. It is, indeed, an element essential to the work of art to have natural shapes for its foundation, seeing that its representation is in the medium of external and therefore of natural phenomena. In painting, for instance, it is an important study to know how to copy with precision the colours in their relations to one another, the effects of light, reflections, etc., and, no less, the forms and figures of objects down to their subtlest characteristics. It is in this respect chiefly that the principle of naturalism in general and of copying nature has recovered its influence in modern times. Its aim is to recall an art which has grown feeble and indistinct to the vigour and crispness of nature, or, again, to invoke against the purely arbitrary and artificial conventionalism, as unnatural as it was inartistic, into which art had strayed, the uniform, direct, and solidly coherent sequences of nature. But however true it is that there is something right in this endeavour from one point of view, yet still the naturalism at which it aims is not as such the substantive and primary concern that underlies fine art. And, therefore, although external appearance in the shape of natural reality constitutes an essential condition of art, yet, nevertheless, neither is the given natural world its *rule*, nor is the mere imitation of external appearances *as* external its *end*.

(*b*) The further question then arises, What *is* the true content of art, and with what aim is this content to be presented? On this subject our consciousness supplies us with the common opinion that it is the task and aim of art to bring in contact with our sense, our feeling, our inspiration, *all* that finds a place in the mind of man. Art, it is thought, should realize in us that familiar saying, *Homo sum: humani nihil a me alienum puto*. Its aim is therefore placed in arousing and animating the slumbering emotions, inclinations, and passions;

in filling the *heart,* in forcing the human being, whether cultured or uncultured, to feel the whole range of what man's soul in its inmost and secret corners has power to experience and to create, and all that is able to move and to stir the human breast in its depths and in its manifold aspects and possibilities; to present as a delight to emotion and to perception all that the mind possesses of real and lofty in its thought and in the Idea—all the splendour of the noble, the eternal, and the true; and no less to make intelligible misfortune and misery, wickedness and crime; to make men realize the inmost nature of all that is shocking and horrible, as also of all pleasure and delight; and, finally, to set imagination roving in idle toyings of fancy, and luxuriating in the seductive spells of sense-stimulating visions. This endlessly varied content, it is held, art is bound to embrace, partly in order to complete the natural experience in which our external existence consists, and partly with the general aim of provoking the passions of our nature, both in order that the experiences of life may not leave us unmoved and because we desire to attain to a receptivity that welcomes all phenomena.

Now, such a stimulus is not given in this sphere by actual experience itself, but can only come by the semblance thereof, by art, that is, deceptively substituting its creations for reality. The possibility of this deception by means of artistic semblance rests on the fact that all reality must, for man, traverse the medium of perception and ideas and cannot otherwise penetrate the feelings and the will. In this process it is quite irrelevant whether his attention is claimed by immediate external reality, or whether this effect is produced by another means—that is, by images, symbols, and ideas, containing or representing *the content* of reality. Man can frame to himself ideas of things that are not actual as though they were actual. Hence it is all the same to our feelings whether external reality or only the semblance of it is the means of bringing in contact with us a situation, a relation, or the import of a life. Either mode suffices to awaken our response to its burden, in grief and in rejoicing, in pathos and in horror, and in traversing the emotions and the passions of wrath, hatred, compassion, of anxiety, fear, love, reverence, and admiration, or of the desire of honour and of fame.

This awakening of all feelings in us, the dragging of the heart through the whole significance of life, the realization of all such inner movements by means of a presented exterior consisting merely in deception—all this was what, from the point of view which we have been considering, constituted the peculiar and pre-eminent power of art.

Now, as this mode of treatment credits art with the vocation of impressing on the heart and on the imagination good and bad alike, and of strengthening man to the noblest, as of enervating him to the most sensuous and selfish emotions, it follows that the task set before art is still purely formal, and so it would have no certain purpose, but would merely furnish the empty form for every possible kind of significance and content.

(c) It is a fact that art does include this formal side, in that it has power to present every possible subject matter in artistic dress before perception and feeling, just exactly as argumentative reflection has the power of manipulating all possible objects and modes of action, and of furnishing them with reasons and justifications. But when we admit so great a variety of content we are at once met by the remark that the manifold feelings and ideas, which art aims at provoking or reinforcing, intersect and contradict, and by mutual interference cancel one another. Indeed, in this aspect, in so far as art inspires men to directly opposite emotions, it only magnifies the contradiction of our feelings and passions, and either sets them staggering like Bacchantes, or passes into sophistry and scepticism, in the same way as argumentation. This diversity of the material of art itself compels us, therefore, not to be content with so formal an aim for it, seeing that rationality forces its way into this wild diversity and demands to see the emergence of a higher and more universal purpose from these elements in spite of their self-contradiction, and to be assured of its being attained. Just in the same way the state

and the social life of men are, of course, credited with the
purpose that in them *all* human capacities and *all* individual
powers are to be developed and to find utterance in *all* directions and with *all* tendencies. But in opposition to so formal
a view there at once arises the question in what *unity* these
manifold formations must be comprehended, and what *single
end* they must have for their fundamental idea and ultimate
purpose.

As such an end, reflection soon suggests the notion that art
has the capacity and the function of mitigating the fierceness
of the desires.

In respect to this first idea, we have only to ascertain in
what feature peculiar to art it is that the capacity lies of
eliminating brutality and taming and educating the impulses,
desires, and passions. Brutality in general has its reason in a
direct selfishness of the impulses, which go to work right
away, and exclusively for the satisfaction of their concupis-
cence. Now, desire is most savage and imperious in proportion as, being isolated and narrow, it occupies the *whole man*,
so that he does not retain the power of separating himself as
a universal being from this determinateness and of becoming
aware of himself as universal. Even if the man in such a case
says, "The passion is stronger than I," it is true that the
abstract I is then separated for consciousness from the particular passion; but still only in a formal way, inasmuch as this
separation is only made in order to pronounce that, against
the power of the passion, the I as such is of no account
whatever. The savageness of passion consists, therefore, in the
oneness of the I as universal with the limited content of its
desires, so that the man has no will outside this particular
passion.

Now, such brutality and untamed violence of passion is
softened through art, to begin with, by the mere fact that it
brings before the man as an idea what in such a state he feels
and does. And even if art restricts itself to merely setting up
pictures of the passions before the mind's eye, or even if it were
actually to flatter them, still this is by itself enough to have a

softening power, inasmuch as the man is thereby at least
made aware of what, apart from such presentation, he simply
is. For then the man observes his impulses and inclinations,
and whereas before they bore him on without power of reflection, he now sees them outside himself, and begins already to be free from them, in so far as they form an object
which he contrasts with himself. Hence it may frequently be
the case with the artist that when attacked by grief he softens
and weakens the intensity of his own feelings in its effect on
his own mind by representing it in art. Tears, even, are
enough to bring comfort; the man who to begin with is utterly sunk and concentrated in grief is able thus, at any rate, to
utter his inner state in a direct fashion. Still more of a relief,
however, is the utterance of what is within in words, images,
pictures, sounds, and shapes. For this reason it was a good
old custom at deaths and funerals to appoint wailing women,
in order to bring the grief before the mind in its utterance.
Manifestations of sympathy, too, hold up the content of a
man's misfortune to his view; when it is much talked about
he is forced to reflect upon it and is thereby relieved. And so
it has always been held that to weep or to speak one's fill is a
means to obtain freedom from the oppressive weight of care,
or at least to find momentary relief for the heart. Hence the
mitigation of the violence of passion has for its universal
reason that man is released from his immediate sunkenness in
a feeling, and becomes conscious of it as of something external to him, towards which he must now enter into an *ideal*
relation.

Art, by means of its representations, while remaining within the sensuous sphere, delivers man at the same time from
the power of sensuousness. Of course we may often hear
those favourite phrases about man's duty being to remain in
immediate oneness with nature, but such oneness in its abstraction is simply and solely coarseness and savagery; and
art, in the very process of dissolving this oneness for man, is
raising him with gentle hand above and away from mere sunkenness in nature. Man's mode of occupying himself with

works of art is always purely contemplative, and educates thereby, in the first place, no doubt, merely attention to the representations themselves, but then, going beyond this, it cultivates attention to their significance, the power of comparison with other contents, and receptivity for the general consideration of them, and for the points of view which it involves.

To the above there attaches itself in natural connection the second characteristic which has been ascribed to art as its essential purpose, viz. the *purification* of the passions, instruction, and *moral* perfecting. For the characteristic that art was to bridle savageness and educate the passions remained quite abstract and general, so that a question must again arise about a *determinate* kind and an essential *end* of this education.

The doctrine of the purification of passion suffers indeed under the same defect as the above doctrine of the mitigation of the desires; yet, when more closely looked at, it at any rate arrives at the point of accentuating the fact that the representations of art may be held to lack a standard by which their worth or unworthiness could be measured. This standard simply means their effectiveness in separating pure from impure in the passions. It therefore requires a content that has capacity to exercise this purifying power, and, in as far as the production of such an effect is taken to constitute the substantive end of art, it must follow that the purifying content must be brought before consciousness in its *universality* and *essentiality*.

In this latter aspect the end of art has been pronounced to be that it should *teach*. Thus, on the one side, the peculiar character of art would consist in the movement of the emotions and in the satisfaction which lies in this movement, even in fear, compassion, in painful pathos and shock—that is to say, in the satisfying engagement of the emotions and passions, and to that extent in a satisfaction, entertainment, and delight in the objects of art, in their representation and effect. But, on the other side, this purpose (of art) is held to find its higher standard only in its instructiveness, in the *fabula docet*,[5] and thus in the useful influence which the work of art succeeds in exerting on the subject. In this respect the Horatian adage, *Et prodesse volunt et delectare poetae* ("Poets aim at utility and entertainment alike"), contains, concentrated in a few words, all that has subsequently been elaborated in infinite degrees and diluted into the uttermost extreme of insipidity as a doctrine of art. As regards such instruction we have, then, to ask whether it is meant to be directly or indirectly, explicitly or implicitly contained in the work of art.

If, speaking generally, we are concerned about a purpose which is universal and not contingent, it follows that this purpose, considering the essentially spiritual nature of art, cannot but be itself spiritual, and indeed, moreover, one which is not contingent, but actual in its nature and for its own sake. Such a purpose in relation to teaching could only consist in bringing before consciousness, by help of the work of art, a really and explicitly significant spiritual content. From this point of view it is to be asserted that the higher art ranks itself, the more it is bound to admit into itself such a content as this, and that only in the essence of such a content can it find the standard which determines whether what is expressed is appropriate or inappropriate. Art has been, in fact, the first *instructress* of peoples.

But the purpose of instruction may be treated as *purpose*, to such a degree that the universal nature of the represented content is doomed to be exhibited and expounded directly and obviously as abstract proposition, prosaic reflection, or general theorem, and not merely in an indirect way in the concrete form of a work of *art*, becomes a mere otiose accessory, a husk which is expressly pronounced to be mere husk, a semblance expressly pronounced to be mere semblance. But thereby the very nature of the work of art is distorted. For the work of art ought to bring a content before the mind's

5. The moral.

eye, not in its generality as such, but with this generality
made absolutely individual and sensuously particularized. If
the work of art does not proceed from this principle but sets
in relief its generalized aspect with the purpose of abstract
instruction, then the imaginative and sensuous aspect is only
an external and superfluous adornment, and the work of art
is a thing divided against itself, in which form and content no
longer appear as grown into one. In that case the sensuously
individual and the spiritually general are become external to
one another.

And further, if the purpose of art is limited to this *didactic*
utility, then its other aspect—that of pleasure, entertainment,
and delight—is pronounced to be in itself *unessential*, and
ought to have its substance merely in the utility of the teaching on which it is attendant. But this amounts to pronoun-
cing that art does not bear its vocation and purpose in itself
and that its conception is rooted in something else, to which
it is a *means*. Art is, in this case, only one among the several
means which prove useful and are applied for the purpose of
instruction. This brings us to the boundary at which art is
made no longer to be an end on its own merits, seeing that it
is degraded into a mere toy of entertainment or a mere means
of instruction.

This boundary becomes most sharply marked when a question is raised, in its turn, about a supreme end and aim for
the sake of which the passions are to be purified and men are
to be instructed. This aim has often, in modern times, been
declared to be *moral* improvement, and the aim of art has
been placed in the function of preparing the inclinations and
impulses for moral perfection, and of leading them to this
goal. This idea combines purification with instruction, inasmuch as art is, by communicating an insight into genuine
moral goodness—that is, by instruction—at the same time to
incite to purification, and in this way alone to bring about
the improvement of mankind as its useful purpose and supreme goal.

Regarding art in reference to moral improvement, the same has prima facie to be said as about the didactic purpose. We may readily grant that art must not as a principle take for its aim the immoral and its furtherance. But it is one thing to take immorality for the express aim of representation, and another to abstain from taking morality. Every genuine work of art may have a good moral drawn from it, but, of course, in doing so much depends on interpretation and on him who draws the moral. Thus one may hear the most immoral representations defended by saying that we must know evil, or sin, in order to act morally; and, conversely, it has been said that the portrayal of Mary Magdalene, the beautiful sinner who afterwards repented, has seduced many into sin, because art makes it look so beautiful to repent, and you must sin before you can repent.

But the doctrine of moral improvement, if consistently carried out, goes in general yet further. It would not be satisfied with the possibility of extracting a moral from a work of art by interpretation, but it would, on the contrary, display the moral instruction as the substantive purpose of the work of art, and, indeed, would actually admit to portrayal none but moral subjects, moral characters, actions, and incidents. For art has the choice among its subjects, in contradistinction to history or the sciences which have their subject matter fixed for them.

In order that we may be able to form a thoroughly adequate estimate of the idea that the aim of art is moral from this point of view, we must inquire first of all for the definite standpoint of the morality on which this doctrine is based. If we look closely at the standpoint of morality as we have to understand it in the best sense at the present day, we soon find that its conception does not immediately coincide with what apart from it we are in the habit of calling in a general way virtue, respectability, uprightness, etc. To be respectable and virtuous is not enough to make a man moral. Morality involves *reflection* and the definite consciousness of that which duty prescribes, and acting out of such a prior con-

sciousness. Duty itself is the law of the will, which man nevertheless lays down freely out of his own self and then is
supposed to determine himself to this duty for duty's and its
fulfilment's sake, by doing good solely from the conviction
which he has attained that it is the good.

Now this law, the duty which is chosen for duty's sake to
be the guide of action, out of free conviction and the inner
conscience, and is then acted upon, is, taken by itself, the
abstract universal of the will, and is the direct antithesis of
nature, the sensuous impulses, the self-seeking interests, the
passions, and of all that is comprehensively entitled the feelings and the heart. In this antagonism the one side is regarded
as *negativing* the other; and, seeing that both are present as
antagonists within the subject (person), he has, as determining himself out of himself, the choice of following the one or
the other. But, according to the view under discussion, a
moral aspect is acquired by such a decision, and by the act
performed in accordance with it, only through the free conviction of duty on the one hand, and, on the other hand,
through the conquest, not only of the particular or separate
will, of the natural motives, inclinations, passions, etc., but
also through that of the nobler emotions and the higher impulses. For the modern moralistic view starts from the fixed
antithesis of the will in its spiritual universality to its sensuous natural particularity, and consists not in the completed
reconciliation of these contrasted sides, but in their conflict
with one another, which involves the requirement that the
impulses which conflict with duty ought to yield to it.

This antithesis does not merely display itself for our consciousness, in the limited region of moral action; but also
emerges as a fundamental distinction and antagonism between that which is real essentially and in its own right,[6] and
that which is external reality and existence. Formulated in
the abstract, it is the contrast of the universal and particular,
when the former is explicitly fixed over against the latter,

---

6. *"An und für sich."*

just as the latter is over against the former. More concretely, it appears in nature as the opposition of the abstract law against the abundance of individual phenomena, each having its own character. Or it appears in the mind, as the sensuous and spiritual in man, as the battle of the spirit against the flesh, of duty for duty's sake, the cold command, with the individual interest, the warm feelings, the sensuous inclinations and impulses, the individual disposition as such; as the hard conflict of inward freedom and of natural necessity. Further, as the contradiction of the dead conception—empty in itself—compared with full concrete vitality, or of theory and subjective thought contrasted with objective existence and experience.

These are antitheses which have not been invented, either by the subtlety of reflection or by the pedantry of philosophy, but which have from all time and in manifold forms preoccupied and disquieted the human consciousness, although it was modern culture that elaborated them most distinctly and forced them up to the point of most unbending contradiction. Intellectual culture and the modern play of understanding create in man this contrast, which makes him an amphibious animal, inasmuch as it sets him to live in two contradictory worlds at once; so that even consciousness wanders back and forward in this contradiction, and, shuttlecocked from side to side, is unable to satisfy itself *as* itself on the one side as on the other. For, on the one side, we see man a prisoner in common reality and earthly temporality, oppressed by want and poverty, hard driven by nature, entangled in matter, in sensuous aims and their enjoyments. On the other side, he exalts himself to eternal ideas, to a realm of thought and freedom, imposes on himself as a *will* universal laws and attributions, strips the world of its living and flourishing reality and dissolves it into abstractions, inasmuch as the mind is put upon vindicating its rights and its dignity simply by denying the rights of nature and maltreating it, thereby retaliating the oppression and violence which itself has experienced from nature.

Such a discrepancy in life and consciousness involves for modern culture and its understanding the demand that the contradiction should be resolved. Yet the understanding cannot release itself from the fixity of these antitheses. The solution, therefore, remains for consciousness a mere *ought,* and the present and reality only stir themselves in the unrest of a perpetual to and fro, which seeks a reconciliation without finding it. Then the question arises of whether such a many-sided and fundamental opposition, which never gets beyond a mere ought and a postulated solution, can be the genuine and complete truth, and, in general, the supreme purpose. If the culture of the world has fallen into such a contradiction, it becomes the task of philosophy to undo or cancel it, i.e. to show that neither the one alternative in its abstraction nor the other in similar one-sidedness possesses truth, but that they are essentially self-dissolving; that truth only lies in the conciliation and mediation of the two, and that this mediation is no mere postulate, but is in its nature and in reality accomplished and always self-accomplishing.

This intuition agrees directly with the natural faith and will, which always has present to the mind's eye precisely this resolved antithesis, and in action makes it its purpose and achieves it. All that philosophy does is to furnish a reflective insight into the essence of the antithesis in as far as it shows that what constitutes truth is merely the resolution of this antithesis, and that not in the sense that the conflict and its aspects in any way *are not,* but in the sense that they *are, in reconciliation.*

(*d*) Now, as an ultimate aim implied a higher standpoint in the case of moral improvement, we shall have to vindicate this higher standpoint for art no less than for morals. Thereby we at once lay aside the false position, which has already been remarked upon, that art has to serve as a means for moral ends, and to conduce to the moral end of the world, as such, by instruction and moral improvement, and thereby has its substantive aim, not in itself, but in something else. If, therefore, we now continue to speak of an aim or purpose, we must, in the first instance, get rid of the perverse idea, which, in asking, "What is the aim?" retains the accessory meaning of the question, "What is the *use*?" The perverseness of this lies in the point that the work of art would then be regarded as aspiring to something else which is set before consciousness as the essential and as what ought to be; so that then the work of art would only have value as a useful instrument in the realization of an end having substantive importance *outside* the sphere of art. Against this it is necessary to maintain that art has the vocation of revealing *the truth* in the form of sensuous artistic shape, of representing the reconciled antithesis just described, and, therefore, has its purpose in itself, in this representation and revelation. For other objects, such as instruction, purification, improvement, pecuniary gain, endeavour after fame and honour, have nothing to do with the work of art as such and do not determine its conception.

It is from this point of view, into which *reflective* consideration of the matter resolves itself, that we have to apprehend the idea of art in its inner necessity, as indeed it was from this point of view, historically speaking, that the true appreciation and understanding of art took its origin. For that antithesis, of which we spoke, made itself felt not only within general reflective culture but no less in philosophy as such, and it was not till philosophy discovered how to overcome this antithesis absolutely that it grasped its own conception and, just in as far as it did so, the conception of nature and of art.

Hence this point of view, as it is the reawakening of philosophy in general, so also is the reawakening of the science of art; and, indeed, it is this reawakening to which alone Aesthetics as a science owes its true origin, and art its higher estimation.

IV

I shall touch briefly upon the historical side of the transition above alluded to, partly for its historical interest, partly because, in doing so, we shall more closely indicate the critical points which are important, and on the foundation of which we mean to continue our structure. In its most general formulation, this basis consists in recognizing artistic beauty as one of the means which resolve and reduce to unity the above antithesis and contradiction between the abstract self-concentrated mind and actual nature, whether that of external phenomena or of the inner subjective feelings and emotions.

1. The Kantian philosophy led the way by not merely feeling the lack of this point of union but attaining definite knowledge of it and bringing it within the range of our ideas. In general, Kant treated as his foundation, for the intelligence as for the will, the self-related rationality or freedom, the self-consciousness that finds and knows itself in itself as infinite. This knowledge of the absoluteness of reason in itself which has brought philosophy to its turning point in modern times, this absolute beginning, deserves recognition even if we pronounce Kant's philosophy inadequate, and is an element in it which cannot be refuted. But, in as far as Kant fell back again into the fixed antithesis of subjective thought and objective things, of the abstract universality and the sensuous individuality of the will, it was he more especially who strained to the highest possible pitch the above-mentioned contradiction called morality, seeing that he moreover exalted the practical side of the mind above the theoretical.

In presence of this fixed antithesis, with its fixity acknowledged by the understanding, he had no course open but to propound the unity merely in the form of subjective ideas of the reason to which no adequate reality could be shown to correspond, or again, to treat it as consisting in postulates which might indeed be deduced from the practical reason, but whose essential nature was not for him knowable by thought, and whose practical accomplishment remained a mere ought deferred to infinity. Thus, then, Kant no doubt brought the reconciled contradiction within the range of our ideas, but he succeeded neither in scientifically unfolding its genuine essence nor in presenting it as the true and sole reality. Kant indeed pressed on still further, inasmuch as he recognized the required unity in what he called the *intuitive understanding*; but here, again, he comes to a standstill in the contradiction of subjectivity and objectivity, so that although he suggests in the abstract a solution of the contradiction of concept and reality, universality and particularity, understanding and sense, and thereby points to the Idea, yet, on the other hand, he makes this solution and reconciliation itself a purely *subjective* one, not one which is true and actual in its nature and on its own merits. In this respect his *Critique of Judgment*, in which he treats of the aesthetic and teleological powers of judgment, is instructive and remarkable. The beautiful objects of nature and art, the rightly adapted products of nature, by connecting which Kant is led to a closer treatment of organic and animated beings, are regarded by him only from the point of view of the reflection which subjectively judges of them. Indeed Kant defines the power of judgment generally as "the power of thinking the particular as contained under the universal"; and he calls the power of judgment *reflective* "when it has only the particular given to it, and has to find the universal under which it comes."

To this end it requires a law, a principle, which it has to impose upon itself; and Kant suggests as this law that of *teleology*. In the idea of freedom that belongs to the practical reason, the accomplishment of the end is left as a mere "ought," but in the teleological judgment dealing with animated beings, Kant hits on the notion of regarding the living organism in the light that in it the concept, the universal, contains the particulars as well. Thus in its capacity as end, it determines the particular and external, the structure of the limbs, not from without, but from within, and in the sense that the particular conforms to the end *spontaneously*. Yet even in such a judgment, again, we are supposed not to know the objective nature of the thing, but only to be enunciating a subjective mode of reflection. Similarly, Kant understands the *aesthetic* judgment as neither proceeding from the understanding as such qua the faculty of ideas, nor from sensuous perception as such with its manifold variety, but from the free play of the understanding and of the imagination. It is in this free agreement of the faculties of knowledge that the thing is related to the subject or person and to his feeling of pleasure and satisfaction.

Now this satisfaction is, in the first place, to be devoid of any interest, i.e. *devoid of relation to our appetitive faculty*. If we have an interest, by way of curiosity for instance, or a sensuous interest on behalf of our sensuous need, a desire of possession and use, then the objects are not important to us for their own sake but for the sake of our need. In that case, what exists has a value only with reference to such a need, and the relation is of such a kind that the object is on the one side, and on the other stands an attribution which is distinct from the object, but to which we relate it. If, for instance, I consume the object in order to nourish myself by it, this interest lies only in me, and remains foreign to the object itself. Now, what Kant asserts is that the relation to the beautiful is not of this kind. The aesthetic judgment allows the external existence to subsist free and independent, giving licence to the object to have its end in itself. This is, as we saw above, an important consideration.

The beautiful, in *the second place*, says Kant, is definable as that which, without a conception, i.e. without a category of the understanding, is perceived as the object of a *universal* delight. To estimate the beautiful requires a cultivated mind; the natural man has no judgment about the beautiful, seeing that this judgment claims universal validity. The universal is, indeed to begin with, *as such* an abstraction; but that which in itself and on its own merits is true bears in itself the attribution and the claim to be valid even universally. In this sense the beautiful, too, ought to be *universally* recognized, although the mere conceptions of the understanding are competent to no judgment thereupon. The good, that which, for instance, is right in particular actions, is subsumed under universal conceptions, and the act is accepted as good when it succeeds in corresponding to these conceptions. Beauty, on the other hand, according to the theory, should awaken a universal delight directly, without any such relation. This amounts to nothing else than that, in contemplating beauty, we are not conscious of the conception and of the subsumption under it and do not permit to take place the severance of the individual object and of the universal conception which in all other cases is present in the judgment.

In the *third* place, the beautiful (Kant says) has the form of teleology, in as far as a teleological character is perceived in the object without the idea of an end. At bottom this only repeats the view which we have just discussed. Any natural product, i.e. a plant or an animal, is organized teleologically, and is so immediately a datum to us in this teleology that we have no separate abstract idea of the end, distinct from its given reality. It is in this way that even *the beautiful* is to be displayed to us as teleological. In finite teleology end and means remain external to one another, inasmuch as the end stands in no essential inner relation to the material medium of its accomplishment. In this case, the idea of the end in its abstraction distinguishes itself from the object in which the end appears as realized. The beautiful, on the other hand, exists as teleological in itself, without means and end revealing themselves in it as distinct aspects. For instance, the purpose of the limbs of an organism is the vitality which exists as actual in the limbs themselves; separated they cease to be limbs. For in the living thing the end and the material medium of the end are so directly united that the existing being only exists so long as its purpose dwells in it. The beautiful, Kant maintains, when considered from this point of view, does not wear its teleology as an external form attached to it; but the teleological correspondence of the inner and outer is the immanent nature of the beautiful object.

Lastly, Kant's treatment determines the beautiful, in the *fourth* place, as being recognized, without a conception, as object of a *necessary* delight. Necessity is an abstract category and indicates an inner essential relation of two aspects; *if* the one is, and *because* the one is, *then (and therefore)* the other is. The one in its nature involves the other as well as itself, just as cause, for example, has no meaning without effect. The delight which the beautiful involves is such a necessary consequence, wholly without relation to conceptions, i.e. to categories of the understanding. Thus, for instance, we are pleased no doubt by what is symmetrical, and this is constructed in accordance with a conception of the understanding. But Kant requires, to give us pleasure, even more than the unity and equality that belong to such a conception of the understanding.

Now, what we find in all these Kantian laws is a nonseverance of that which in all other cases is presupposed in our consciousness to be distinct. In the beautiful this severance finds itself cancelled, inasmuch as universal and particular, end and means, conception and object thoroughly interpenetrate one another. And thus, again, Kant regards the beautiful in *art* as an agreement in which the particular itself *is* in accordance with the conception. Particulars, as such, are prima facie contingent, both as regards one another and as regards the universal, and this very contingent element, sense, feeling, temper, inclination, is now in the beauty of art not merely *subsumed* under universal categories of the understanding and *controlled* by the conception of feeling in its abstract universality, but so united with the universal that it reveals itself as inwardly and in its nature and realization adequate thereto. By this means the beauty of art becomes embodiment of a thought, and the material is not externally determined by this thought, but exists itself in its freedom. For in this case the natural, sensuous, the feelings, and so forth have *in themselves* proportion, purpose, and agreement; while perception and feeling are exalted into spiritual universality, and thought itself, not content with renouncing its hostility to nature, finds cheerfulness therein. Thus feeling, pleasure, and enjoyment are justified and sanctified, so that nature and freedom, sensuousness and the idea, find their warrant and their satisfaction all in *one*. Yet even this apparently complete reconciliation is ultimately inferred by Kant to be, nevertheless, merely subjective in respect of our appreciation as in respect of our production, and not to be the naturally and completely true and real.

These we may take as the main results of the Kantian criticism, so far as they have interest for us in our present inquiry. This criticism forms the starting point for the true conception of artistic beauty. Yet this conception had to overcome the Kantian defects before it could assert itself as the higher grasp of the true unity of necessity and freedom, of the particular and the universal, of the sensuous and the rational.

2. It must then be admitted that the artistic sense of a profound, and, at the same time, philosophic mind was ahead of philosophy as such, in demanding and enunciating the principle of totality and reconciliation as against that abstract endlessness of reflective thought, that duty for duty's sake, that intelligence devoid of plastic shape, which apprehend nature and reality, sensation and feeling as a mere *limit*, and as an absolutely hostile element. For Schiller must be credited with the great merit of having broken through the Kantian subjectivity and abstractness of thought and having dared the attempt to transcend these limits by intellectually grasping the principles of unity and reconciliation as the truth, and realizing them in art. Schiller, in his aesthetic discussions, did not simply adhere to art and its interest without concerning himself about its relation to philosophy proper, but compared his interest in artistic beauty with the principles of philosophy; and it was only by starting from the latter, and by their help, that he penetrated the profounder nature and notion of the beautiful. Thus we feel it to be a feature in one period of his works that he has busied himself with thought— more perhaps than was conducive to their unsophisticated beauty as works of art. The intentional character of abstract reflection and even the interest of the philosophical idea are noticeable in many of his poems. This has been made a ground of censure against him, especially by way of blaming

and depreciating him in comparison with Goethe's agreeable straightforwardness and objectivity. But in this respect Schiller, as poet, did but pay the debt of his time; and the reason lay in a perplexity which turned out only to the honour of that sublime soul and profound character, and to the profit of science and knowledge.

At the same epoch the same scientific stimulus withdrew Goethe, too, from poetry, his proper sphere. Yet just as Schiller immersed himself in the study of the inner depths of the *mind*, so Goethe's idiosyncrasy led him to the *physical* side of art, to external nature, to animal and vegetable organisms, to crystals, to cloud formation, and to colour. To such scientific research Goethe brought the power of his great mind, which in these regions put to rout the science of mere understanding with its errors, just as Schiller, on the other side, succeeded in asserting the idea of the free totality of beauty against the understanding's science of volition and thought. A whole set of Schiller's productions is devoted to this insight of his into the nature of art, especially the "Letters upon Aesthetic Education." In these letters the central point from which Schiller starts is that every individual human being has within him the capacity of an ideal humanity. This genuine human being, he says, is represented by the state, which he takes to be the objective, universal, or, so to speak, normal form in which the diversity of particular subjects or persons aims at aggregating and combining itself into a unity. There were, then, he considered, two imaginable ways in which the human being in time (in the actual course of events) might coincide with the human being in the Idea: on the one hand, by the state, qua genus or class idea of morality, law, and intelligence, incorporating individuality; on the other hand, by the individual raising himself to the level of his genus, i.e. by the human being that lives in time ennobling himself into the human being of the Idea. Now reason, he thinks, demands unity as such, the generic character, but nature demands diversity and individuality; and both these legislative authorities have simultaneous claims on man.

In presence of the conflict between these antagonistic elements, aesthetic education simply consists in realizing the requirement of mediation and reconciliation between them. For the aim of this education is, according to Schiller, to give such form to inclination, sensuousness, impulse, and heart that they may become rational in themselves, and by the same process reason, freedom, and spirituality may come forward out of their abstraction and, uniting with the natural element, now rationalized throughout, may in it be invested with flesh and blood. Beauty is thus pronounced to be the unification of the rational and the sensuous, and this unification to be the genuinely real.

This notion of Schiller's may be readily recognized in the general views of *Anmuth und Würde*,[7] and in his poems more particularly from the fact that he makes the praise of women his subject matter; because it was in their character that he recognized and held up to notice the spontaneously present combination of the spiritual and natural.

Now this *unity* of the universal and particular, of freedom and necessity, of the spiritual and the natural, which Schiller grasped from a scientific point of view as the principle and essence of art, and laboured indefatigably to evoke into actual existence by help of art and aesthetic culture, was considered, by a further advance, *as the Idea itself*, and was thus constituted the principle of knowledge and of existence, while the Idea in this sense was recognized as the sole truth and reality. By means of this recognition, science, in Schelling's philosophy, attained its absolute standpoint, and although art had previously begun to assert its peculiar nature and dignity in relation to the highest interests of humanity, yet it was now that the actual *notion* of art and its place in scientific theory were discovered. Art was now accepted, even if erroneously in one respect, which this is not the place to discuss, yet in its higher and genuine vocation. No doubt

---

7. *Ueber Anmuth und Würde*, "Of Grace and Dignity," a work of Schiller's that appeared in 1793.

before this time so early a writer as Winckelmann had been
inspired by his observation of the ideals of the ancients in a
way that led him to develop a new sense for the contemplation of art, to rescue it from the notions of commonplace
aims and of mere mimicry of nature, and to exert an immense influence in favour of searching out the Idea of art in
the works of art and in its history. For Winckelmann should
be regarded as one of the men who have succeeded in furnishing the mind with a new organ and new methods of study in
the field of art. On the theory, however, and the scientific
knowledge of art his view has had less influence.

3. To touch briefly on the further course of the subject,
A. W. and Friedrich von Schlegel, in proximity to the renaissance of philosophy, being covetous of novelty and with a
thirst for what was striking and extraordinary, appropriated
as much of the philosophical Idea as their natures, which
were anything but philosophical, and essentially of the critical stamp, were capable of absorbing. Neither of them can
claim the reputation of a speculative thinker. But it was they
who, armed with their critical understanding, set themselves
somewhere near the standpoint of the Idea, and with great
plainness of speech and audacity of innovation, though with
but a poor admixture of philosophy, directed a clever po-
lemic against the traditional views. And thus they undoubtedly introduced in several branches of art a new standard of
judgment in conformity with notions which were higher than
those that they attacked. As, however, their criticism was not
accompanied by the thorough philosophical comprehension
of their standard, this standard retained a character of indefiniteness and vacillation, with the result that they sometimes
did too much and sometimes too little. No doubt they are to
be credited with the merit of bringing afresh to light and
extolling in a loving spirit much that was held obsolete and
was inadequately esteemed by their age, e.g. the work of the
older painters of Italy and the Netherlands, the "Nibelungen
Lied," etc.; and, again, they endeavoured with zeal to learn
and to teach subjects that were little known, such as the

Indian poetry and mythology. Nevertheless, they attributed too high a value to the productions of such epochs, and sometimes themselves fell into the blunder of admiring what was but mediocre, e.g. Holberg's comedies, and attaching a universal importance to what had only relative value, or even boldly showing themselves enthusiasts for a perverse tendency and subordinate standpoint as if it were something supreme.

Out of this tendency, and especially out of the sentiments and doctrines of Friedrich von Schlegel, there further grew in all its manifold shapes the so-called *irony*. This idea had its deeper root, if we take it in one of its aspects, in Fichte's philosophy, in so far as the principles of his philosophy were applied to art. Friedrich von Schlegel, as also Schelling, started from Fichte's point of view; Schelling, to pass wholly beyond it, Friedrich von Schlegel to develop it in a peculiar fashion and to tear himself loose from it. As regards the intimate connection of Fichte's principles with one tendency (among others) of this irony, we need only lay stress on the following point: that Fichte establishes the I as the absolute principle of all knowledge, of all reason and cognition; and that in the sense of the I which is, and is no more than, utterly abstract and formal. For this reason, in the second place, this I is in itself absolutely simple, and, on the one hand, every characteristic, every attribute, every content is negated therein—for every positive matter is annihilated by absorption into this abstract freedom and unity; on the other side, every content which is to be of value for the I is given position and recognition only by favour of the I. Whatever is, is only by favour of the I, and what is by my favour I am in turn able to annihilate.

Now, if we abide by these utterly empty forms which have their origin in the absoluteness of the abstract I, then nothing has value in its real and actual nature, and regarded in itself, but only as produced by the subjectivity of the I. But if so, it follows that the I is able to remain lord and master of everything, and in no sphere of morality or legality, of things human or divine, profane or sacred, is there anything that would not have to begin by being given position by the I, and that might not, therefore, just as well be in turn annihilated thereby. This amounts to making all that is actual in its own right a mere *semblance* not true and real for its own sake and by its own means, but a mere appearance due to the I, within whose power and caprice it remains, and at its free disposal. To admit it or to annihilate it stands purely in the pleasure of the I which has attained absoluteness in itself and simply as I.

In the third place,[8] then, the I is a *living* active individual, and its life consists in bringing its individuality to its own consciousness as to that of others, in uttering itself and taking shape in phenomena. For every human being while he lives, seeks to realise himself, and does realise himself. With respect to beauty and art this receives the meaning of living as artist and forming one's life *artistically*. But, according to the principle before us, I live as artist when all my action and utterance in general, whenever it has to do with any content, is for me on the level of mere *semblance*, and assumes a shape which is wholly in my power. So I am not really in *earnest*, either about this content, or generally, about its utterance and realisation. For genuine earnest comes into being only by means of a substantial interest, a matter that has something in it, truth, morality, and so forth; by means of a content which, as such (without my help), is enough to have value for me as something essential, so that I myself only become essential in my own eyes in as far as I have immersed myself in such a matter and have come to be in conformity with it in my whole knowledge and action. At the standpoint according to which the artist is the I that binds and looses of its own power, for whom no content of consciousness counts as absolute and as essentially real, but only as itself an artificial and dissoluble semblance, such earnestness can never come into being, as nothing has validity ascribed to it but the formalism of the I.

8. The three points are (1) The I is abstract. (2) Everything is a semblance for it. (3) Its own acts, even, are a semblance.

By others, indeed, my self-display in which I present myself to them may be taken seriously, inasmuch as they interpret me as though I were really concerned about the matter
in hand; but therein they are simply deceived, poor *borné*
creatures, without talent and capacity to apprehend and to
attain my standpoint. And this shows me that not everyone is
so free (*formally* free, that is) as to see in all that usually has
value, dignity, and sanctity for mankind simply a product of
his own power of caprice, whereby he is able to set his seal
on the value of such matters and to determine himself and
obtain a content by their means, or not. And then this skill in
living an ironical artist life apprehends itself as a *godlike geniality*, for which every possible thing is a mere dead creature,
to which the free creator, knowing himself to be wholly unat-
tached, feels in no way bound, seeing that he can annihilate
as well as create it. He who has attained such a standpoint of
godlike geniality looks down in superiority on all mankind
besides, for they are pronounced *borné* and dull in as far as
law, morality, and so forth retain for them their fixed, obligatory, and essential validity. And the individual who thus lives
his artist life assigns himself indeed relation to others, lives
with friends, mistresses, etc., but as genius he sets no value on
this relation to his determinate reality and particular actions,
or to what is universal in its own right; that is, he assumes an
ironical attitude towards it.

This is the universal import of the genial godlike irony, as
that concentration of the I into itself for which all bonds are
broken, and which will only endure to live in the bliss of
self-enjoyment. This irony was the invention of Friedrich von
Schlegel, and many followed him in prating about it then, or
are prating of it afresh just now.

The proximate form of this negativity which displays itself
as irony is, then, on the one hand the vanity of all that is
matter of fact, or moral and of substantive import in itself;
the nothingness of all that is objective, and that has essential
and actual value. If the I remains at this point of view, all
appears to it as worth nothing and as vain, excepting its own

subjectivity, which thereby becomes hollow and empty, and itself mere conceit. But on the other hand, the reverse may happen, and the I may also find itself unsatisfied in its enjoyment of itself, and may prove insufficient to itself, so as in consequence to feel a craving for the solid and substantial, for determinate and essential interests. Out of this there arises misfortune and contradiction, in that the subject desires to penetrate into truth and has a craving for objectivity, but yet is unable to abandon its isolation and retirement into itself, and to strip itself free of this unsatisfied abstract inwardness (of mind), and so has a seizure of sickly yearning which we have also seen emanate from Fichte's school.

The discontent of this quiescence and feebleness—which does not like to act or to touch anything for fear of surrendering its inward harmony, and, for all its craving after the absolute, remains none the less unreal and empty, even though pure in itself—is the source of morbid saintliness and yearning. For a true saintly soul acts and is a reality. But all that craving is the feeling of the nullity of the empty futile subject or person, which lacks the strength to escape this its futility, and to fill itself with something of substantial value.

Insofar, however, as the irony was treated as a form of art, it did not content itself with conferring artistic shape upon the life and particular individuality of the artist. In addition to the works of art presented by his own actions, etc., the artist was bound to produce external works of art as creations of his imagination. The principle of these productions, which for the most part can only come to the birth in poetical form, is, in due course, the representation of the divine as the ironical. The ironical, as "genial" individuality, consists in the self-annihilation of what is noble, great, and excellent; and thus even the objective shapes of art will have to represent the mere principle of absolute subjectivity, by displaying what has value and nobleness for man as null in its self-annihilation. This implies not merely that we are not to be serious about the right, the moral, and the true, but that the highest and best of all has nothing in it, inasmuch as in its exhibition

through individuals, characters, and actions it refutes and annihilates itself, and so is irony at its own expense. This mode,
taken in the abstract, borders closely on the principle of
comedy; but yet within this affinity the comic must be essentially distinguished from the ironical. For the comic must be
limited to bringing to nothing what is in itself null, a false
and self-contradictory phenomenon; for instance, a whim, a
perversity, or particular caprice, set over against a mighty passion; or even a *supposed* reliable principle or rigid maxim
may be shown to be null. But it is quite another thing when
what is in reality moral and true, any substantial content as
such, exhibits itself as null in an individual and by his means.
Such an individual is then null and despicable in character,
and weakness and want of character are thus introduced into
the representation.

In this distinction between the ironical and the comic it is
therefore an essential question what import that has which is
brought to nothing. In the case supposed they are wretched
worthless subjects, persons destitute of the power to abide by
their fixed and essential purpose but ready to surrender it
and let it be destroyed in them. The "irony" loves this irony
of the characterless. For true character involves on the one
hand an essential import in its purpose and, on the other
hand, adherence to that purpose, such that the individuality
would be robbed of its whole existence if forced to desist
from and to abandon it. This stability and substance constitute the keynote of character. Cato can live only as Roman
and as republican. Now, if irony is taken as the keynote of
the representation, this means that the supremely inartistic is
taken as the true principle of the work of art. For the result
is in part insipid figures; in part shapes void of import and of
conduct, seeing that their substantive nature turns out to be a
nullity; and in part, finally, those yearning moods and unre-
solved contradictions of the heart that attach themselves to
such conceptions.

Representations of this kind can awake no genuine interest. And for this reason it is from the irony that we have

eternal lamentations over the lack of profound feeling, artistic insight, and genius in the public, inasmuch as it does not
understand these heights of irony. That is to say, the public
does not like all this mediocrity, half grotesque and half characterless. And it is well that these unsubstantial languishing
natures afford no pleasure; it is a comfort that such insincer-
ity and hypocrisy are not approved, and that, on the contrary, man has a desire no less for full and genuine interests than
for characters which remain true to the weighty purposes of
their lives.

It may be added as an historical remark that those who
more particularly adopted irony as the supreme principle of
art were Solger and Ludwig Tieck.

This is not the place to speak of Solger at the length which
is due to him, and I must content myself with a few observations. Solger was not like the others, satisfied with superficial
philosophical culture, but the genuine speculative need of his
innermost nature impelled him to descend into the depths of
the philosophic Idea. And therein he hit upon the dialectical
element of the Idea, the point to which I give the name of
"infinite absolute negativity," the activity of the Idea in that
it negates itself as the infinite and universal, so as to become
finiteness and particularity, and just as really cancels this
negation in turn, establishing thereby the universal and infinite in the finite and particular. Solger got no further than
this negativity, and it is no doubt an element in the speculative Idea, but yet when conceived as this mere dialectic unrest and dissolution both of infinite and of finite *no more
than* an element; not, as Solger maintains, *the entire Idea*.
Unhappily Solger's life was too soon interrupted for him to
have achieved the concrete development of the philosophical
Idea. And so he never got beyond this aspect of negativity,
which has affinity with the dissolution that irony effects of
what is determinate and of what has substantive value in
itself, a negativity in which he saw the principle of artistic
activity. Yet in his actual life, considering the solidity, seriousness, and strength of his character, he neither was himself,

in the sense above depicted, an ironical artist, nor was his profound feeling for genuine works of art, developed in protracted art studies, in this respect of an ironical nature. So much in vindication of Solger, whose life, philosophy, and art merit to be distinguished from the previously mentioned apostles of irony.

As regards Ludwig Tieck, his culture, too, dates from that period in which for some time Jena was the literary centre. Tieck and others of these distinguished people display great familiarity with the phrases in question, but without telling us what they mean by them. Thus, Tieck indeed always says there ought to be irony; but when he himself approaches the criticism of great works of art, though his recognition and portrayal of their greatness is excellent, yet, if we fancy that now is the best opportunity to explain where the irony is, e.g. in such a work as *Romeo and Juliet*, we are taken in—for we hear no more about the irony.

V

1. After the above introductory remarks, it is now time to pass to the study of our subject matter. But we are still in the introduction, and an introduction cannot do more than lay down, for the sake of explanation, the general sketch of the entire course which will be followed by our subsequent scientific considerations. As, however, we have spoken of art as proceeding from the absolute Idea, and have even assigned as its end the sensuous representation of the absolute itself, we shall have to conduct this review in a way to show, at least in general, how the particular divisions of the subject spring from the conception of artistic beauty as the representation of the absolute. Therefore we must attempt to awaken a very general idea of this conception itself.

It has already been said that the content of art is the Idea, and that its form lies in the plastic use of images accessible to sense. These two sides art has to reconcile into a full and united totality. The *first* attribution which this involves is the requirement that the content, which is to be offered to artistic representation, shall show itself to be in its nature worthy of such representation. Otherwise we only obtain a bad combination, whereby a content that will not submit to plasticity and to external presentation is forced into that form, and a matter which is in its nature prosaic is expected to find an appropriate mode of manifestation in the form antagonistic to its nature.

The *second* requirement, which is derivable from this first, demands of the content of art that it should not be anything abstract in itself. This does not mean that it must be concrete as the sensuous is concrete in contrast to everything spiritual and intellectual, these being taken as in themselves simple and abstract. For everything that has genuine truth in the mind as well as in nature is concrete in itself, and has, in spite of its universality, nevertheless, both subjectivity and particularity within it. If we say, for example, that God is simply *One*, the supreme being as such, we have only enunciated a lifeless abstraction of the irrational understanding. Such a God, as he himself is not apprehended in his concrete truth, can afford no material for art, least of all for plastic art. Hence the Jews and the Turks have not been able to represent their God, who does not even amount to such an abstraction of the understanding, in the positive way in which Christians have done so. For God in Christianity is conceived in his truth, and therefore, as in himself thoroughly concrete, as a person, as a subject, and more closely determined, as mind or spirit. What he is as spirit unfolds itself to the religious apprehension as the Trinity of Persons, which at the same time in relation with itself is *One*. Here is essentiality, universality, and particularity, together with their reconciled unity; and it is only such unity that constitutes the concrete. Now, as a content in order to possess truth at all must be of this concrete nature, art demands the same concreteness, because a mere abstract universal has not in itself the vocation to advance to particularity and phenomenal manifestation and to unity with itself therein.

If a true and therefore concrete content is to have corresponding to it a sensuous form and modelling, this sensuous form must, in the third place, be no less emphatically something individual, wholly concrete in itself, and one. The character of concreteness as belonging to both elements of art, to the content as to the representation, is precisely the point in which both may coincide and correspond to one another; as, for instance, the natural shape of the human body is such a sensuous concrete as is capable of representing spirit, which is concrete in itself, and of displaying itself in conformity therewith. Therefore we ought to abandon the idea that it is a mere matter of accident that an actual phenomenon of the external world is chosen to furnish a shape thus conformable to truth. Art does not appropriate this form either because it simply finds it existing or because there is no other. The concrete content itself involves the element of external and actual, we may say indeed of sensible manifestation. But in compensation this sensuous concrete, in which a content essentially belonging to mind expresses itself, is in its own nature addressed to the inward being. Its external element of shape, whereby the content is made perceptible and imaginable, has the aim of existing purely for the heart and mind. This is the only reason for which content and artistic shape are fashioned in conformity with each other. The *mere* sensuous concrete, external nature as such, has not this purpose for its exclusive ground of origin. The birds' variegated plumage shines unseen, and their song dies away unheard, the torch thistle which blossoms only for a night withers without having been admired in the wilds of southern forests, and these forests, jungles of the most beautiful and luxuriant vegetation, with the most odorous and aromatic perfumes, perish and decay no less unenjoyed. The work of art has not such a naïve self-centered being, but is essentially a question, an address to the responsive heart, an appeal to affections and to minds.

Although the artistic bestowal of sensuous form is in this respect not accidental, yet on the other hand it is not the

highest mode of apprehending the spiritually concrete.
Thought is a higher mode than representation by means of
the sensuous concrete. Although in a relative sense abstract,
yet it must not be one-sided but concrete thinking, in order
to be true and rational. Whether a given content has sensuous
artistic representation for its adequate form, or in virtue of
its nature essentially demands a higher and more spiritual
embodiment, is a distinction that displays itself at once, if,
for instance, we compare the Greek gods with God as conceived according to Christian ideas. The Greek god is not
abstract but individual and is closely akin to the natural human shape; the Christian God is equally a concrete personality, but in the mode of pure spiritual existence, and is to be
known as *mind*[9] and in mind. His medium of existence is
therefore essentially inward knowledge and not external natural form, by means of which he can only be represented
imperfectly, and not in the whole depth of his Idea.

But inasmuch as the task of art is to represent the Idea to
direct perception in sensuous shape, and not in the form of
thought or of pure spirituality as such, and seeing that this
work of representation has its value and dignity in the correspondence and the unity of the two sides, i.e. of the Idea and
its plastic embodiment, it follows that the level and excellen-
cy of art in attaining a realization adequate to its Idea must
depend upon the grade of inwardness and unity with which
Idea and shape display themselves as fused into one.

Thus the higher truth is spiritual being that has attained a
shape adequate to the conception of spirit. This is what furnishes the principle of division for the science of art. For
before the mind can attain the true notion of its absolute
essence, it has to traverse a course of stages whose ground is
in this Idea itself; and to this evolution of the content with
which it supplies itself, there corresponds an evolution, immediately connected therewith, of the plastic forms of art,

9. Or "as spirit and in spirit."

under the shape of which the mind as artist presents to itself the consciousness of itself.

This evolution within the art spirit has again in its own nature two sides. In the *first* place the development itself is a spiritual and universal one, in so far as the graduated series of definite *conceptions of the world* as the definite but comprehensive consciousness of nature, man and God, gives itself artistic shape. And, in the *second* place, this *universal* development of art is obliged to provide itself with external existence and sensuous form, and the definite modes of the sensuous art existence are themselves a totality of necessary distinctions in the realm of art—which are *the several arts*. It is true, indeed, that the necessary kinds of artistic representation are on the one hand qua spiritual of a very general nature, and not restricted to any one material; while sensuous existence contains manifold varieties of matter. But as this latter, like the mind, has the Idea potentially for its inner soul, it follows from this that particular sensuous materials have a close affinity and secret accord with the spiritual distinctions and types of art presentation.

In its completeness, however, our science divides itself into three principal portions.

First, we obtain a *general part*. It has for its content and object the universal Idea of artistic beauty—this beauty being conceived as the Ideal—together with the nearer relation of the latter both to nature and to subjective artistic production.

Secondly, there develops itself out of the idea of artistic beauty a *particular* part, in as far as the essential differences which this idea contains in itself evolve themselves into a scale of *particular* plastic forms.

In the *third* place there results a *final* part, which has for its subject the individualization of artistic beauty, which consists in the advance of art to the sensuous realization of its shapes and its self-completion as a system of the several arts and their genera and species.

2. With respect to the first and second parts, we must begin by recalling to mind, in order to make the sequel intelligible, that the Idea qua the beautiful in art is not the Idea as such, in the mode in which a metaphysical logic apprehends it as the absolute, but the Idea as developed into concrete form fit for reality, and as having entered into immediate and adequate unity with this reality. For the *Idea as such*, although it is the essentially and actually true, is yet the truth only in its generality which has not yet taken objective shape; but the *Idea* as the *beautiful in art* is at once the Idea when specially determined as in its essence individual reality, and also an individual shape of reality essentially destined to embody and reveal the Idea. This amounts to enunciating the requirement that the Idea and its plastic mould as concrete reality are to be made completely adequate to one another. When reduced to such form the Idea, as a reality moulded in conformity with the conception of the Idea, is the *Ideal*. The problem of this conformity might, to begin with, be understood in the sense that any Idea would serve, so long as the actual shape, it did not matter what shape, represented this particular Idea and no other. But if so, the required truth of the Ideal is confounded with mere correctness, which consists in the expression of any meaning whatever in appropriate fashion so that its import may be readily recognized in the shape created. The Ideal is not to be thus understood. Any content whatever may attain to being represented quite adequately, judged by the standard of its own nature, but it does not therefore gain the right to claim the artistic beauty of the Ideal. Compared indeed with ideal beauty, even the presentation will in such a case appear defective. From this point of view we must remark to begin with what cannot be proved till later: that the defects of a work of art are not to be regarded simply as always due, for instance, to individual *defectiveness of content.*

So, for example, the Chinese, Indians, and Egyptians in their artistic shapes, their forms of deities, and their idols never got beyond a formless phase, or one of a bad and false definiteness of form, and were unable to attain genuine beauty; because their mythological ideas, the content and thought of their works of art, were as yet indeterminate in themselves, or of a bad determinateness, and did not consist in the content that is absolute in itself. The more that works of art excel in true beauty of presentation, the more profound is the inner truth of their content and thought. And in dealing with this point, we have not to think merely perhaps of the greater or lesser skill with which the natural forms as given in external reality are apprehended and imitated. For in certain stages of art consciousness and of representation, the distortion and disfigurement of natural structures is not unintentional technical inexpertness and want of skill but intentional alteration, which emanates from the content that is in consciousness, and is required thereby. Thus, from this point of view, there is such a thing as imperfect art, which may be quite perfect, both technically and in other respects, *in its determinate* sphere, yet reveals itself to be defective when compared with the conception of art as such, and with the Ideal.

Only in the highest art are the Idea and the representation genuinely adequate to one another, in the sense that the outward shape given to the Idea is in itself essentially and actually the true shape, because the content of the Idea, which that shape expresses, is itself the true and real content. It is a corollary from this, as we indicated above, that the Idea must be defined in and through itself as concrete totality, and thereby possess in itself the principle and standard of its particularization and determination in external appearance. For example, the Christian imagination will be able to represent God only in human form and with man's intellectual expression, because it is herein that God himself is completely known in himself as mind. Determinateness is, as it were, the bridge to phenomenal existence. Where this determinateness is not totality derived from the Idea itself, where the Idea is not conceived as self-determining and self-particularizing, the Idea remains abstract and has its determinateness, and therefore the principle that dictates its particular and exclusively appropriate mode of presentation, not in itself but external to it. Therefore, the Idea when still abstract has even its shape external, and not dictated by itself. The Idea, however, which is concrete in itself bears the principle of its mode of manifestation within itself and is by that means the free process of giving shape to itself. Thus it is only the truly concrete Idea that can generate the true shape, and this correspondence of the two is the Ideal.

3. Now because the Idea is in this fashion concrete unity, it follows that this unity can enter into the art consciousness only by the expansion and reconciliation of the particularities of the Idea, and it is through this evolution that artistic beauty comes to possess a *totality of particular stages and forms*. Therefore, after we have studied the beauty of art in itself and on its own merits, we must see how beauty as a whole breaks up into its particular determinations. This gives, as our *second part, the doctrine of the types of art*. These forms find their genesis in the different modes of grasping the Idea as artistic content, whereby is conditioned a difference of the form in which it manifests itself. Hence the types of art are nothing but the different relations of content and shape, relations which emanate from the Idea itself, and furnish thereby the true basis of division for this sphere. For the principle of division must always be contained in *that* conception whose particularization and division is in question.

We have here to consider *three* relations of the Idea to its outward shaping:

First, the Idea gives rise to the beginning of art when, being itself still in its indistinctness and obscurity, or in bad untrue determinateness, it is made the import of artistic creations. As indeterminate it does not yet possess in itself that individuality which the Ideal demands; its abstractness and one-sidedness leave its shape to be outwardly bizarre and defective. The first form of art is therefore rather a mere search after plastic portrayal than a capacity of genuine representation. The Idea has not yet found the true form even within itself, and therefore continues to be merely the struggle and aspiration thereafter. In general terms we may call this form the *symbolic* form of art. In it the abstract Idea has its outward shape external to itself in natural sensuous matter, with which the process of shaping begins, and from which, qua outward expression, it is inseparable.

Natural objects are thus primarily left unaltered, and yet at the same time invested with the substantial Idea as their significance, so that they receive the vocation of expressing it, and claim to be interpreted as though the Idea itself were present in them. At the root of this is the fact that natural objects have in them an aspect in which they are capable of representing a universal meaning. But as an adequate correspondence is not yet possible, this reference can only concern *an abstract attribute*, as when a lion is used to mean strength.

On the other hand, this abstractness of the relation brings to consciousness no less strongly the foreignness of the Idea to natural phenomena; and the Idea, having no other reality to express it, issues forth in all these shapes, seeks itself in them in all their unrest and disproportion, but nevertheless does not find them adequate to itself. Then it proceeds to exaggerate the natural shapes and the phenomena of reality into indefiniteness and disproportion, to intoxicate itself in them, to seethe and ferment in them, to do violence to them, to distort and explode them into unnatural shapes, and strives by the variety, hugeness, and splendour of the forms employed to exalt the phenomenon to the level of the Idea. For the Idea is here still more or less indeterminate and nonplastic, but the natural objects are in their shape thoroughly determinate.

Hence, in view of the unsuitability of the two elements to each other, the relation of the Idea to objective reality becomes a *negative* one, for the former, as in its nature inward, is unsatisfied with such an externality, and as being its inner universal substance persists in exaltation or *sublimity* beyond and above all this inadequate abundance of shapes. In virtue of this sublimity the natural phenomena and the human shapes and incidents are accepted, and left as they were, though at the same time understood to be inadequate to their significance, which is exalted far above every earthly content.

These aspects may be pronounced in general terms to constitute the character of the primitive artistic pantheism of the East, which either charges even the meanest objects with the absolute import, or again coerces nature with violence into the expression of its view. By this means it becomes bizarre, grotesque, and tasteless, or turns the infinite but abstract freedom of the substantive Idea disdainfully against all phenomenal being as null and evanescent. By such means the import cannot be completely embodied in the expression, and in spite of all aspiration and endeavour the reciprocal inadequacy of shape and Idea remains insuperable. This may be taken as the first form of art—symbolic art with its aspiration, its disquiet, its mystery, and its sublimity.

In the second form of art, which we propose to call "classical," the double defect of symbolic art is cancelled. The plastic shape of symbolic art is imperfect, because, in the first place, the Idea in it only enters into consciousness in *abstract* determinateness or indeterminateness, and, in the second place, this must always make the conformity of shape to import defective, and in its turn merely abstract. The classical form of art is the solution of this double difficulty; it is the free and adequate embodiment of the Idea in the shape that, according to its conception, is peculiarly appropriate to the Idea itself. With it, therefore, the Idea is capable of entering into free and complete accord. Hence, the classical type of art is the first to afford the production and intuition of the completed Ideal and to establish it as a realized fact.

The conformity, however, of notion and reality in classical art must not be taken in the purely *formal* sense of the agreement of a content with the external shape given to it, any more than this could be the case with the Ideal itself.

Otherwise every copy from nature, and every type of coun-
tenance, every landscape, flower, or scene, etc., which forms
the purport of any representation, would be at once made
classical by the agreement which it displays between form
and content. On the contrary, in classical art the peculiarity
of the content consists in being itself concrete idea, and, as
such, the concrete spiritual; for only the spiritual is the truly
inner self. To suit such a content, then, we must search out
that in nature which on its own merits belongs to the essence
and actuality of the mind. It must be the absolute or original
notion that *invented* the shape appropriate to concrete mind,
so that the *subjective* notion—in this case the spirit of art—
has merely *found* it, and brought it, as an existence possessing natural shape, into accord with free individual spirituality. This shape, with which the Ideas as spiritual—as individually determinate spirituality—invests itself when manifested as a temporal phenomenon, is *the human form.*
Personification and anthropomorphism have often been
decried as a degradation of the spiritual; but art, insofar as its
end is to bring before perception the spiritual in sensuous
form, must advance to such anthropomorphism, as it is only
in its proper body that mind is adequately revealed to sense.
The migration of souls is in this respect a false abstraction,
and physiology ought to have made it one of its axioms that
life had necessarily in its evolution to attain to the human
shape, as the sole sensuous phenomenon that is appropriate
to mind.

The human form is employed in the classical type of art
not as mere sensuous existence, but exclusively as the existence and physical form corresponding to mind, and is therefore exempt from all the deficiencies of what is merely
sensuous, and from the contingent finiteness of phenomenal
existence. The outer shape must be thus purified in order to
express in itself a content adequate to itself; and again, if the
conformity of import and content is to be complete, the
spiritual meaning which is the content must be of a particular
kind. It must, that is to say, be qualified to express itself

completely in the physical form of man, without projecting
into another world beyond the scope of such an expression in
sensuous and bodily terms. This condition has the effect that
Mind is by it at once specified as a particular case of mind, as
human mind, and not as simply absolute and eternal, inasmuch as mind in this latter sense is incapable of proclaiming
and expressing itself otherwise than as intellectual being.

Out of this latter point arises, in its turn, the defect which
brings about the dissolution of classical art, and demands a
transition into a third and higher form, viz. into the *romantic*
form of art.

The romantic form of art destroys the completed union of
the Idea and its reality, and recurs, though in a higher phase,
to that difference and antagonism of two aspects which was
left unvanquished by symbolic art. The classical type attained
the highest excellence of which the sensuous embodiment of
art is capable; and if it is in any way defective, the defect is in
art as a whole, i.e. in the limitation of its sphere. This
limitation consists in the fact that art as such takes for its
object mind—the conception of which is *infinite* concrete
universality—in the shape of *sensuous* concreteness, and in
the classical phase sets up the perfect amalgamation of spiritual and sensuous existence as a *conformity* of the two. Now,
as a matter of fact, in such an amalgamation mind cannot be
represented according to its true notion. For mind is the
infinite subjectivity of the Idea, which, as absolute inwardness, is not capable of finding free expansion in its true
nature on condition of remaining transposed into a bodily
medium as the existence appropriate to it.

As *an escape from such a condition* the romantic form of
art in its turn dissolves the inseparable unity of the classical
phase, because it has won a significance which goes beyond
the classical form of art and its mode of expression. This
significance—if we may recall familiar ideas—coincides with
what Christianity declares to be true of God as Spirit, in
contradistinction to the Greek faith in gods which forms the
essential and appropriate content for classical art. In Greek

art the concrete import is potentially, but not explicitly, the unity of the human and divine nature; a unity which, just because it is purely *immediate* and *not explicit*, is capable of adequate manifestation in an immediate and sensuous mode. The Greek god is the object of naïve intuition and sensuous imagination. His shape is, therefore, the bodily shape of man. The circle of his power and of his being is individual and individually limited. In relation with the subject, he is, therefore, an essence and a power with which the subject's inner being is merely in latent unity, not itself possessing this unity as inward subjective knowledge. Now the higher stage is the *knowledge* of this *latent* unity, which as latent is the import of the classical form of art, and capable of perfect representation in bodily shape. The elevation of the latent or potential into self-conscious knowledge produces an enormous difference. It is the infinite difference which, for example, separates man as such from the animals. Man is animal, but even in his animal functions he is not confined within the latent and potential as the animal is, but becomes conscious of them, learns to know them, and raises them—as, for instance, the process of digestion—into self-conscious science. By this means man breaks the boundary of merely potential and immediate consciousness, so that just for the reason that he knows himself to be animal, he ceases to be animal, and, as *mind*, attains to self-knowledge.

If in the above fashion the unity of the human and divine nature, which in the former phase was potential, is raised from an *immediate* to a *conscious* unity, it follows that the true medium for the reality of this content is no longer the sensuous immediate existence of the spiritual, the human bodily shape, but *self-conscious inward intelligence*. Now, Christianity brings God before our intelligence *as spirit* or mind—not as particularized individual spirit, but as absolute, in *spirit* and in truth. And for this reason Christianity retires from the sensuousness of imagination into intellectual inwardness, and makes this, not bodily shape, the medium and actual existence of its significance. So, too, the unity of the human and divine nature is a conscious unity, only to be realized by *spiritual* knowledge and in *spirit*. Thus the new content, won by this unity, is not inseparable from sensuous representation, as if that were adequate to it, but is freed from this immediate existence, which has to be posited as negative, absorbed, and reflected into the spiritual unity. In this way, romantic art must be considered as art transcending itself, while remaining within the artistic sphere and in artistic form.

Therefore, in short, we may abide by the statement that in this third stage the object (of art) is *free*, concrete intellectual being, which has the function of revealing itself as spiritual existence for the inward world of spirit. In conformity with such a subject matter, art cannot work for sensuous perception. It must address itself to the inward mind, which coalesces with its object simply and as though this were itself, to the subjective inwardness, to the heart, the feeling, which, being spiritual, aspires to freedom within itself, and seeks and finds its reconciliation only in the spirit within. It is this *inner* world that forms the content of the romantic, and must therefore find its representation as such inward feeling, and in the show or presentation of such feeling. The world of inwardness celebrates its triumph over the outer world, and actually in the sphere of the outer and in its medium manifests this its victory, owing to which the sensuous appearance sinks into worthlessness.

But, on the other hand, this type of art, like every other, needs an external vehicle of expression. Now the spiritual has withdrawn into itself out of the external and its immediate oneness therewith. For this reason, the sensuous externality of concrete form is accepted and represented, as in symbolic art, as something transient and fugitive. And the same measure is dealt to the subjective finite mind and will, even including the peculiarity or caprice of the individual, of character, action, etc., or of incident and plot. The aspect of external existence is committed to contingency and left at the mercy of freaks of imagination, whose caprice is no more likely to mirror what is given *as* it is given than to throw the shapes of the outer world into chance medley, or distort them into grotesqueness. For this external element no longer has its notion and significance, as in classical art, in its own sphere, and in its own medium. It has come to find them in the feelings, the display of which is *in themselves* instead of being in the external and *its* form of reality, and which have the power to preserve or to regain their state of reconciliation with themselves, in every accident, in every unessential circumstance that takes independent shape, in all misfortune and grief, and even in crime.

Owing to this, the characteristics of symbolic art, in difference, discrepancy, and severance of Idea and plastic shape, are here reproduced, but with an essential difference. In the sphere of the romantic, the Idea, whose defectiveness in the case of the symbol produced the defect of external shape, has to reveal itself in the medium of spirit and feelings as perfected in itself. And it is because of this higher perfection that it withdraws itself from any adequate union with the external element, inasmuch as it can seek and achieve its true reality and revelation nowhere but in itself.

This we may take as in the abstract the character of the symbolic, classical, and romantic forms of art, which represent the three relations of the Idea to its embodiment in the sphere of art. They consist in the aspiration after, and the attainment and transcendence of, the Ideal as the true Idea of beauty.

4. The third part of our subject, in contradistinction to the two just described, presupposes the conception of the Ideal, and the general types of art, inasmuch as it simply consists of their realization in particular sensuous media. Hence we have no longer to do with the inner development of artistic beauty in conformity with its general fundamental principles. What we have to study is how these principles pass into actual existence, how they distinguish themselves in their external aspect, and how they give actuality to every element contained in the idea of beauty, separately and by

itself *as a work of art*, and not merely as a general type. Now, what art transfers into external existence are the differences proper to the idea of beauty and immanent therein. Therefore, the general types of art must reveal themselves in this third part, as before, in the character of the fundamental principle that determines the arrangement and definition of the *several arts*; in other words, the species of art contain in themselves the same essential modifications as those with which we become acquainted as the general types of art. External objectivity, however, to which these forms are introduced through the medium of a sensuous and therefore *particular* material, affects these types in the way of making them *separate* into independent and so particular forms embodying their realization. For each type finds its definite character in some one definite external material, and its adequate actuality in the mode of portrayal which that prescribes. But, moreover, these types of art, being for all their determinateness its *universal* forms, break the bounds of *particular* realization by a determinate form of art, and achieve existence in other arts as well, although in subordinate fashion. Therefore, the particular arts belong each of them specifically to *one* of the general types of art, and constitute *its adequate* external actuality; and also they represent, each of them after its own mode of external plasticity, the totality of the types of art.

Then, speaking generally, we are dealing in this third principal division with the beautiful of art, as it unfolds itself in the several arts and in their creations into a *world* of actualized beauty. The content of this world is the beautiful, and the true beautiful, as we saw, is spiritual being in concrete shape, the Ideal; or, more closely looked at, the absolute mind, and the truth itself. This region, that of divine truth artistically represented to perception and to feeling, forms the centre of the whole world of art. It is the independent, free, and divine plasticity, which has thoroughly mastered the external elements of form and of medium, and wears them simply as a means to manifestation of itself. Still, as the beautiful unfolds itself in this region in the character of *objective* reality, and in so doing distinguishes within itself its individual aspects and elements, permitting them independent particularity, it follows that this centre erects its extremes, realized in their peculiar actuality, into its own antitheses. Thus one of these extremes comes to consist in an objectivity as yet devoid of mind, in the merely natural vesture of God. At this point the external element takes plastic shape as something that has its spiritual aim and content, not in itself, but in another.

The other extreme is the divine as inward, as something known, as the variously particularized *subjective* existence of the Deity. It is the truth as operative and vital in sense, heart, and mind of individual subjects, not persisting in the mould of its external shapes, but as having returned into subjective, individual inwardness. In such a mode, the Divine is at the same time distinguished from its first manifestation as Deity, and passes thereby into the diversity of particulars which belongs to all subjective knowledge—emotion, perception, and feeling. In the analogous province of religion, with which art at its highest stage is immediately connected, we conceive this same difference as follows: *First*, we think of the earthly natural life in its finiteness as standing on one side; but, then, *secondly*, consciousness makes God its object, in which the distinction of objectivity and subjectivity is done away. And at last, *thirdly*, we advance from God as such to the devotion of the *community*, that is, to God as living and present in the subjective consciousness. Just so these three chief modifications present themselves in the world of art in independent development.

The *first* of the particular arts with which, according to their fundamental principle, we have to begin, is architecture considered as a fine art. Its task lies in so manipulating external inorganic nature that it becomes cognate to mind, as an artistic outer world. The material of architecture is matter itself in its immediate externality as a heavy mass subject to mechanical laws, and its forms do not depart from the forms

of inorganic nature, but are merely set in order in conformity
with relations of the abstract understanding, i.e. with relations of symmetry. In this material and in such forms, the
ideal as concrete spirituality does not admit of being realized.
Hence the reality which is represented in them remains contrasted with the Idea, as something external which it has not
penetrated, or has penetrated only to establish an abstract
relation. For these reasons, the fundamental type of the fine
art of building is the *symbolical* form of art. It is architecture
that pioneers the way for the adequate realization of the
God, and in this its service bestows hard toil upon existing
nature, in order to disentangle it from the jungle of finitude
and the abortiveness of chance. By this means it levels a space
for the God, gives form to his external surroundings, and
builds him his temple as a fit place for concentration of
spirit, and for its direction to the mind's absolute objects. It
raises an enclosure round the assembly of those gathered
together, as a defence against the threatening of the storm,
against rain, the hurricane, and wild beasts, and reveals the
will to assemble, although externally, yet in conformity with
principles of art. With such import as this it has power to
inspire its material and its forms more or less effectively, as
the determinate character of the content on behalf of which
it sets to work is more or less significant, more concrete or
more abstract, more profound in sounding its own depths, or
more dim and more superficial. So much, indeed, may architecture attempt in this respect that it may even create an
adequate artistic existence for such an import in its shapes
and in its material. But in such a case it has already over-
stepped its own boundary and is leaning to sculpture, the
phase above it. For the limit of architecture lies precisely in
this point, that it retains the spiritual as an inward existence
over against the external forms of the art, and consequently
must refer to what has soul only as to something other than
its own creations.

Architecture, however, as we have seen, has purified the
external world and endowed it with symmetrical order and

with affinity to mind; and the temple of the God, the house of his community, stands ready. Into this temple, then, in the *second* place, the God enters in the lightning flash of individuality, which strikes and permeates the inert mass, while the infinite and no longer merely symmetrical form belonging to mind itself concentrates and gives shape to the corresponding bodily existence. This is the task of *sculpture*. In as far as in this art the spiritual inward being which architecture can but indicate makes itself at home in the sensuous shape and its external matter, and in as far as these two sides are so adapted to one another that neither is predominant, sculpture must be assigned the *classical form of art* as its fundamental type. For this reason the sensuous element itself has here no expression which could not be that of the spiritual element, just as, conversely, sculpture can represent no spiritual content which does not admit throughout of being adequately presented to perception in bodily form. Sculpture should place the spirit before us in its bodily form and in immediate unity therewith at rest and in peace; and the form should be animated by the content of spiritual individuality. And so the external sensuous matter is here no longer manipulated, either in conformity with its mechanical quality alone, as a mass possessing weight, nor in shapes belonging to the inorganic world, nor as indifferent to colour, etc.; but it is wrought in ideal forms of the human figure, and, it must be remarked, in all three spatial dimensions.

In this last respect we must claim for sculpture that it is in it that the inward and spiritual are first revealed in their eternal repose and essential self-completeness. To such repose and unity with itself there can correspond only that external shape which itself maintains its unity and repose. And this is fulfilled by shape in its abstract spatiality. The spirit which sculpture represents is that which is solid in itself, not broken up in the play of trivialities and of passions; and hence its external form too is not abandoned to any manifold phases of appearance but appears under this one aspect only, as the abstraction of space in the whole of its dimensions.

Now, after architecture has erected the temple, and the hand of sculpture has supplied it with the statue of the God, then, in the third place, this god present to sense is confronted in the spacious halls of his house by the *community*. The community is the spiritual reflection into itself of such sensuous existence and is the animating subjectivity and inner life which brings about the result that the determining principle for the content of art, as well as for the medium which represents it in outward form, comes to be particularization (dispersion into various shapes, attributes, incidents, etc.), individualization, and the subjectivity which they require. The solid unity which the God has in sculpture breaks up into the multitudinous inner lives of individuals, whose unity is not sensuous, but purely ideal.

It is only in this stage that God himself comes to be really and truly spirit—the spirit in his community; for he here begins to be a to-and-fro, an alternation between his unity within himself and his realization in the individual's knowledge and in its separate being, as also in the common nature and union of the multitude. In the community, God is released from the abstractness of unexpanded self-identity, as well as from the simple absorption in a bodily medium, by which sculpture represents him. And he is thus exalted into spiritual existence and into knowledge, into the reflected appearance which essentially displays itself as inward and as subjectivity. Therefore the higher content is now the spiritual nature, and that in its absolute shape. But the dispersion of which we have spoken reveals this at the same time as particular spiritual being and as individual character.

Now, what manifests itself in this phase as the main thing is not the serene quiescence of the God in himself, but appearance as such, being which is *for* another, self-manifestation. And hence, in the phase we have reached, all the most manifold subjectivity in its living movement and operation—as human passion, action, and incident, and, in general, the wide realm of human feeling, will, and its negation—is for its own sake the object of artistic representation. In conformity with this content, the sensuous element of art has at once to show itself as made particular in itself and as adapted to subjective inwardness.

Media that fulfil this requirement we have in colour, in musical sound, and finally in sound as the mere indication of inward perceptions and ideas; and as modes of realising the import in question by help of these media we obtain painting, music, and poetry. In this region the sensuous medium displays itself as subdivided in its own being and universally set down as ideal. Thus it has the highest degree of conformity with the content of art, which, as such, is spiritual, and the connection of intelligible import and sensuous medium develops into closer intimacy than was possible in the case of architecture and sculpture. The unity attained, however, is a more inward unity, the weight of which is thrown wholly on the subjective side, and which, in as far as form and content are compelled to particularize themselves and give themselves merely ideal existence, can only come to pass at the expense of the objective universality of the content and also of its amalgamation with the immediately sensuous element.

The arts, then, of which form and content exalt themselves to ideality, abandon the character of symbolic architecture and the classical ideal of sculpture, and therefore borrow their type from the romantic form of art, whose mode of plasticity they are most adequately adapted to express. And they constitute a *totality* of arts, because the romantic type is the most concrete in itself.

The articulation of this *third sphere* of the individual arts may be determined as follows: The *first* art in it, which comes next to sculpture, is painting. It employs as a medium for its content and for the plastic embodiment of that content visibility as such in as far as it is specialized in its own nature, i.e. as developed into colour. It is true that the material employed in architecture and sculpture is also visible and coloured; but it is not, as in painting, visibility as such, not the simple light which, differentiating itself in virtue of its contrast with darkness, and in combination with the latter, gives rise to colour. This quality of visibility, made subjective in itself and treated as ideal, needs neither, like architecture, the abstractly mechanical attribute of mass as operative in the properties of heavy matter, nor, like sculpture, the complete sensuous attributes of space, even though concentrated into organic shapes. The visibility and the rendering visible which belong to painting have their differences in a more ideal form, in the several kinds of colour, and they liberate art from the sensuous completeness in space which attaches to material things, by restricting themselves to a plane surface.

On the other hand, the content also attains the most comprehensive specification. Whatever can find room in the human heart, as feeling, idea, and purpose, whatever it is capable of shaping into act—all this diversity of material is capable of entering into the varied content of painting. The whole realm of particular existence, from the highest embodiment of mind down to the most isolated object of nature, finds a place here. For it is possible even for finite nature, in its particular scenes and phenomena, to make its appearance in the realm of art, if only some allusion to an element of mind endows it with affinity to thought and feeling.

The *second* art in which the romantic type realizes itself is contrasted with painting, and is music. Its medium, though still sensuous, yet develops into still more thorough subjectivity and particularization. Music, too, treats the sensuous as ideal, and does so by negating, and idealizing into the individual isolation of a single point, the indifferent externality of space, whose complete semblance is accepted and imitated by painting. The single point, qua such a negativity (excluding space), is in itself a concrete and active process of positive negation within the attributes of matter, in the shape of a motion and tremor of the material body within itself and in its relation to itself. Such an inchoate ideality of matter, which appears no longer as under the form of space, but as temporal ideality, is sound, the sensuous set down as negated, with its abstract visibility converted into audibility, inasmuch as sound, so to speak, liberates the ideal content from its immersion in matter.

This earliest inwardness of matter and inspiration of soul into it furnishes the medium for the mental inwardness—itself as yet indefinite—and for the soul into which mind concentrates itself; and finds utterance in its tones for the heart with its whole gamut of feelings and passions. Thus music forms the centre of the romantic arts, just as sculpture represents the central point between architecture and the arts of romantic subjectivity. Thus, too, it forms the point of transition between abstract spatial sensuousness, such as painting employs, and the abstract spirituality of poetry. Music has within itself, like architecture, a relation of quantity conformable to the understanding, as the antithesis to emotion and inwardness; and has also as its basis a solid conformity to law on the part of the tones, of their conjunction, and of their succession.

As regards the *third* and most spiritual mode of representation of the romantic art type, we must look for it in *poetry*. Its characteristic peculiarity lies in the power with which it subjects to the mind and to its ideas in the sensuous element from which music and painting in their degree began to liberate art. For sound, the only external matter which poetry retains, is in it no longer the feeling of the sonorous itself, but is a *sign* which by itself is void of import. And it is a sign of the idea which has become concrete in itself, and not merely of indefinite feeling and of its nuances and grades. This is how sound develops into the *word*, as voice articulate in itself, whose import it is to indicate ideas and notions. The merely negative point up to which music had developed now makes its appearance as the completely concrete point, the point which is mind, the self-conscious individual, which, producing out of itself the infinite space of its ideas, unites it with the temporal character of sound. Yet this sensuous element, which in music was still immediately one with inward feeling, is in poetry separated from the content of consciousness. In poetry the mind determines this content for its own sake, and apart from all else, into the shape of ideas, and though it employs sound to express them, yet treats it solely as a symbol without value or import. Thus considered, sound may just as well be reproduced by a mere letter, for the audible, like the visible, is thus reduced to a mere indication of mind. For this reason the proper medium of poetical representation is the poetical imagination and intellectual portrayal itself. And as this element is common to all types of art, it follows that poetry runs through them all and develops itself independently in each. Poetry is the universal art of the mind which has become free in its own nature, and which is not dependent for its realisation on external sensuous matter, but issues forth in the inner space and inner time of ideas and feelings. Yet just in this, its highest phase, art ends by transcending itself, inasmuch as it abandons the medium of a harmonious embodiment of mind in sensuous form and passes from the poetry of imagination into the prose of thought.

5. Such we may take to be the articulated totality of the particular arts, viz. the external art of architecture, the objective art of sculpture, and the subjective art of painting, music, and poetry. Many other classifications have been attempted, for a work of art presents so many aspects, that, as has often been the case, first one and then another is made the basis of classification. For instance, one might take the sensuous medium. Thus architecture is treated as crystallization; sculpture, as the organic modelling of the material in its sensuous and spatial totality; painting, as the coloured surface and line; while in music, space, as such, passes into the point of time possessed of content within itself, until finally the external medium is in poetry reduced to complete insignificance. Or, again, these differences have been considered with reference to their purely abstract attributes of space and time. Such abstract peculiarities of works of art may, like their material medium, be consistently explored in their characteristic traits; but they cannot be worked out as the ultimate and

fundamental law, because any such aspect itself derives its origin from a higher principle, and must therefore be subordinate thereto.

This higher principle we have found in the types of art—symbolic, classical, and romantic—which are the universal stages or elements of the Idea of beauty itself.

For *symbolic art* attains its most adequate reality and most complete application in *architecture*, in which it holds sway in the full import of its notion and is not yet degraded to be, as it were, the inorganic nature dealt with by another art. The *classical* type of art, on the other hand, finds adequate realisation in sculpture, while it treats architecture only as furnishing an enclosure in which it is to operate, and has not acquired the power of developing painting and music as absolute forms for its content. The *romantic* type of art, finally, takes possession of painting and music, and in like manner of poetic representation, as substantive and unconditionally adequate modes of utterance. Poetry, however, is conformable to all types of the beautiful, and extends over them all, because the artistic imagination is its proper medium, and imagination is essential to every product that belongs to the beautiful, whatever its type may be.

And, therefore, what the particular arts realise in individual works of art are, according to their abstract conception, simply the universal types which constitute the self-unfolding Idea of beauty. It is as the external realisation of this Idea that the wide pantheon of art is being erected, whose architect and builder is the spirit of beauty as it awakens to self-knowledge, and to complete which the history of the world will need its evolution of ages.

On Religion

The work below is a translation of G.W.F. Hegel's *(Vorlesungen über die Philosophie der Religion, Erster Band).* The Introduction reprinted here is from the translation by E.B. Speirs and J. Burdon Sanderson in *Lectures on the Philosophy of Religion* (London: Routledge & Kegan Paul, Ltd., 1895), pp. 1-85. It has been edited by J. Glenn Gray for the Torchbook edition.

It has appeared to me to be necessary to make religion by itself the object of philosophical consideration and to add on this study of it, in the form of a special part, to philosophy as a whole. By way of introduction I shall, however, first of all (a) give some account of the severance, or division, of consciousness, which awakens the need our science has to satisfy, and describe the relation of this science to philosophy and religion, as also to the prevalent principles of the religious consciousness. Then, after I have (b) touched upon some preliminary questions which follow from those relations, I shall give (c) the division of the subject.

To begin with, it is necessary to recollect generally what object we have before us in the philosophy of religion, and what is our ordinary idea of religion. We know that in religion we withdraw ourselves from what is temporal and that religion is for our consciousness that region in which all the enigmas of the world are solved, all the contradictions of deeper-reaching thought have their meaning unveiled, and where the voice of the heart's pain is silenced—the region of eternal truth, of eternal rest, of eternal peace. Speaking generally, it is through thought, concrete thought, or, to put it more definitely, it is by reason of his being spirit that man

128

is man. And from man as spirit proceed all the many developments of the sciences and arts, the interests of political life, and all those conditions which have reference to man's freedom and will. But all these manifold forms of human relations, activities, and pleasures, and all the ways in which these are intertwined, all that has worth and dignity for man, all wherein he seeks his happiness, his glory, and his pride, finds its ultimate centre in religion, in the thought, the consciousness, and the feeling of God. Thus God is the beginning of all things and the end of all things. As all things proceed from this point, so all return back to it again. He is the centre which gives life and quickening to all things and which animates and preserves in existence all the various forms of being. In religion man places himself in a relation to this center, in which all other relations concentrate themselves, and in so doing he rises up to the highest level of consciousness and to the region which is free from relation to what is other than itself, to something which is absolutely self-sufficient, the unconditioned, what is free, and is its own object and end.

Religion, as something which is occupied with this final object and end, is therefore absolutely free and is its own end; for all other aims converge in this ultimate end, and in presence of it they vanish and cease to have value of their own. No other aim can hold its ground against this, and here alone all find their fulfilment. In the region where the spirit occupies itself with this end, it unburdens itself of all finiteness, and wins for itself final satisfaction and deliverance; for here the spirit relates itself no longer to something that is other than itself, and that is limited, but to the unlimited and infinite, and this is an infinite relation, a relation of freedom, and no longer of dependence. Here its consciousness is absolutely free, and is indeed true consciousness, because it is consciousness of absolute truth. In its character as feeling, this condition of freedom is the sense of satisfaction which we call blessedness, while as activity it has nothing further to do than to manifest the honour of God and to reveal his glory, and in this attitude it is no longer with himself that

man is concerned—with his own interests or his empty pride—
but with the absolute end. All the various peoples feel that it
is in the religious consciousness that they possess truth, and
they have always regarded religion as constituting their true
dignity and the Sabbath of their life. Whatever awakens in us
doubt and fear, all sorrow, all care, all the limited interests of
finite life, we leave behind on the shores of time; and as from
the highest peak of a mountain, far away from all definite
view of what is earthly, we look down calmly upon all the
limitations of the landscape and of the world, so with the
spiritual eye man, lifted out of the hard realities of this actual
world, contemplates it as something having only the semblance of existence, which seen from this pure region bathed
in the beams of the spiritual sun, merely reflects back its
shades of colour, its varied tints and lights, softened away
into eternal rest. In this region of spirit flow the streams of
forgetfulness from which Psyche drinks, and in which she drowns
all sorrow, while the dark things of this life are softened away
into a dreamlike vision and become transfigured until they are
a mere framework for the brightness of the Eternal.

This image of the absolute may have a more or less present
vitality and certainty for the religious and devout mind and
be a present source of pleasure; or it may be represented as
something longed and hoped for, far off, and in the future.
Still it always remains a certainty, and its rays stream as
something divine into this present temporal life, giving the
consciousness of the active presence of truth, even amidst the
anxieties which torment the soul here in this region of time.
Faith recognises it as the truth, as the substance of actual
existing things; and what thus forms the essence of religious
contemplation, is the vital force in the present world, makes
itself actively felt in the life of the individual, and governs his
entire conduct. Such is the general perception, sensation,
consciousness, or however we may designate it, of religion.
To consider, to examine, and to comprehend its nature is the
object of the present lectures.

We must first of all, however, definitely understand, in

reference to the end we have in view, that it is not the concern of philosophy to produce religion in any individual. Its existence is, on the contrary, presupposed as forming what is fundamental in every one. So far as man's essential nature is concerned, nothing new is to be introduced into him. To try to do this would be as absurd as to give a dog printed writings to chew, under the idea that in this way you could put mind into it. He who has not extended his spiritual interests beyond the hurry and bustle of this finite world, nor succeeded in lifting himself above this life through aspiration, through the anticipation, through the feeling of the Eternal, and who has not gazed upon the pure ether of the soul, does not possess in himself that element which it is our object here to comprehend.

It may happen that religion is awakened in the heart by means of philosophical knowledge, but it is not necessarily so. It is not the purpose of philosophy to edify, and quite as little is it necessary for it to make good its claims by showing in any particular case that it must produce religious feeling in the individual. Philosophy, it is true, has to develop the necessity of religion in and for itself, and to grasp the thought that spirit must of necessity advance from the other modes of its will in conceiving and feeling to this absolute mode; but it is the universal destiny of spirit which is thus accomplished. It is another matter to raise up the individual subject to this height. The self-will, the perversity, or the indolence of individuals may interfere with the necessity of their universal spiritual nature; individuals may deviate from it, and attempt to get for themselves a standpoint of their own, and hold to it. This possibility of letting oneself drift, through inertness, to the standpoint of untruth, or of lingering there consciously and purposely, is involved in the freedom of the subject, while planets, plants, and animals cannot deviate from the necessity of their nature—from their truth —and become what they ought to be. But in human freedom what is and what ought to be are separate. This freedom brings with it the power of free choice, and it is possible for it to sever itself from its necessity, from its laws, and to work in opposition to its true destiny. Therefore, although philosophical knowledge should clearly perceive the necessity of the religious standpoint, and though the will should learn in the sphere of reality the nullity of its separation, all this does not hinder the will from being able to persist in its obstinacy, and to stand aloof from its necessity and truth.

There is a common and shallow manner of arguing against cognition or philosophical knowledge, as when, for instance, it is said that such and such a man has a knowledge of God, and yet remains far from religion, and has not become godly. It is not, however, the aim of knowledge to lead to this, nor is it meant to do so. What knowledge must do is to know religion as something which already exists. It is neither its intention nor its duty to induce this or that person, any particular empirical subject, to be religious if he has not been so before, if he has nothing of religion in himself, and does not wish to have.

But the fact is, no man is so utterly ruined, so lost, and so bad, nor can we regard anyone as being so wretched, that he has no religion whatever in him, even if it were only that he has the fear of it, or some yearning after it, or a feeling of hatred towards it. For even in this last case he is inwardly occupied with it, and cannot free himself from it. As man, religion is essential to him, and is not a feeling foreign to his nature. Yet the essential question is the relation of religion to his general world outlook, and it is with this that philosophical knowledge connects itself, and upon which it essentially works. In this relation we have the source of the division which arises in opposition to the primary absolute tendency of the spirit toward religion, and here, too, all the manifold forms of consciousness, and their most widely different connections with the main interest of religion, have sprung up. Before the philosophy of religion can sum itself up in its own peculiar conception, it must work itself through all those ramifications of the interests of the time which have at present concentrated themselves in the widely extended sphere of religion. At first the movement of the principles of the time has its place outside of philosophical study, but this movement pushes on to the point at which it comes into contact, strife, and antagonism with philosophy. We shall consider this opposition and its solution when we have examined the opposition as it still maintains itself outside of philosophy, and have seen it develop until it reaches that completed state where it involves philosophical knowledge in itself.

THE RELATION OF THE PHILOSOPHY OF RELIGION TO ITS PRESUPPOSITIONS AND TO THE PRINCIPLES OF THE TIME

The Severance of Religion from the Free Worldly Consciousness

1. In the relation in which religion, even in its immediacy, stands to the other forms of the consciousness of man, there already lie germs of division, since both sides are conceived of as in a condition of separation relative to each other. In their simple relation they already constitute two kinds of pursuits, two different regions of consciousness, and we pass to and fro from the one to the other *alternately* only. Thus man has in his actual worldly life a number of working days during which he occupies himself with his own special interests, with worldly aims in general, and with the satisfaction of his needs; and then he has a Sunday, when he lays all this aside, collects his thoughts, and, released from absorption in finite occupations, lives to himself and to the higher nature which is in him, to his true essential being. But into this separateness of the two sides there enters at once a double modification.

Let us consider first of all the religion of the godly man; that is, of one who truly deserves to be so called. Faith is still presupposed as existing irrespective of, and without opposition to, anything else. To believe in God is thus in its simplicity something different from that where a man, with reflection and with the consciousness that something else stands opposed to this faith, says, "I *believe* in God." Here the need of justification, of inference, of controversy, has already come in. Now that religion of the simple, godly man is not kept shut off and divided from the rest of his existence and life, but, on the contrary, it breathes its influence over all his feelings and actions, and his consciousness brings *all* the aims and objects of his worldly life into relation to God, as to its infinite and ultimate source. Every moment of his finite existence and activity, of his sorrow and joy, is lifted up by him out of his limited sphere, and by being thus lifted up produces in him the idea and sense of his eternal nature. The rest of his life, in like manner, is led under the conditions of confidence, of custom, of dutifulness, of habit; he *is* that which circumstances and nature have made him, and he takes his life, his circumstances, and rights as he receives everything, namely, as a lot or destiny which he does not understand. *It is so.* In regard to God, he either takes what is His and gives thanks, or else he offers it up to Him freely as a gift of free grace. The rest of his conscious life is thus subordinated, without reflection, to that higher region.

From the worldly side, however, the distinction involved in this relation develops until it becomes opposition. It is true that the development of this side does not seem to affect religion injuriously, and all action seems to limit itself strictly to that side in the matter. Judging from what is expressly acknowledged, religion is still looked upon as what is highest; but as a matter of fact it is not so, and starting from the worldly side, ruin and disunion creep over into religion. The development of this distinction may be generally designated as the maturing of the understanding and of human aims. While understanding awakens in human life and in science, and reflection has become independent, the will sets before itself absolute aims; for example, justice, the state, objects which are to have absolute worth, to be in and for themselves. Thus research recognises the laws, the constitution, the order, and the peculiar characteristics of natural things, and of the activities and productions of spirit. Now these experiences and forms of knowledge, as well as the willing and actual carrying out of these aims, is a work of man, both of his understanding and will. In them he is in presence of *what is his own*. Although he sets out from what *is* from what he finds, yet he *is* no longer merely one who knows, who *has* these rights; but what he *makes* out of that which is given in knowledge and in will is *his* affair, *his* work, and he has the consciousness that he has produced it. Therefore these productions constitute his glory and his pride, and provide for him an immense, an infinite wealth—that world of his intelligence, of his knowledge, of his external possession, of his rights and deeds.

Thus the spirit has entered into the condition of opposition—as yet, it is true, artlessly, and without at first knowing it—but the opposition comes to be a conscious one, for the spirit now moves between two sides, of which the distinction has actually developed itself. The one side is that in which the spirit knows itself to be its own, where it lives in its own aims and interests, and determines itself on its own authority as independent and self-sustaining. The other side is that where the spirit recognises a higher power—absolute duties, duties without rights belonging to them, and what the spirit receives for the accomplishment of its duties is always regarded as grace alone. In the first instance it is the independence of the spirit which is the foundation, there its attitude is that of humility and dependence. Its religion is accordingly distinguished from what we have in that region of independence by this, that it restricts knowledge, science, to the *worldly side,* and leaves for the sphere of religion, feeling and faith.

Notwithstanding, that aspect of independence involves this also, that its action is conditioned, and knowledge and will must have experience of the fact that it is thus conditioned. Man demands his right; whether or not he actually gets it is something independent of his efforts, and he is referred in the matter to an Other. In the act of knowledge he sets out from the organisation and order of nature, and this is something *given*. The content of his sciences is a material outside of him. Thus the two sides, that of independence and that of conditionality, enter into relation with each other, and this relation leads man to the avowal that everything is made by God—all things which constitute the content of his knowledge, which he takes possession of, and uses as means for his ends, as well as he himself, the spirit and the spiritual faculties of which he, as he says, makes use, in order to attain to that knowledge.

But this admission is cold and lifeless, because that which constitutes the vitality of this consciousness, in which it is "at home with itself," and is self-consciousness, this insight, this knowledge are wanting in it. All that is determined comes, on the contrary, to be included in the sphere of knowledge, and of human, self-appointed aims, and here, too, it is only the activity belonging to self-consciousness which is present. Therefore that admission is unfruitful too, because it does not get beyond the abstract universal, that is to say, it stops short at the thought that all is a work of God, and with regard to objects which are absolutely different (as, for example, the course of the stars and their laws, ants, or men), that relation continues for it fixed at one and the same point, namely this, that God has made all. Since this religious relation of particular objects is always expressed in the same monotonous manner, it would become tedious and burdensome if it were repeated in reference to each individual thing. Therefore the matter is settled with the *one* admission, that God has made everything, and this religious side is thereby satisfied *once for all*, and then in the progress of knowledge and the pursuit of aims nothing further is thought of the matter. It would accordingly appear that this admission is made simply and solely in order to get rid of the whole business, or perhaps it may be to get protection for the religious side as it were relatively to what is without. In short, such expressions may be used either in earnest or not.

Piety does not weary of lifting up its eyes to God on all and every occasion, although it may do so daily and hourly in the same manner. But as religious feeling, it really rests *in singleness* or single instances; it is in every moment *wholly* what it is, and is without reflection and the consciousness which compares experiences. It is here, on the contrary, where knowledge and self-determination are concerned, that this comparison, and the consciousness of that sameness, are essentially present, and then a general proposition is enunciated once for all. On the one side we have understanding playing its part, while over against it is the religious feeling of dependence.

2. Even piety is not exempt from the fate of falling into a state of division or dualism. On the contrary, division is already present in it implicitly, in that its actual content is only a manifold, accidental one. These two attitudes, namely, that of piety and of the understanding that compares, however different they seem to be, have this in common: that in them the relation of God to the other side of consciousness is undetermined and general. The second of these attitudes has indicated and pronounced this unhesitatingly in the expression already quoted, "God has created all things."

The manner of looking at things, however, which is followed by the religious man, and whereby he gives a greater completeness to his reflection, consists in the contemplation of the constitution and arrangement of things according to the *relations of ends*, and similarly in regarding all the circumstances of individual life, as well as the great events of history, as proceeding from divine purposes, or else as directed and leading back to such. The universal divine relation is thus not adhered to here. On the contrary, this becomes a definite relation, and consequently a more strictly defined content is introduced—for the manifold materials are placed in relation to one another, and God is then considered as the one who brings about these relations. Animals and their surroundings are accordingly regarded as beings definitely regulated, in that they have food, nurture their young, are provided with weapons as a defence against what is hurtful, stand the winter, and can protect themselves against enemies. In human life it is seen how man is led to happiness, whether it be eternal or temporal, by means of this or that apparent accident, or perhaps misfortune. In short, the action, the will of God, is contemplated here in definite dealings, conditions of nature, occurrences, and such-like.

But this content itself, these ends, representing thus a finite content, are accidental, are taken up only for the moment, and even directly disappear in an inconsistent and illogical fashion. If, for example, we admire the wisdom of God in nature because we see how animals are provided with weapons, partly to obtain their food and partly to protect them against enemies, yet it is presently seen in experience that these weapons are of no avail, and that those creatures which have been considered as ends are made use of by others as means.

It is therefore really progressive knowledge which has depreciated and supplanted this external contemplation of ends; that higher knowledge, namely, which, to begin with, at least demands *consistency*, and recognises ends of this kind, which are taken as divine ends, as subordinate and finite—as something which proves itself in the very same experience and observation to be worthless and not to be an object of the eternal, divine Will.

If that manner of looking at the matter be accepted, and if, at the same time, its inconsistency be disregarded, yet it still remains indefinite and superficial, for the very reason that all and every content—no matter what it be—may be included in it; for there is nothing, no arrangement of nature, no occurrence, which, regarded in some aspect or other, might not be shown to have some use. Religious feeling is, in short, here no longer present in its naïve and experimental character. On the contrary, it proceeds from the universal thought of an end, of a good, and makes inferences, inasmuch as it subsumes present things under these universal thoughts. But this argumentation, this inferential process, brings the religious man into a condition of perplexity, because however much he may point to what serves a purpose, and is useful in this immediate world of natural things, he sees, in contrast to all this, just as much that does not serve a purpose and is injurious. What is profitable to one person is detrimental to another, and therefore does not serve a purpose. The preservation of life and of the interests bound up with existence, which in the one case is promoted, is in the other case just as much endangered and put a stop to. Thus an implicit dualism or division is involved here, for in contradiction to God's eternal manner of operation, finite things are elevated to the rank of essential ends. The idea of God and of his manner of operation as universal and necessary is contradicted by this inconsistency, which is even destructive of that universal character.

Now, if the religious man considers external ends and the externality of the whole matter in accordance with which these things are profitable for an Other, the natural determinateness, which is the point of departure, appears indeed to be only *for an Other*. But this, more closely considered, is its own relation, its own nature, the immanent nature of what is related, its necessity, in short. Thus it is that the actual transition to the other side, which was formerly designated as the moment of selfness, comes about for ordinary religious thought.

Religious feeling, accordingly, is forced to abandon its argumentative process; and now that a beginning has once been made with thought, and with the relations of thought, it becomes necessary, above all things to thought, to demand and to look for that which belongs to itself; namely, first of all consistency and necessity, and to place itself in opposition to that standpoint of contingency. And with this, the principle of selfness at once develops itself completely. "I," as simple, universal, as thought, am really relation; since I am for myself, am self-consciousness, the relations too are to be for me. To the thoughts, ideas which I make my own, I give the character which I myself am. I am this simple point, and that which is for me I seek to apprehend in this unity.

Knowledge so far aims at that which *is,* and the *necessity* of it, and apprehends this in the relation of cause and effect, reason and result, power and manifestation; in the relation of the universal, of the species and of the individual existing things which are included in the sphere of contingency. Knowledge, science, in this manner places the manifold material in mutual relation, takes away from it the contingency which it has through its immediacy, and while contemplating the relations which belong to the wealth of finite phenomena, encloses the world of finiteness in itself so as to form a system of the universe, of such a kind that knowledge requires nothing for this system outside of the system itself. For what a thing *is,* what it is in its essential determinate character, is disclosed when it is perceived and made the subject of observation. From the constitution of things, we proceed to their connections in which they stand in relation to an Other; not, however, in an accidental relation but in a determinate relation, and in which they point back to the original source from which they are a deduction. Thus we inquire after the reasons and causes of things; and the meaning of inquiry here is that what is desired is to know the *special* causes.

Thus it is no longer sufficient to speak of God as the cause of the lightning, or of the downfall of the Republican system of government in Rome, or of the French Revolution; here it is perceived that this cause is only an entirely general one, and does not yield the desired explanation. What we wish to know regarding a natural phenomenon, or regarding this or that law as effect or result, is the reason as the reason of this particular phenomenon, that is to say, not the reason which applies to all things, but only and exclusively to this definite thing. And thus the reason must be that of such special phenomena, and such reason or ground must be the most immediate, must be sought and laid hold of in the *finite,* and must itself be a finite one. Therefore this knowledge does not go above or beyond the sphere of the finite, nor does it desire to do so, since it is able to apprehend all in its finite sphere, is conversant with everything, and knows its course of action. In this manner science forms a universe of knowledge, to which God is not necessary, which lies outside of religion, and has absolutely nothing to do with it. In this kingdom, knowledge spreads itself out in its relations and connections, and in so doing has all determinate material and content on its side; and for the other side, the side of the infinite and the eternal, nothing whatever is left.

Thus both sides have developed themselves completely in their opposition. On the side of religion the heart is filled with what is divine, but without freedom or self-consciousness and without consistency in regard to what is determinate, this latter having, on the contrary, the form of contingency. Consistent connection of what is determinate belongs to the side of knowledge, which is at home in the finite and moves freely in the thought determinations of the manifold connections of things, but can only create a system which is without absolute substantiality—without God. The religious side gets the absolute material and purpose, but only as something abstractly positive. Knowledge has taken possession of all finite material and drawn it into its territory, all determinate content has fallen to its share; but although it gives it a necessary connection, it is still unable to give it the absolute connection. Since finally science has taken possession of knowledge, and is the consciousness of the necessity of the finite, religion has become devoid of knowledge, and has shrivelled up into simple feeling, into the contentless or empty elevation of the spiritual to the Eternal. It can, however, affirm nothing regarding the Eternal, for all that could be regarded as knowledge would be a drawing down of the Eternal into the sphere of the finite and of finite connections of things.

Now when two aspects of thought that are so developed in this way enter into relation with one another, their attitude is one of mutual distrust. Religious feeling distrusts the finiteness which lies in knowledge, and it brings against science the charge of futility, because in it the subject clings to itself, is in itself, and the "I" as the knowing subject is independent in relation to all that is external. On the other hand, knowledge has a distrust of the totality in which feeling entrenches itself and in which it confounds together all extension and development. It is afraid to lose its freedom should it comply with the demand of feeling and unconditionally recognise a truth which it does not definitely understand. And when religious feeling comes out of its universality, sets ends before itself, and passes over to the determinate, knowledge can see nothing but arbitrariness in this, and if it were to pass in a similar way to anything definite, would feel itself given over to mere contingency. When, accordingly, reflection is fully developed and has to pass over into the domain of religion, it is unable to hold out in that region, and becomes impatient with regard to all that peculiarly belongs to it.

3. Now that the opposition has arrived at this stage of development, where the one side, whenever it is approached by the other, invariably thrusts it away from it as an enemy, the necessity for an adjustment comes in, of such a kind that the infinite shall appear in the finite, and the finite in the infinite, and each no longer form a separate realm. This would be the reconciliation of religious, genuine simple feeling with knowledge and intelligence. This reconciliation must correspond with the highest demands of *knowledge*, and of the concept, for these can surrender nothing of their dignity. But just as little can anything of the absolute content be given up and that content be brought down into the region of finiteness; and when face to face with it knowledge must give up its finite form.

In the Christian religion, more than in other religions, the need of this reconciliation has of necessity come into prominence, for the following reasons:

The Christian religion has its very beginning in absolute dualism or division, and starts from that sense of suffering in which it rends the natural unity of the spirit asunder and destroys natural peace. In it man appears as evil from his birth and is thus in his innermost life in contradiction with himself, and the spirit, as it is driven back into itself, finds itself separated from the infinite, absolute Essence.

The *reconciliation*, the need of which is here intensified to the uttermost degree, appears in the first place for faith, but not in such a way as to allow of faith being of a merely ingenuous kind. For the spirit has left its natural simplicity behind and entered upon an internal conflict; it is, as sinful, an Other in opposition to the truth; it is withdrawn, estranged from it. "I," in this condition of schism, am not the truth, and this is therefore given as an independent content of ordinary thought, and the truth is in the first instance put forward upon authority.

When, however, by this means I am transplanted into an intellectual world in which the nature of God, the characteristics and modes of action which belong to God, are presented to knowledge, and when the truth of these rests on the witness and assurance of others, yet I am at the same time referred *into myself*, for thought, knowledge, reason are *in me*, and in the feeling of sinfulness, and in reflection upon this, my freedom is plainly revealed to me. Rational knowledge, therefore, is an essential element in the Christian religion itself.

In the Christian religion I am to retain my freedom, or rather, in it I am to become free. In it the subject, the salvation of the soul, the redemption of the individual as an individual, and not only the species, is an essential end. This subjectivity, this *selfness* (not selfishness), is just the principle of rational knowledge itself.

Rational knowledge being thus a fundamental characteristic in the Christian religion, the latter gives development to its content, for the ideas regarding its general subject matter are implicitly or in themselves thoughts, and must as such develop themselves. On the other hand, however, since the content is something which exists essentially for the mind as forming ideas, it is distinct from unreflecting opinion and sense knowledge, and as it were passes right beyond the distinction. In short, it has in relation to subjectivity the value of an absolute content existing in and for itself. The Christian religion therefore touches the antithesis between feeling and immediate perception on the one hand, and reflection and knowledge on the other. It contains rational knowledge as an essential element, and has supplied to this rational knowledge the occasion for developing itself to its full logical issue as Form and as a world of form, and has thus at the same time enabled it to place itself in opposition to this content as it appears in the shape of given truth. It is from this that the discord which characterises the thought of the present day arises.

Hitherto we have considered the progressive growth of the antitheses only in the form in which they have not yet developed into actual philosophy, or in which they still stand outside of it. Therefore the questions which primarily come before us are these: (1) How does philosophy in general stand related to religion? (2) How does the Philosophy of Religion stand related to philosophy? and (3) What is the relation of the philosophical study of religion to positive religion?

The Position of the Philosophy of Religion Relative to Philosophy and to Religion

The Attitude of Philosophy to Religion Generally

In saying above that philosophy makes religion the subject of consideration, and when further this consideration of it appears to be in the position of something which is different from its object, it would seem as if we are still occupying that attitude in which both sides remain mutually independent and separate. In taking up such an attitude in thus considering the subject, we should accordingly come out of that region of devotion and enjoyment which religion is, and the object and the consideration of it as the movement of thought would be as different as, for example, the geometrical figures in mathematics are from the mind which considers them. Such is only the relation, however, as it at first appears, when knowledge is still severed from the religious side, and is finite knowledge. On the contrary, when we look more closely, it becomes apparent that as a matter of fact the content, the need, and the interest of philosophy represent something which it has in common with religion.

The object of religion as well as of philosophy is eternal truth in its objectivity, God and nothing but God, and the explication of God. Philosophy is not a wisdom of the world, but is knowledge of what is not of the world; it is not knowledge which concerns external mass, or empirical existence and life, but is knowledge of that which is eternal, of what God is, and what flows out of his nature. For this his nature must reveal and develop itself. Philosophy, therefore, only unfolds itself when it unfolds religion, and in unfolding itself it unfolds religion. As thus occupied with eternal truth which exists on its own account, or is in and for itself, and, as in fact, a dealing on the part of the thinking spirit, and not of individual caprice and particular interest, with this object, it is the same kind of activity as religion is. The mind insofar as it thinks philosophically immerses itself with like living interest in this object and renounces its particularity in that it permeates its object, in the same way, as religious consciousness does, for the latter also does not seek to have anything of its own, but desires only to immerse itself in this content.

Thus religion and philosophy come to be one. Philosophy is itself, in fact, worship; it is religion, for in the same way it renounces subjective notions and opinions in order to occupy itself with God. Philosophy is thus identical with religion, but the distinction is that it is so in a peculiar manner, distinct from the manner of looking at things which is commonly called religion as such. What they have in common is that they are religion; what distinguishes them from each other is merely the kind and manner of religion we find in each. It is in the peculiar way in which they both occupy themselves with God that the distinction comes out. It is just here, however, that the difficulties lie which appear so great, that it is even regarded as an impossibility that philosophy should be one with religion. Hence comes the suspicion with which philosophy is looked upon by theology, and the antagonistic attitude of religion and philosophy. In accordance with this antagonistic attitude (as theology considers it to be) philosophy seems to act injuriously, destructively, upon religion, robbing it of its sacred character, and the way in which it occupies itself with God seems to be absolutely different from religion. Here, then, is the same old opposition and contradiction which had already made its appearance among the Greeks. Among that free democratic people, the Athenians, philosophical writings were burnt, and Socrates was condemned to death. Now, however, this opposition is held to be an acknowledged fact, more so than that unity of religion and philosophy just asserted.

Old though this opposition is, however, the combination of philosophy and religion is just as old. Already to the neo-Pythagoreans and neo-Platonists, who were as yet within the heathen world, the gods of the people were not gods of imagination but had become gods of thought. That combination had a place, too, among the most eminent of the Fathers of the Church, who in their religious life took up an essentially intellectual attitude inasmuch as they set out from the presupposition that theology is religion together with conscious thought and comprehension. It is to their philosophical culture that the Christian Church is indebted for the first beginnings of a content of Christian doctrine.

This union of religion and philosophy was carried out to a still greater extent in the Middle Ages. So little was it believed that the knowledge which seeks to comprehend is hurtful to faith that it was even held to be essential to the further development of faith itself. It was by setting out from philosophy that those great men Anselm and Abelard further developed the essential characteristics of faith.

Knowledge in constructing its world for itself, without reference to religion, had only taken possession of the finite contents; but since it has developed into the true philosophy, it has the same content as religion.

If we now look provisionally for the distinction between religion and philosophy as it presents itself in this unity of content, we find it takes the following form:

(a) A speculative philosophy is the consciousness of the Idea, so that everything is apprehended as Idea; the Idea, however, is the True in thought, and not in mere sensuous contemplation or in ordinary conception. The True in thought, to put it more precisely, means that it is something concrete, posited as divided in itself, and in such a way, indeed, that the two sides of what is divided are *opposed characteristics of thought*, and the Idea must be conceived of as the unity of these. To think speculatively means to resolve anything real into its parts and to oppose these to each other in such a way that the distinctions are set in opposition in accordance with the characteristics of thought and the object is apprehended as unity of the two.

In sense perception or picture thought we have the object before us as a whole, our reflection distinguishes, apprehends different sides, recognises the diversity in them, and severs them. In this act of distinguishing, reflection does not keep firm hold of their unity. Sometimes it forgets the wholeness, sometimes the distinctions; and if it has both before it, it yet separates the properties from the object, and so places both so that that in which the two are one becomes a third, which is different from the object and its properties. In the case of mechanical objects which appear in the region of externality, this relation may have a place, for the object is only the lifeless substratum for the distinctions, and the quality of oneness is the gathering together of external aggregates. In the true object, however, which is not merely an aggregate, an externally united multiplicity, the object is one, although it has characteristics which are distinguished from it, and it is speculative thought which first gets a grasp of the unity in this very antithesis as such. It is in fact the business of speculative thought to apprehend all objects of pure thought, of nature and of spirit, in the form of thought, and thus as the unity of the difference.

(b) Religion, then, is itself the standpoint of the consciousness of the True, which is in and for itself, and is consequently the stage of spirit at which the speculative content generally is object for consciousness. Religion is not consciousness of this or that truth in individual objects, but of the absolute truth, of truth as the universal, the all-comprehending, outside of which there lies nothing at all. The content of its consciousness is further the Universally True, which exists on its own account or in and for itself, which determines itself, and is not determined from without. While the finite required an Other for its determinateness, the True has its determinateness, the limit, its end in itself; it is not limited through an Other, but the Other is found in itself. It is this speculative element which comes to consciousness in religion. Truth is, indeed, contained in every other sphere, but not the highest absolute truth, for this exists only in perfect universality of characterisation or determination, and in the fact of being determined in and for itself, which is not simple determinateness having reference to an Other but contains the Other, the difference, in its very self.

(c) Religion is accordingly this speculative element in the form, as it were, of a state of consciousness, of which the aspects are not simple categories of thought but are concretely filled up. These moments can be no other than the moment of thought, active universality, thought in operation, and reality as immediate, particular self-consciousness.

Now, while in philosophy the rigidity of these two sides loses itself through reconciliation in thought, because both sides are thoughts, and the one is not pure universal thought, and the other of an empirical and individual character, religion only arrives at the enjoyment of unity by lifting these two rigid extremes out of this state of severance, by rearranging them, and bringing them together again. But by thus stripping off the form of dualism from its extremes, rendering the opposition in the element of universality fluid, and bringing it to reconciliation, religion remains always akin to thought, even in its form and movement; and philosophy, as simply active thought, and thought which unites opposed elements, has approached closely to religion.

The contemplation of religion in thought has thus raised the determinate moments of religion to the rank of thoughts, and the question is how this contemplation of religion in thought is related generally to philosophy as forming an organic part in its system.

The Relation of the Philosophy of Religion to the System of Philosophy

1. In philosophy, the highest is called the absolute, the Idea; it is superfluous to go further back here, and to mention that this highest was in the Wolfian philosophy called *ens*, thing; for that at once proclaims itself an abstraction, which corresponds very inadequately to our idea of God. In the more recent philosophy, the absolute is not so complete an abstraction, but yet it has not on that account the same signification as is implied in the term "God." In order even to make the difference apparent, we must in the first place consider what the word "signify" itself signifies. When we ask, "What does this or that signify?" we are asking about two kinds of things, and, in fact, about things which are opposed. In the first place, we call what we are thinking of, the meaning, the end or intention, the general thought of this or that expression, work of art, etc.; if we ask about its intrinsic character, it is essentially the *thought* that is in it of which we wish to have an idea. When we thus ask, "What is God?" "What does the expression God signify?" it is the thought involved in it that we desire to know; the idea we possess already. Accordingly, what is signified here is that we have got to specify the notion, and thus it follows that the *notion* is the signification; it is the absolute, the nature of God as grasped by thought, the logical knowledge of this, to which we desire to attain. This, then, is the one signification

of signification, and so far, that which we call the absolute has a meaning identical with the expression "God."

2. But we put the question again, in a second sense, according to which it is the opposite of this which is sought after. When we begin to occupy ourselves with pure thought determinations, and not with outward ideas, it may be that the mind does not feel satisfied, is not at home, in these, and asks what this pure thought determination signifies. For example, everyone can understand for himself what is meant by the terms unity, objective, subjective, etc., and yet it may very well happen that the specific form of thought we call the unity of subjective and objective, the unity of real and ideal, is not understood. What is asked for in such a case is the meaning in the very opposite sense from that which was required before. Here it is an idea or a pictorial conception of the thought determination which is demanded, an example of the content, which has as yet only been given in thought. If we find a thought content difficult to understand, the difficulty lies in this: that we possess no pictorial idea of it; it is by means of an example that it becomes clear to us and that the mind first feels at home with itself in this content.

When, accordingly, we start with the ordinary conception of God, the philosophy of religion has to consider its signification—this, namely, that God is the Idea, the absolute, the essential reality, which is grasped in thought and in the concept, and this it has in common with logical philosophy; the logical Idea is God as he is in himself. But it is just the nature of God that he should not be implicit or in himself only. He is as essentially for himself, the absolute spirit, not only the being who keeps himself within thought, but who also manifests himself, and gives himself objectivity.

3. Thus, in contemplating the Idea of God, in the philosophy of religion, we have at the same time to do with the manner of his manifestation or presentation to us; he simply makes himself apparent, represents himself to himself. This is the aspect of the determinate being or existence of the absolute. In the philosophy of religion we have thus the

absolute as object; not, however, merely in the form of thought, but also in the form of its manifestation. The universal Idea is thus to be conceived of with the purely concrete meaning of essentiality in general, and is also to be regarded from the point of view of its activity in displaying itself, in appearing, in revealing itself. Popularly speaking, we say God is the Lord of the natural world and of the realm of spirit. He *is* the absolute harmony of the two, and it is he who produces and carries on this harmony. Here neither thought and concept nor their manifestation—determinate being or existence—are wanting. This aspect, thus represented by determinate being, is itself, however, to be grasped again in thought, since we are here in the region of philosophy.

Philosophy to begin with contemplates the absolute as logical Idea, the Idea as it is in thought, under the aspect in which its content is constituted by the specific forms of thought. Further, philosophy exhibits the absolute in its activity, in its creations. This is the manner in which the absolute becomes actual or "for itself," becomes spirit, and God is thus the result of philosophy. It becomes apparent, however, that this is not merely a result, but is something which eternally creates itself and which precedes all else. The one-sidedness of the result is abrogated and absorbed in the very result itself.

Nature, finite spirit, the world of consciousness, of intelligence, and of will, are embodiments of the divine Idea, but they are definite shapes, special modes of the appearance of the Idea, forms, in which the Idea has not yet penetrated to itself, so as to be absolute spirit.

In the philosophy of religion, however, we do not contemplate the implicitly existing logical Idea merely, in its determinate character as pure thought, nor in those finite determinations where its mode of appearance is a finite one, but as it is in itself or implicitly in thought, and at the same time as it appears, manifests itself, and thus in infinite manifestation as spirit, which reflects itself in itself; for spirit which does not appear *is* not. In this characteristic of appearance *finite* appearance is also included—that is, the world of nature and the world of finite spirit—but spirit is regarded as the power or force of these worlds, as producing them out of itself, and out of them producing itself.

This, then, is the position of the philosophy of religion in relation to the other parts of philosophy. Of the other parts, God is the result; here, this End is made the Beginning, and becomes our special Object, as the simply concrete Idea, with its infinite manifestations; and this characteristic concerns the content of the philosophy of religion. We look at this content, however, from the point of view of rational thought, and this concerns the form, and brings us to consider the position of the philosophy of religion with regard to religion as this latter appears in the shape of positive religion.

The Relation of the Philosophy of Religion to Positive Religion

It is well known that the faith of the Church, more especially of the Protestant Church, has taken a fixed form as a system of doctrine. This content has been universally accepted as truth; and as the description of what God is, and of what man is in relation to God, it has been called the *Creed*, that is, in the subjective sense that which is believed, and objectively, what is to be known as content, in the Christian Church, and what God has revealed himself to be. Now as universal established doctrine this content is partly laid down in the Apostolic *Symbolum* or Apostles' Creed, partly in later symbolical books. And moreover, in the Protestant Church the Bible has always been characterised as the essential foundation of doctrine.

1. Accordingly, in the apprehension and determination of the content of doctrine, the influence of reason, as "argumentation" has made itself felt. At first indeed, this was so much the case that the doctrinal content, and the Bible as its positive foundation, were to remain unquestioned, and thought was only to take up the thoughts of the Bible as exegesis. But as a matter of fact understanding had previously

established its opinions and its thoughts for itself, and then attention was directed towards observing how the words of Scripture could be explained in accordance with these. The words of the Bible are a statement of truth which is not systematic; they are Christianity as it appeared in the beginning; it is spirit which grasps the content, which unfolds its meaning. This exegesis having thus taken counsel with reason, the result has been that a so-called theology of reason[1] has now come into existence, which is put in opposition to that doctrinal system of the Church, partly by this theology itself and partly by that doctrinal system to which it is opposed. At the same time, exegesis takes possession of the written word, interprets it, and pretends only to lay stress on the understanding of the word, and to desire to remain faithful to it.

But whether it be chiefly to save appearances, or whether it is really and in downright earnest that the Bible is made the foundation, it is inherent in the very nature of any explanation which interprets that thought should have its part in it. Thought explicitly contains categories, principles, and premises which must make their influence felt in the work of interpretation. If interpretation be not mere explanation of words but explanation of the sense, the thoughts of the interpreter must necessarily be put into the words which constitute the foundation. Mere word interpretation can only amount to this, that for one word another coextensive in meaning is substituted; but in the course of explanation further categories of thought are combined with it. For a development is advance to further thoughts. In appearance the sense is adhered to, but in reality further thoughts are developed. Commentaries on the Bible do not so much make us acquainted with the content of the Scriptures as with the manner in which things were conceived in the age in which they were written. It is, indeed, the sense contained in the words which is supposed to be given. The giving of the sense

1. *Vernunft Theologie.*

means, however, the bringing forward of the sense into consciousness, into the region of ideas; and these ideas, which get
determinate character elsewhere, then assert their influence
in the exposition of the sense supposed to be contained in
the words. It is the case even in the presentation of a
philosophical system which is already fully developed, as, for
example, that of Plato or of Aristotle, that the presentation
takes a different form, according to the definite kind of idea
which those who undertake thus to expound it have already
formed themselves. Accordingly, the most contradictory
meanings have been exegetically demonstrated by means of
theology out of the Scriptures, and thus the so-called Holy
Scriptures have been made into a nose of wax. All heresies
have, in common with the church, appealed to the Scriptures.

2. The theology of reason, which thus came into existence, did not, however, limit itself to being merely an
exegesis which kept to the Bible as its foundation, but in its
character as free, rational knowledge assumed a certain relation to religion and its content generally. In this more general
relation the dealing with the subject and the result can
amount to nothing more than the taking possession by such
knowledge of all that, in religion, has a determinate character. For the doctrine concerning God goes on to that of the
characteristics, the attributes, and the actions of God. Such
knowledge takes possession of this determinate content, and
would make it appear that it belongs to it. It, on the one
hand, conceives of the Infinite in its own finite fashion, as
something which has a determinate character, as an *abstract*
infinite, and then on the other hand finds that all special
attributes are inadequate to this Infinite. By such a mode of
proceeding the religious content is annihilated, and the absolute object reduced to complete poverty. The finite and
determinate which this knowledge has drawn into its territory, points indeed to a Beyond as existing for it, but even
this Beyond is conceived of by it in a *finite* manner, as an
abstract, supreme being, possessing no character at all. "Enlightenment"—which is that consummation of finite knowl-

edge just described—intends to place God very high when it speaks of him as the Infinite, with regard to which all predicates are inadequate and are unwarranted anthropomorphisms. In reality, however, it has, in conceiving God as the supreme being, made him hollow, empty, and poor.

3. If it should now seem as if the philosophy of religion rested on the same basis as this theology of reason, or theology of enlightenment, and was consequently in the same condition of opposition to the content of religion, further reflection shows that this is merely an appearance of resemblance which vanishes directly it is examined into.

For God was conceived by that rationalistic way of looking at religion, which was only the abstract metaphysic of the understanding, as an abstraction which is empty ideality, and as against which the finite stands in an external fashion, and thus too from this point of view morals constituted, as a special science, the knowledge of that which was held to belong to the actual subject as regards general actions and conduct. The fact of the relation of man to God, which represents the one side, occupied a separate and independent position. Thinking reason, on the contrary, which is no longer abstract, but which sets out from the faith of man in the dignity of his spirit, and is actuated by the courage of truth and freedom, grasps the truth as something *concrete*, as fulness of content, as Ideality, in which determinateness—the finite—is contained as a moment. Therefore, to thinking reason, God is not emptiness, but spirit; and this characteristic of spirit does not remain for it a word only, or a superficial characteristic; on the contrary, the nature of spirit unfolds itself for rational thought, inasmuch as it apprehends God as essentially the Triune God. Thus God is conceived of as making himself an object to himself, and further, the object remains in this distinction in identity with God; in it God loves himself. Without this characteristic of trinity, God would not be spirit, and spirit would be an empty word. But if God be conceived as spirit, then this conception includes the *subjective* side in itself or even develops itself so as to reach to that side, and the philosophy of religion, as the contemplation of religion by thought, binds together again the determinate content of religion in its entirety.

With regard, however, to that form of contemplation in thought which adheres to the words of Holy Scripture, and asserts that it explains them by the aid of reason, it is only in appearance that the philosophy of religion stands on the same basis with it. For that kind of contemplation by its own sovereign power lays down *its* argumentations as the foundation of Christian doctrine; and although it still leaves the biblical words standing, yet the particular meaning remains as the principal determination, and to this the assumed biblical truth must subordinate itself. This argumentation accordingly *retains* its assumptions, and moves within the relations of the understanding, which belong to reflection, without subjecting these to criticism. But the philosophy of religion, as being rational knowledge, is opposed to the arbitrariness of this argumentative process, and is the reason of the universal, which presses forward to unity.

Philosophy is therefore very far removed from being on the common highway on which this theology of reason and this exegetical argumentative process move, the truth rather being that it is these tendencies chiefly which combat it, and seek to bring it under suspicion. They protest against philosophy, but only in order to reserve to themselves the arbitrariness of their argumentative process. Philosophy is called something special and particular, although it is nothing else than rational, truly universal thought. Philosophy is regarded as a something ghostly, of which we know nothing, and about which there is something uncanny; but this idea only shows that these rationalistic theologians find it more convenient to keep to their unregulated arbitrary reflections, to which philosophy attaches no validity. If, then, those theologians, who busy themselves with their argumentations in exegesis, and appeal to the Bible in connection with all their notions, when they deny as against philosophy the possibility of knowledge, have brought matters to such a pass, and have so greatly depreciated the reputation of the Bible, that if the truth were as they say, and if according to the true explanation of the Bible, no knowledge of the nature of God were possible, the spirit would be compelled to look for another source in order to acquire such truth as should be substantial or full of content.

The philosophy of religion cannot, therefore, in the fashion of that metaphysic of the understanding, and exegesis of inferences, put itself in opposition to positive religion, and to such doctrine of the Church as has still preserved its content. On the contrary, it will become apparent that it stands infinitely nearer to positive doctrine than it seems at first sight to do. Indeed, the re-establishment of the doctrines of the Church, reduced to a minimum by the understanding, is so truly the work of philosophy, that it is decried by that so-called theology of reason, which is merely a theology of the understanding, as a darkening of the mind, and this just because of the true content possessed by it. The fears of the understanding, and its hatred of philosophy, arise from a feeling of apprehension, based on the fact that it perceives how philosophy carries back its reflecting process to its foundation, that is, to the affirmative in which it perishes, and yet that philosophy arrives at a content, and at a knowledge of the nature of God, after all content seemed to be already done away with. Every content appears to this negative tendency to be a darkening of the mind, its only desire being to continue in that nocturnal darkness which it calls enlightenment, and hence the rays of the light of knowledge must be necessarily regarded by it as hostile.

It is sufficient here merely to observe, regarding the supposed opposition of the philosophy of religion and positive religion, that there cannot be two kinds of reason and two kinds of spirit; there cannot be a divine reason and a human, there cannot be a Divine Spirit and a human, which are *absolutely different*. Human reason—the consciousness of one's being—is indeed reason; it is the divine in man, and spirit, insofar as it is the spirit of God, is not a spirit beyond the stars, beyond the world. On the contrary, God is present, omnipresent, and exists as spirit in all spirits. God is a living God, who is acting and working. Religion is a product of the Divine Spirit; it is not a discovery of man but a work of divine operation and creation in him. The expression that God as reason rules the world would be irrational if we did not assume that it has reference also to religion, and that the Divine Spirit works in the special character and form assumed by religion. But the development of reason as perfected in thought does not stand in opposition to this spirit, and consequently it cannot be absolutely different from the work which the Divine Spirit has produced in religion. The more a man in thinking rationally lets the true thing or fact[2] itself hold sway with him, renounces his particularity, acts as universal consciousness, while his reason does not seek its own in the sense of something special, the less will he, as the embodiment of this reason, get into that condition of opposition; for it, namely, reason, is itself the essential fact or thing, the spirit, the Divine Spirit. The Church or the theologians may disdain this aid, or may take it amiss when their doctrine is made reasonable; they may even repel the exertions of philosophy with proud irony, though these are not directed in a hostile spirit against religion, but, on the contrary, seek to fathom its truth; and they may ridicule the "manufactured" truth—but this scorn is no longer of any avail, and is, in fact, idle when once the need of true rational knowledge, and the sense of discord between it and religion, have been awakened. The intelligence has here its rights, which can in no way be longer denied to it, and the triumph of knowledge is the reconciliation of the opposition.

Although then, philosophy, as the philosophy of religion, is so very different from those tendencies of the understanding, which are at bottom hostile to religion, and is in no way such a spectral thing as it has usually been represented to be, yet even at the present day we still see the belief in the

2. Die Sache.

absolute opposition between philosophy and religion made one of the shibboleths of the time. All those principles of the religious consciousness which have been developed at the present time, however widely distinguished their forms may be from one another, yet agree in this, that they are at enmity with philosophy, and endeavour at all hazards to prevent it from occupying itself with religion; and the work that now lies before us is to consider philosophy in its relation to these *principles of the time*. From this considera-tion of the subject we may confidently promise ourselves success, all the more that it will become apparent how, in presence of all that enmity which is shown to philosophy, from however many sides it may come—indeed, it comes from almost every side of consciousness in its present form— the time has nevertheless arrived when philosophy can, partly in an unprejudiced and partly in a favourable and successful manner, occupy itself with religion. For the opposition takes one or another of those forms of the divided consciousness which we considered above. They occupy partly the stand-point of the metaphysic of the understanding, for which God is emptiness, and content has vanished, partly the standpoint of feeling, which after the loss of absolute content has withdrawn itself into its empty subjectivity, but is in accord with that metaphysic in coming to the result that every characterisation is inadequate to the eternal content—for this indeed is only an abstraction. Or we may even see that the assertions of the opponents of philosophy contain nothing else than what philosophy itself contains as its principle, and as the foundation of its principle. This contradiction, namely, that the opponents of philosophy are the opponents of religion who have been overcome by it, and that they yet implicitly possess the principle of philosophical knowledge in their reflections, has its foundation in this: that they repre-sent the historical element out of which philosophical thought in its complete shape has been formed.

The Relation of the Philosophy of Religion to the Current Principles of the Religious Consciousness

If at the present day philosophy be an object of enmity because it occupies itself with religion, this cannot really surprise us when we consider the general character of the time. Everyone who attempts to deal with the knowledge of God, and by the aid of thought to comprehend his nature, must be prepared to find, that either no attention will be paid to him or that people will turn against him and combine to oppose him.

The more the knowledge of finite things has increased— and the increase is so great that the extension of the sciences has become almost boundless, and all regions of knowledge are enlarged to an extent which makes a comprehensive view impossible—so much the more has the sphere of the knowledge of God become contracted. There was a time when all knowledge was knowledge of God. Our own time, on the contrary, has the distinction of knowing about all and everything, about an infinite number of subjects, but nothing at all of God. Formerly the mind found its supreme interest in knowing God, and searching into his nature. It had and it found no rest unless in thus occupying itself with God. When it could not satisfy this need it felt unhappy. The spiritual conflicts to which the knowledge of God gives rise in the inner life were the highest which the spirit knew and experienced in itself, and all other interests and knowledge were lightly esteemed. Our own time has put this need, with all its toils and conflicts, to silence; we have done with all this, and got rid of it. What Tacitus said of the ancient Germans, that they were *securi adversus deos*, we have once more become in regard to knowledge, *securi adversus deum*.

It no longer gives our age any concern that it knows nothing of God; on the contrary, it is regarded as a mark of the highest intelligence to hold that such knowledge is not even possible. What is laid down by the Christian religion as the supreme, absolute commandment, "Ye shall know God," is regarded as a piece of folly. Christ says, "Be ye perfect, as My Father in heaven is perfect." This lofty demand is to the wisdom of our time an empty sound. It has made of God an infinite phantom, which is far from us, and in like manner has made human knowledge a futile phantom of finiteness, or a mirror upon which fall only shadows, only phenomena. How, then, are we any longer to respect the commandment, and grasp its meaning, when it says to us, "Be ye perfect, as My Father in heaven is perfect," since we know nothing of the Perfect One, and since our knowing and willing are confined solely and entirely to appearance, and the truth is to be and to remain absolutely and exclusively a something beyond the present? And what, we must further ask, what else would it be worthwhile to comprehend, if God is incomprehensible?

This standpoint must, judged by its content, be considered as the last stage of the degradation of man, in which at the same time he is, it is true, all the more arrogant inasmuch as he thinks he has proved to himself that this degradation is the highest possible state, and is his true destiny. Such a point of view is, indeed, directly opposed to the lofty nature of the Christian religion, for according to this we ought to know God, his nature, and his essential being, and to esteem this knowledge as something which is the highest of all. (The distinction as to whether this knowledge is brought to us by means of faith, authority, revelation, or reason is here of no importance.) But although this is the case, and although this point of view has come to dispense both with the content which revelation gives of the divine nature, and with what belongs to reason, yet it has not shrunk, after all its abject gropings, in that blind arrogance which is proper to it, from turning against philosophy. And yet it is philosophy which is the liberation of the spirit from that shameful degradation, and which has once more brought religion out of the stage of intense suffering which it had to experience when occupying the standpoint referred to. Even the theologians, who are at home in that region of vanity, have ventured to charge philosophy with its destructive tendency—theologians who have no longer anything left of that substantial element which could possibly be destroyed.

In order to repel these not merely groundless, but, what is more, frivolous and unprincipled objections, we need only observe cursorily how theologians have, on the contrary, done everything in their power to do away with what is definite in religion, in that they have (1) thrust dogmas into the background, or pronounced them to be unimportant; or (2) consider them only as extraneous definitions given by others, and as mere phenomena of a past history. When we have reflected in this manner upon the aspect presented by the content, and have seen how this last is re-established by philosophy, and placed in safety from the devastations of theology, we shall (3) reflect upon the form of that standpoint, and shall see here how the tendency which, taking its departure from the form, is at enmity with philosophy, is so ignorant of what it is, that it does not even know that it contains in itself the very principle of philosophy.

Philosophy and the Prevalent Indifference
to Definite Dogmas

If, then, it be made a reproach to philosophy in its relation to religion that the content of the doctrine of revealed positive religion, and more expressly of the Christian religion, is depreciated by it, and that it subverts and destroys its dogmas, yet this hindrance is taken out of the way, and by the new theology itself, in fact. There are very few dogmas of the earlier system of Church confessions left which have any longer the importance formerly attributed to them, and in their place no other dogmas have been set up. It is easy to convince oneself, by considering what is the real value now attached to ecclesiastical dogmas, that into the religious world generally there has entered a widespread, almost universal, indifference towards what in earlier times were held to be essential doctrines of the faith. A few examples will prove this.

Christ still indeed continues to be made the central point of faith, as Mediator, Reconciler, and Redeemer; but what was known as the work of redemption has received a very prosaic and merely psychological signification, so that although the edifying words have been retained, the very thing that was essential in the old doctrine of the Church has been expunged.

"Great energy of character, steadfast adherence to conviction for the sake of which He regarded not His life"—these are the common categories through which Christ is brought down, not indeed to the plane of ordinary everyday life, but to that of human action in general and moral designs, and into a moral sphere into which even heathens like Socrates were capable of entering. Even though Christ be for many the central point of faith and devotion in the deeper sense, yet Christian life as a whole restricts itself to this devotional bent, and the weighty doctrines of the Trinity, of the resurrection of the body, as also the miracles in the Old and New Testaments, are neglected as matters of indifference, and have lost their importance. The divinity of Christ, dogma, what is peculiar to the Christian religion is set aside, or else reduced to something of merely general nature. It is not only by the Enlightenment that Christianity has been thus treated, but even by pious theologians themselves. These latter join with the men of the Enlightenment in saying that the Trinity was brought into Christian doctrine by the Alexandrian school, by the neo-Platonists. But even if it must be conceded that the fathers of the Church studied Greek philosophy, it is in the first instance a matter of no importance whence that doctrine may have come; the only question is whether it be essentially, inherently, true; but that is a point which is not examined into, and yet that doctrine is the keynote of the Christian religion.

If an opportunity were given to a large number of these theologians to lay their hand on their heart, and say whether

they consider faith in the Trinity to be indispensably necessary to salvation, and whether they believe that the absence
of such faith leads to damnation, there can be no doubt what
the answer would be.

Even the words "eternal happiness" and "eternal damnation" are such as cannot be used in good society; such
expressions are regarded as ἀρρητα, as words which one
shrinks from uttering. Even though a man should not wish to
deny these doctrines, he would, in case of his being directly
appealed to, find it very difficult to express himself in an
affirmative way.

In the doctrinal teaching of these theologians, it will be
found that dogmas have become very thin and shrunken,
although they are talked about a great deal.

If any one were to take a number of religious books, or
collections of sermons, in which the fundamental doctrines
of the Christian religion are supposed to be set forth, and
attempt to sift the greater part of those writings con-
scientiously in order to ascertain whether, in a large proportion of such literature, the fundamental doctrines of Christianity are to be found contained and stated in the orthodox
sense, without ambiguity or evasion, the answer is again not a
doubtful one.

It would appear that the theologians themselves, in accordance with the general training which most of them have
received, only attribute that importance which they formerly
assigned to the principle and doctrines of positive Christianity—when these were still regarded as such—to these doctrines when they are veiled in a misty indefiniteness. Thus if
philosophy has always been regarded as the opponent of the
doctrines of the Church, it cannot any longer be such, since
these doctrines, which it seemed to threaten with destruction, are no longer regarded by general conviction as of
importance. A great part of the danger which threatens
philosophy from this side when she considers these dogmas in
order to comprehend them ought to be thus taken away, and
so philosophy can take up a more untrammelled attitude

with regard to dogmas which have so much sunk in interest with theologians themselves.

The Historical Treatment of Dogmas

The strongest indication, however, that the importance of these dogmas has declined, is to be perceived in the fact that they are treated principally in a historical manner, and are regarded in the light of convictions which belong to *others*, as matters of history, which do not go on in our own mind as such, and which do not concern the needs of our spirit. The real interest here is to find out how the matter stands so far as others are concerned, what part others have played, and centres in this accidental origin and appearance of doctrine. The question as to what is a man's own personal conviction only excites astonishment. The absolute manner of the origin of these doctrines out of the depths of spirit, and thus the necessity, the truth, which they have for *our* spirits too, is shoved on one side by this historical treatment. It brings much zeal and erudition to bear on these doctrines. It is not with their essential substance, however, that it is occupied, but with the externalities of the controversies about them, and with the passions which have gathered around this external mode of the origin of truth. Thus theology is by her own act put in a low enough position.

If the philosophical knowledge of religion is conceived of as something to be reached historically only, then we should have to regard the theologians who have brought it to this point as clerks in a mercantile house, who have only to keep an account of the wealth of strangers, who only act for others without obtaining any property for themselves. They do, indeed, receive salary, but their reward is only to serve, and to register that which is the property of others. Theology of this kind has no longer a place at all in the domain of thought; it has no longer to do with infinite thought in and for itself, but only with it as a finite fact, as opinion, ordinary thought, and so on. History occupies itself with truths which *were* truths—namely, for others, not with such as would come to be the possession of those who are occupied with them. With the true content, with the knowledge of God, such theologians have no concern. They know as little of God as a blind man sees of a painting, even though he handles the frame. They only know how a certain dogma was established by this or that council; what grounds those present at such a council had for establishing it, and how this or that opinion came to predominate. And in all this, it is indeed religion that is in question, and yet it is not religion itself which here comes under consideration. Much is told us of the history of the painter of the picture, and of the fate of the picture itself, what price it had at different times, into what hands it came, but we are never permitted to see anything of the picture itself.

It is essential in philosophy and religion, however, that the spirit should *itself* enter with supreme interest into an inner relation, should not only occupy itself with a thing that is foreign to it, but should draw its content from that which is essential, and should regard itself as worthy of such knowledge. For here man is concerned with the value of his *own* spirit, and he is not at liberty humbly to remain outside and to wander about at a distance.

Philosophy and Immediate Knowledge

In consequence of the emptiness of the standpoint just considered, it might appear as if we only mentioned the reproaches which it casts upon philosophy in order to pronounce expressly against such a point of view, and that our aim, which we do not relinquish, is to do the opposite of that which it holds to be the highest of all aims—namely, to know God. Yet this standpoint has an aspect belonging to its form in which it must really have a rational interest for us, and regarded from this side, the recent attitude of theology is more favourable for philosophy. For with the thought that all objective determinateness has converged in the inwardness of subjectivity, the conviction is bound up that God gives revelation in an immediate way in man; that religion consists just in this, that man has immediate knowledge of God. This immediate knowing is called reason, and also faith, but in a sense other than that in which the Church takes faith. All knowledge, all conviction, all piety, regarded from the point of view which we are considering, is based on the principle that in the spirit, as such, the consciousness of God exists immediately with the consciousness of itself.

1. This statement taken in a direct sense, and as not implying that any polemical attitude has been taken up to philosophy, passes for one which needs no proof, no confirmation. This universal idea, which is now matter of assumption, contains this essential principle—namely, that the highest, the religious content shows itself in the spirit itself, that spirit manifests itself in spirit, and in fact *in this my spirit*, that this faith has its source, its root in my deepest personal being, and that it is what is most peculiarly my own, and as such is inseparable from the consciousness of pure spirit.

Inasmuch as this knowledge exists immediately in myself, all external authority, all foreign attestation is cast aside; what is to be of value to me must be verified in my own spirit, and in order that I may believe I must have the witness of my spirit. It may indeed come to me from without, but any such external origin is a matter of indifference; if it is to be valid, this validity can only build itself up upon the foundation of all truth, in the *witness of the spirit*.

This principle is the simple principle of philosophical knowledge itself, and philosophy is so far from rejecting it that it constitutes a fundamental characteristic in philosophy itself. Thus it is to be regarded as a gain, a kind of happy circumstance, that fundamental principles of philosophy live even in general popular conceptions, and have become general assumptions, for in this way the philosophical principle may expect the more easily to obtain the general consent of the educated. As a result of this general disposition of the spirit of our time, philosophy has not only won a position which is externally favourable—with what is external it is never concerned, and least of all where it, and active interest in it, takes the form of an institution of the state—but is favoured inwardly, since its principle already lives in the minds and in the hearts of men as an assumption. For philosophy has this in common with the form of culture referred to: that reason is regarded as that part of the spirit in which God reveals himself to man.

2. But the principle of immediate knowledge does not rest satisfied with this simple determinateness, this natural and ingenuous content; it does not only express itself affirmatively, but takes up a directly polemical attitude to philosophical knowledge, and directs its attacks especially against the philosophical knowledge and comprehension of God. Not only does it teach that we are to believe and to know in an immediate manner, not only is it maintained that the consciousness of God is bound up with the consciousness of self, but that the relation to God is *only* an immediate one. The immediateness of the connection is taken as excluding the other characteristic of mediateness, and philosophy, because it is mediated knowledge, is said to be only a finite knowledge of that which is finite.

Thus this knowledge in its immediacy is to get no further than this, that we know that God is, but not what he is; the content, the filling up of the idea of God, is negated. By philosophical knowledge or cognition we mean that we know not only that an object is, but also what it is; and that to know what it is, is not only to know it to the extent of possessing a certain knowledge, certainty, of what it is; but more than this, this knowledge must relate to its characteristics, to its content, and it must be complete and full and proved knowledge, in which the necessary connection of these characteristics is a matter of knowledge.

If we consider more closely what is involved in the assertion of immediate knowledge, it is seen to mean that the consciousness so relates itself to its content that it itself and this content—God—are inseparable. It is this relation, in fact

–knowledge of God–and this inseparableness of consciousness from this content, which we call religion. Further,
however, it is of the essence of this assertion that we are to
limit ourselves to the consideration of religion as such, and to
keep strictly to the consideration of the relation to God, and
are not to proceed to the knowledge of God, that is, of the
divine content–of what the divine content essentially is in
itself.

In this sense it is stated, further, that we can only know
our relation to God, not what God himself is; and that it is
only our relation to God which is embraced in what is
generally called religion. Thus it happens that at the present
time we only hear religion spoken of and do not find that
investigation is made regarding the nature of God, what he is
in himself, and how the nature of God must be determined.
God, as God, is not even made an object of thought; knowledge does not trench upon that object, and does not exhibit
distinct attributes in him, so as to make it possible that he
himself should be conceived of as constituting the relation of
these attributes, and as relation in himself. God is not before
us as an object of knowledge, but only our relation with God,
our relation to him; and while discussions of the nature of
God have become fewer and fewer, it is now only required of
a man that he should be religious, that he should abide by
religion, and we are told that we are not to proceed further
to get a knowledge of any divine content.

3. If, however, we bring out what is inherent in the
principle of immediate knowing–that is, what is directly
affirmed in it–we find it to be just this, that God is spoken
of in relation to consciousness in such a way that this relation
is something inseparable, or, in other words, that we must of
necessity contemplate *both*. It implies, in the first place, the
essential distinction which the conception of religion contains: on the one side, subjective consciousness, and on the
other, God recognised as Object in himself, or implicitly. At
the same time, however, it is stated that there is an essential
relation between the two, and that it is this inseparable

relation of religion which is the real point, and not the notions which one may have concerning God.

What is really contained in this position, and really constitutes its true kernel, is the philosophical Idea itself, only that this Idea is confined by immediate knowledge within limitations which are abolished by philosophy, and which are by it exhibited in their one-sidedness and untruth. According to the philosophical conception, God is spirit, is concrete; and if we inquire more closely what spirit is, we find that the whole of religious doctrine consists in the development of the fundamental conception of spirit. For the present, however, it may suffice to say that spirit is essentially self-manifestation—its nature is *to be for spirit*. Spirit is for spirit, and not, be it observed, only in an external, accidental manner. On the contrary, spirit is only spirit insofar as it is for spirit; this constitutes the conception or notion of spirit itself. Or, to express it more theologically, God is essentially spirit, so far as he is in his church. It has been said that the world, the material universe, must have spectators, and must be for spirit, or mind; how much more, then, must God be for spirit.

We cannot, consequently, view the matter in a one-sided way, and consider the subject merely according to its finiteness, to its contingent life, but inasmuch too as it has the infinite absolute object as its content. For if the subject be considered by itself, it is considered within the limits of finite knowledge, of knowledge which concerns the finite. It is also maintained, on the other hand, that God, in like manner, must not be considered for himself, for man only knows of God in relation to consciousness; and thus the unity and inseparability of the two determinations—of the knowledge of God and self-consciousness—even presupposes what is expressed in identity, and that dreaded identity itself is contained in it.

As a matter of fact, we thus find the fundamental conception which belongs to philosophy already existing as an universal element in the cultured thought of the present day.

And here it becomes apparent, too, that philosophy does not stand above its age as if it were something absolutely different from the general character of the time, but that it is one spirit which pervades both the actual world and philosophical thought, and that this last is only the true self-comprehension of what is actual. Or, in other words, it is one movement upon which both the age and its philosophy are borné, the distinction being only that the character of the time still appears to present itself as accidental, and is not rationally justified, and may thus even stand in an unreconciled, hostile attitude towards the truly essential content; while philosophy, as the justification of principles, is at the same time the universal peace bringer and universal reconciliation. As the Lutheran Reformation carried faith back to the first centuries, so the principle of immediate knowledge has carried Christian knowledge back to the primary elements. If, however, this process at first causes the essential content to evaporate, yet it is philosophy which recognises this very principle of immediate knowledge as representing content, and as being such carries it forward to its true expansion within itself.

The want of sound sense which marks the arguments advanced against philosophy knows no bounds. The very opinions which are supposed by those who hold them to militate against philosophy, and to be in the sharpest antagonism to it, upon examination of their content exhibit essential agreement with that which they combat. Thus the result of the study of philosophy is that these walls of separation, which are supposed to divide absolutely, become transparent; and that when we go to the root of things we find that there is absolute accordance where it was believed that there was the greatest opposition.

PRELIMINARY QUESTIONS

Before we can proceed to the treatment of our subject itself, it appears to be indispensable to solve several preliminary questions, or rather to institute an investigation into these with the view of showing that the possibility of any such treatment of the subject, and of a rational knowledge of religion, is made dependent on the result of this investigation. It appears to be absolutely necessary to examine and to answer these questions, for this reason: that they have very specially engaged the interest of thinking men in our day, both in a philosophical and in a popular connection, and because they have to do with the principles upon which prevalent opinions regarding the religious content, or substantial element of religion, as also regarding the knowledge of it, are based. If we omit such examination, it will at least be necessary to prove that this omission is not accidental, and that we possess the right to do this, since the essential element of any such examination is included in the science of philosophy itself, and all those questions can only find their solution there.

Here, therefore, we have only to look in the face the hindrances which the culture and opinion of the time, as hitherto considered, put in the way of our exercising the right to get an intellectual grasp of religion.

1. In the first place, it is not religion in general that we have before us, but *positive* religion, regarding which it is acknowledged that it is the gift of God, which rests on higher than human authority and therefore appears to be outside the sphere of human reason and to be elevated above it. The first hindrance in this connection is that we should be called upon, before proceeding further, to verify the competence and capability of reason to deal with the truth and doctrine of a religion which is supposed to be withdrawn from the sphere of human reason. Rational or philosophical knowledge comes, however, and must of necessity come, into relation with positive religion. It has been said, indeed, and is said still, that positive religion is "for itself," or stands on its own basis. We do not question its doctrines; we respect them, and hold them in honour; on the other side stands reason, thought, which seeks to grasp its object intellectually, and these two are supposed not to come into relation; reason is

not to interfere with these doctrines. Formerly, it was imagined that the freedom of philosophical investigation could be guarded in this way. It was then said that it was a thing by itself, which was not to do any harm to positive religion, and its result, moreover, also was subordinated to the teaching of positive religion. We do not wish, however, to place the present investigation on this footing. It is a false idea that these two, faith and free philosophical investigation, can subsist quietly side by side. There is no foundation for maintaining that faith in the content or essential element of positive religion can continue to exist, if reason has convinced itself of the opposite. The Church has, therefore, consistently and justly refused to allow that reason might stand in opposition to faith and yet be placed under subjection to it. The human spirit in its inmost nature is not something so divided up that two contradictory elements might subsist together in it. If discord has arisen between intellectual insight and religion, and is not overcome in knowledge, it leads to despair, which comes in the place of reconciliation. This despair is reconciliation carried out in a one-sided manner. The one side is cast away, the other alone held fast; but a man cannot win true peace in this way. The one alternative is for the divided spirit to reject the demands of the intellect and try to return to simple religious feeling. To this, however, the spirit can only attain by doing violence to itself, for the independence of consciousness demands satisfaction, and will not be thrust aside by force; and to renounce independent thought, is not within the power of the healthy mind. Religious feeling becomes yearning, hypocrisy, and retains the moment of nonsatisfaction. The other alternative is a one-sided attitude of indifference toward religion, which is either left unquestioned and let alone, or is ultimately attacked and opposed. That is the course followed by shallow spirits.

This, then, is the first preliminary question in virtue of which the right of reason to occupy itself with the doctrines of religion has to be proved.

2. In the sphere above referred to, it is only maintained that reason cannot apprehend the truth of the nature of God: the possibility of apprehending other truths is not denied to it; it is only the highest truth which is said to be beyond its knowledge. According to another position, however, it is entirely denied to reason to know truth at all. It is asserted that philosophical knowledge, when it deals with spirit in its true essence, in and for itself, with life, with the infinite, only produces mistakes, and that reason must renounce all claim to grasp anything of the infinite in an affirmative manner; the infinite is destroyed by thought, is brought down to the level of the finite. This result, in regard to reason, this negation of reason, is even said to be a result of rational knowledge itself. Thus it would be necessary first to examine reason itself in order to ascertain whether the capability of knowing God, and consequently the possibility of a philosophy of religion, is inherent in it.

3. It follows from this that the knowledge of God is not to be placed in the reason which seeks to comprehend its object, but that the consciousness of God springs only *out of feeling*; and that the relation of man to God lies within the sphere of feeling only and is not to be brought over into thought. If God be excluded from the region of rational intelligence or insight, of necessary, substantial subjectivity, nothing indeed is left but to assign to him the region of accidental subjectivity, that of feeling, and in this case it may well be a subject of wonder that objectivity is ascribed to God at all. In this respect, materialistic views, or by whatever other name you choose to designate them, empirical, historical, naturalistic, have been at least more consistent, in that they have taken spirit and thought for something material and imagine they have traced the matter back to sensations, even taking God to be a product of feeling, and denying to him objectivity. The result has, in this case, been atheism. God would thus be an historical product of weakness, of fear, of joy, or of interested hopes, cupidity, and lust of power. What has its root only in my feelings, is only for me; it is

mine, but not its own; it has no independent existence in and for itself. Therefore it appears to be necessary, before going further, to show that God is not rooted in feeling merely, is not merely *my* God. For this reason the older metaphysic has always demonstrated first of all that a God is, and not merely that there is a feeling of God, and thus the philosophy of religion too finds the demand made upon it to demonstrate God.

It might seem as if the other sciences had the advantage over philosophy, inasmuch as their material is already acknowledged, and they are exempted from the necessity of proving the existence of this material. To arithmetic the fact of numbers, to geometry that of space, to medicine that of human bodies and diseases, is granted from the very beginning, and it is not required of them to prove, for example, that space, bodies, diseases, exist. Philosophy, however, seems to labour under the disadvantage of being obliged, before beginning, to guarantee an existence to its objects; if it be granted without challenge that there *is* a world, yet no sooner does philosophy go on to assume the reality of the immaterial in general, of a thought and spirit free from what is material, and still more the reality of God, than it is at once taken to task. The object with which philosophy occupies itself is not, however, of such a character as to be something merely hypothetical, and it is not to be regarded as such. Were it so, philosophy, and especially the philosophy of religion, would have in the first place to verify its object for itself. It would have to direct its efforts toward showing it to be necessary that before it exist it prove that it is; it would have before its existence to prove its existence.

These, then, are the preliminary questions which it seems would have to be solved beforehand, as in their solution the very possibility of a philosophy of religion would lie. For, if such points of view be valid, then any philosophy of religion is absolutely impossible, since in order to prove its possibility these obstacles must in the first place be removed. So it appears at first sight. We nevertheless leave them on one side, and for what reason we do so will, so far as the principal points are concerned, be briefly explained, in order that this difficulty may be met.

The first demand is that reason, the faculty of knowledge, should be examined to begin with, before we advance to knowledge. Knowledge is thus conceived of as if it were to be got at by means of an instrument, with which the truth is to be laid hold of. When looked at more closely, however, the demand that this instrument should first be known is a clumsy one. Criticism of the faculty of knowledge is a position of the Kantian philosophy, and one which is general in the present time and in the theology of the day. It was believed to be a great discovery, but as so often happens in the world, this belief proved to be self-deception. For it is commonly the case that when people have a notion which they consider to be a very clever one, it is in connection with it that they show themselves most foolish, and their satisfaction consists in having found a splendid outlet for their folly and ignorance. Indeed they are inexhaustible in finding such outlets when it is a question of keeping a good conscience in the face of their indolence and of getting quit of the whole affair.

Reason is to be examined, but how? It is to be rationally examined, to be known; this is, however, only possible by means of rational thought; it is impossible in any other way, and consequently a demand is made which cancels itself. If we are not to begin philosophical speculation without having attained rationally to a knowledge of reason, no beginning can be made at all, for in getting to know anything in the philosophical sense, we comprehend it rationally; we are, it seems, to give up attempting this, since the very thing we have to do is first of all to know reason. This is just the demand which was made by that Gascon, who would not go into the water until he could swim. It is impossible to make any preliminary examination of rational activity without being rational.

Here in the philosophy of religion it is more especially

God, reason in fact, that is the object; for God is essentially rational, rationality, which as spirit is in and for itself. Now in speculating philosophically upon reason, we investigate knowledge, only we do it in such a way as to imply that we do not suppose we would want to complete this investigation beforehand outside of the object; on the contrary, the knowledge of reason is precisely the object with which we are concerned. It is of the very essence of spirit to be for spirit. That is just what spirit is, and this consequently implies that finite spirit has been posited, and the relation of finite spirit, of finite reason to the divine, originates of itself within the philosophy of religion itself and must be treated of there, and indeed in the very place where it first originates. It is this which constitutes the difference between a science and conjectures about a science; the latter are accidental; insofar, however, as they are thoughts, which relate to the matter itself, they must be included in its treatment, and they are in this case no longer mere chance bubbles of thought.

Spirit in making itself an object gives itself essentially the form of appearance or manifestation, as something which comes in a higher manner to the finite spirit; and it is essentially owing to this that the finite spirit arrives at a positive religion. Spirit becomes for itself or actual in the form of mental representation or idea, in the form of the Other, and for that other for which it is, religion is produced as something positive. Thus, too, there is inherent in religion that characteristic of reason in virtue of which it involves knowledge, in virtue of which it is activity of comprehension and of thought. This standpoint of knowledge is included in religion, and so, too, is the standpoint of feeling. Feeling is the subjective element; that which belongs to me as this individual, and because of which it is to myself that I appeal. The standpoint of feeling, too, in so far as God gives himself this ultimate individualisation of *This One*, of one who feels, has its place in the development of the conception of religion, because this feeling has in it a spiritual relation, has spirituality in it. The determination, too, that God *is*, is a

determination which is essentially included in the consideration of religion.

Religion, however, speaking generally, is the ultimate and
the highest sphere of human consciousness, whether it be
opinion, will, idea, ordinary knowledge, or philosophical
knowledge. It is the absolute result—it is the region into
which man passes over, as into the domain of absolute truth.

By reason of this universal character of religion, consciousness must, when in this sphere, have already raised itself
above all that is finite—above finite existence, conditions,
ends, and interests, as well as above finite thoughts, finite
relations of all kinds. To be actually within the sphere of
religion, it is necessary to have laid these aside.

Yet although even for the ordinary consciousness religion
is the act of rising up above the finite, it usually happens
when philosophy in general, and especially the philosophy
which deals with God, with religion, is attacked, that in
support of this polemical attitude, finite thoughts, relations
belonging to limitation, categories and forms of the finite are
brought forward to the disregard of this fundamental characteristic. Such forms of the finite are made points of departure
from which to oppose philosophy, especially the highest
philosophy, the philosophy of religion.

We shall only touch briefly upon this. Immediacy of knowledge—the fact of consciousness—is, for example, such a finite
form; such finite categories are the antitheses of finite and
infinite, subject and object. But these antitheses, finite *or*
infinite, subject *or* object, are abstract forms, which are out
of place in such an absolutely rich, concrete content as
religion is. In spirit, soul—that which has to do with religion—
quite other qualities are present than finiteness, etc.; and on
such qualities is based all that is essential in religion. These
forms must indeed be employed, since they are moments of
the essential relation which lies at the foundation of religion,
but it is of primary importance that their nature should have
been examined and recognised long before. This logical
knowledge, which comes first, must lie behind us when we

have to deal with religion scientifically; such categories must have long ago been done with. But the usual thing is to employ these as weapons against the concept, the Idea; against rational knowledge. Those categories are used entirely without criticism, in a quite artless way, just as if Kant's *Critique of Pure Reason* did not exist, which at least attacked these forms, and after its own fashion reached the result that it is only phenomena which can be known by means of these categories. In religion it is not, however, with phenomena that we have to do, it is with an absolute content. But those who employ this argumentative kind of reasoning seem to think the Kantian philosophers have existed only to afford opportunity for the more unblushing use of those categories.

It is entirely out of place, it is indeed preposterous, to bring forward these categories, such as immediacy, facts of consciousness, in *opposition* to philosophy, and to meet philosophy with the reply that the finite is different from the infinite, and the object from the subject, as if there were anyone, any philosopher whatever, who did not know this, or had still to learn such trivialities. Yet people are not ashamed to parade triumphantly cleverness of this sort, as if they had made a new discovery.

We shall here remark only that such characteristics as finite and infinite, subject and object—and this is what always constitutes the foundation of that very knowing and overwise talk—are undoubtedly different, but are at the same time inseparable too. We have an example of this in physics, in the north and south pole of the magnet. It is often said "those characteristics are as different as heaven and earth." That is quite correct; they are absolutely different, but as is already suggested by the figure just mentioned, they are inseparable. Earth cannot be shown without heaven, and vice versa.

It is difficult to enter into discussion with those who wage war on the philosophy of religion and think they have triumphed over it, for they tell us so bluntly that immediacy, after all, "is something quite different from mediation." At the same time they show an incredible ignorance, and a

complete want of acquaintance with the forms and categories
by means of which they make their attacks and pronounce a
final judgment upon philosophy. They make their affirma-
tions quite artlessly, without having thought over these subjects or made any thorough observation of external nature
and of the inner experience of their consciousness—of their
minds—and of the manner in which these qualities present
themselves there. Reality is not for them something present,
but is something strange and unknown. The hostile language
which they direct against philosophy is therefore mere
scholastic pedantry—the chatter of the schools—which
entangles itself in empty, unsubstantial categories, while in
philosophy we are not in the so-called school, but are in the
world of reality; and in the wealth of its qualities we do not
find a yoke under which we are in bondage, but have in them
free movement. And then, those who attack and disparage
philosophy are, owing to their finite style of thinking, incapable of even grasping a philosophical proposition; and though
they may perhaps repeat its words, they have given it a wrong
meaning, for they have not grasped its infiniteness, but have
introduced their finite conditions into it.

Thus philosophy is indefatigable, so to speak, and imposes
upon itself the great labour of carefully investigating what its
opponents have to say. Indeed that is its necessary course,
being in accordance with its conception, and it can only
satisfy the inward impulse of its notion or conception by
getting a knowledge both of itself and of what is opposed to
it (*verum index sui et falsi*), but it ought to be able to expect
as a recompense that the opposition should now, by way of a
reciprocal service, relinquish its hostility and calmly comprehend its essential nature. But that is certainly not the result
in this case, and the magnanimity which desires to recognise
in a friendly way the adversary, and which heaps coals of fire
on his head, does not help philosophy in the least, for the
adversary will not keep quiet, but persists in his attacks.
When *we* perceive, however, that the antithesis vanishes like a
phantom and dissolves into mist, we shall at the same time

only render to ourselves and to philosophical thought what is due, and shall not seek merely to carry our point as against the other. And indeed to convince that "other" to exert this personal influence upon him is impossible, since he remains wedded to his limited categories.

The thinking spirit must have got beyond all these forms of reflection; it must know their nature, the true relation involved in them, the infinite relation—that is to say, that in which their finiteness is done away with. Then it will become apparent, too, that immediate knowledge, like mediated knowledge, is entirely one-sided. What is true is their unity, an immediate knowledge which is likewise mediated, something mediated which is likewise simple in itself, which is immediate reference to itself. Inasmuch as the one-sidedness is done away with by means of such combination, it is a condition of infiniteness. Here is union, in which the difference of those characteristics is done away with,[3] while they at the same time being preserved ideally have the higher destiny of serving as the pulse of vitality, the impulse, movement, unrest of the spiritual, as of the natural life.

Since it is with religion, with what is supreme and ultimate, that we are to be occupied in the following dissertation, we ought now to be in a position to assume that the futility of those relations has long ago been overcome. But at the same time, since we do not begin at the very beginning of the science, but are considering religion per se, regard must be also had when dealing with it to such relations of understanding as are wont to come principally under consideration in connection with it.

With this reference to the following dissertation itself, we shall now proceed to give the general survey, the synopsis, or division, of our science.

3. *Aufgehoben* = abrogated, annulled, done away with, but also "preserved," as below. This is an example of the use of the word in the second phase of its double meaning.

Division Of The Subject

There can be but one method in all science, since the method is the self-unfolding notion (*Begriff*) and nothing else, and this latter is only one.

In accordance, therefore, with the moments of the concept, the exposition and development of religion will be presented in three parts. In the first place, the notion or conception of religion will be considered in its universal aspect, then, secondly, in its particular form as the self-dividing and self-differentiating notion, that is, under the aspect of judgment,[4] of limitation, of difference, and of finiteness; and thirdly, we shall consider the notion, which encloses itself within itself, the syllogism, or the return of the notion to itself out of the particularity in which it is unequal to itself, so that it arrives at equality with its form and does away with its limitation. This is the rhythm, the pure eternal life of spirit itself; and had it not this movement, it would be something dead. It is of the essential nature of spirit to have itself as object, and thence arises its manifestation. But here spirit is to begin with in the relation of objectivity, and in this relation it is something finite. The third stage is reached when it is object to itself in such a way that it reconciles itself with itself in the object, is "with itself," and in being so has attained its freedom. For freedom means to be self-contained, or at home with oneself.

But this rhythm, within which our science as a whole and the entire development of the notion moves, reappears in each of the three moments specified, since each of these is potentially totality in its determinateness, until this totality is made explicit as such in the final moment. Therefore, when the notion first appears in the form of universality, then in the form of particularity, and lastly, in the form of individuality, or when the movement of our science as a whole is that in which the notion becomes judgment and completes

4. *Ur-theil* = separation of subject from predicate.

itself in the syllogism, in every sphere of this movement the same development of the moments will show itself, only that in the first sphere it is held together within the determinate character of universality, in the second sphere within that of particularity, where it exhibits the moments independently, and it is only on arriving at the sphere of individuality that it returns to the real syllogism, which mediates itself in the totality of determinations.

Such, then, is the division of the subject, representing the movement, nature, and action of spirit itself, of which we, so to speak, are only spectators. It is necessitated by the concept; the necessity of the progression has, however, to present, explicate, prove itself in the development itself. The division, the different parts and content of which we shall now indicate in a more definite way, is therefore simply historical

The General Notion[5]
or Conception of Religion

What comes first is the notion in its universal aspect, what follows in the second place is the determinateness of the notion, the notion in its definite forms; these are indissolubly united with the notion itself, for in the philosophical mode of treatment it is not the case that the universal, the notion, is put into prominence, to do it honour, as it were. There are indeed notions or conceptions of Right and of nature, which are general definitions and are given a prominent place, and as to which there is, to tell the truth, room for doubt. These are not, however, taken seriously, and so we feel that it is not these that are of importance, but the particular content itself, the particular subjects. What is in this connection called the notion has no further influence upon this content beyond pointing out in a general way what the ground is upon which we stand in dealing with these subjects and preventing the introduction of content from any other sphere. The content, for example, magnetism, electricity, answers to the subject

5. *Begriff.*

matter itself,[6] the notion to the formal element. The conception or notion which is placed in the foreground (as, for example, that of Right) may, however, in connection with such a mode of considering the subject, become a mere name for the most abstract, uncertain content.

For the philosophical way of looking at things, too, the notion occupies the first place, but here the notion is the content itself, the absolute subject matter, the substance, as in the case of the germ, out of which the whole tree develops itself. All specifications or determinations are contained in this, the whole nature of the tree, the kind of sap it has, the way in which the branches grow; but in a spiritual manner, and not preformed so that a microscope could reveal its boughs, its leaves, in miniature. It is thus that the notion contains the whole nature of the object, and knowledge itself is nothing else but the development of the notion, of that which is implicitly contained in the notion and has not yet come into existence, has not been unfolded, displayed. Thus we begin with the notion or conception of religion.

The Moment of Universality

In the notion or conception of religion the purely universal, again, does indeed take the first place; that is, the moment of thought in its complete universality. It is not this or that that is thought, but *thought thinks itself*. The object is the universal, which, as active, is thought. As the act of rising up to the true, religion is a departing from sensuous, finite objects. If this becomes merely an advance to an "Other," it is the false progressive process *ad infinitum*, and is that kind of talk which does not make progress. Thought, however, is a rising up from the limited to the absolutely universal, and religion is only through thought, and in thought. God is not the highest emotion, but the highest thought. Although he is lowered down to popular conception, yet the content of this conception belongs to the realm

6. *Sache.*

of thought. The opinion that thought is injurious to religion, and that the more thought is abandoned the more secure the position of religion is, is the maddest error of our time. This misunderstanding originates in a fundamental misconception of the higher spiritual relations. Thus in regard to Right, good will for itself (or as an independent motive) is taken as something which stands in contrast to intelligence, and men are given the more credit for true good will the less they think. Right and morality, on the contrary, consist in this alone, that I am a thinking being; that is to say, in the fact that I do not look upon my freedom as that of my empirical personality, which belongs to me as this *individual*, and in which I might subjugate my neighbour by means of stratagem or force, but in my regarding freedom as something that has its being in and for itself, or exists on its own account, that is, as something universal.

If we now say that religion has the moment of thought in its complete universality in itself, and that the unlimited-universal is supreme absolute thought, we do not as yet make the distinction here between subjective and objective thought. The universal is object, and is thought pure and simple, but thought not as yet developed and made determinate in itself. All distinctions are as yet absent and exist potentially only. In this ether of thought all that is finite has passed away, everything has disappeared, while at the same time everything is included in it. But this element of the universal has not as yet taken those more explicit forms. Out of this liquid element, and in this transparency, nothing has as yet fashioned itself into distinct shape.

Now the further advance consists in this: that this universal determines itself for itself, and this self-determination constitutes the development of the Idea of God. In the sphere of universality the Idea itself is, to begin with, the material of determination, and the progress is revealed in divine figures, but as yet the second element—form—is retained in the divine Idea, which is still in its substantiality,

and under the character of eternity it remains in the bosom
of the universal.

The Moment of Particularity, or the Sphere of Differentiation

The particularisation, therefore, which is as yet retained in
the sphere of the universal, when it actually manifests itself
outwardly as such, constitutes the Other as against the
extreme of universality, and this other extreme is consciousness in its individuality as such. It is the subject in its
immediacy, and with its needs, conditions, sins—in fact, in its
wholly empirical, temporal character.

In religion, I am myself the *relation* of the two sides as
thus determined. I who think, who am that which lifts myself
up, the active universal, and ego, the immediate subject, are
one and the same "I." And further, the *relation* of these two
sides which are so sharply opposed—the absolutely finite
consciousness and being on the one hand, and the infinite on
the other—exists in religion for *me*. In thinking I lift myself
up to the absolute above all that is finite, and am infinite
consciousness, while I am at the same time finite consciousness, and indeed am such in accordance with my whole
empirical character. Both sides, as well as their relation, exist
for me. Both sides seek each other, and both flee from each
other. At one time, for example, I accentuate my empirical,
finite consciousness, and place myself in opposition to infiniteness; at another I exclude myself from myself, condemn
myself, and give the preponderance to the infinite consciousness. The middle term contains nothing else than the characteristics of both the extremes. They are not pillars of Her-
cules, which confront each other sharply. I am, and it is *in
myself* and for myself that this conflict and this conciliation
take place. In myself, I as infinite am against or in contrast
with myself as finite, and as finite consciousness I stand over
against my thought as infinite. I am the feeling, the perception, the idea alike of this unity and this conflict, and am
what holds together the conflicting elements, the effort put

forth in this act of holding together, and represent the labour of heart and soul to obtain the mastery over this opposition.

I am thus the relation of these two sides, which are not abstract determinations, as "finite and infinite." On the contrary, each is itself totality. Each of the two extremes is itself "I," what relates them; and the holding together, the relating, is itself this which is at once in conflict with itself and brings itself to unity in the conflict. Or, to put it differently, I am the conflict, for the conflict is just this antagonism, which is not any indifference of the two as different, but is their being bound together. I am not *one* of those taking part in the strife, but I am both the combatants, and am the strife itself. I am the fire and the water which touch each other, and am the contact and union of what flies apart, and this very contact itself is this double, essentially conflicting relation, as the relation of what is now separated, severed, and now reconciled and in unity with itself.

As representing the forms of the relation of the two extremes, we shall make ourselves acquainted with (1) feeling; (2) sense perception;[7] (3) idea,[8] or ordinary thought.

Before entering upon this subject, it will be necessary to get a knowledge of the entire sphere of these relations in its necessity, in so far as it contains, as elevation of the finite consciousness to the absolute, the forms of religious consciousness. In investigating this necessity of religion, we are obliged to conceive religion as posited through what is other than itself.

In this mediation, indeed, when it opens for us the way into the sphere of those forms of consciousness, religion will present itself already as a result which at once does away with itself as a result; consequently it will present itself as the primary thing, through which all is mediated, and on which all else depends. We shall thus see in what is mediated the counterimpact, the reciprocal action of the movement and of necessity, which both goes forwards and pushes backwards.

7. *Anschauung.*
8. *Vorstellung.*

But this mediation of necessity is now to be posited within religion itself too, so that in fact the relation and the essential connection of the two sides, which are comprised in the religious spirit, may be known as necessary. The forms of feeling, of sense perception, and of idea or mental representation, as they necessarily proceed one out of the other, are now forced of themselves into that sphere in which the inward mediation of their moments proves itself to be necessary—that is to say, into the sphere of thought in which religious consciousness will get a grasp of itself in its notion. These two mediations of necessity, therefore, of which one leads to religion and the other takes place within religious consciousness itself, comprise the forms of religious consciousness as it *appears* as feeling, sense perception, and idea or ordinary thought.

The Annulling of the Differentiation, or Worship
(Cultus)

The movement in the preceding sphere is just that of the notion of God, of the Idea, in becoming objective to itself. We have this movement before us in the language of ordinary thought, in the expression "God is a spirit." Spirit is not something having a single existence, but is spirit only in being objective to itself, and in beholding itself in the "Other," as itself. The highest characteristic of spirit is self-consciousness, which includes this objectivity in itself. God, as Idea, is subjective for what is objective and is objective for what is subjective. When the moment of subjectivity defines itself further, so that the distinction is made between God as object and the knowing spirit, the subjective side defines itself in this distinction as that which belongs to the side of finiteness, and the two stand at first so contrasted, that the separation constitutes the antithesis of finiteness and infiniteness. This infinitude, however, being still encumbered with this opposition, is not the true infinitude; to the subjective side, which exists for itself, the absolute object remains still an Other, and the relation in which it stands to it is not

self-consciousness. Such an attitude, however, also involves
the relation which is expressed by saying, that the finite
knows itself as a nullity in its state of separation, and knows
its object as the absolute, as its substance. And here the first
attitude toward the absolute object is that of fear; for individuality knows itself as in regard to the absolute object only
as accidental, or as something which is transient and
vanishing.

But this standpoint of separation is not the true relation.
On the contrary, it is what knows itself to be a nullity, and,
therefore, something which is to be done away with and
absorbed; and its attitude is not merely a negative one, but is
in itself, or implicitly, positive. The subject recognises the
absolute substance, in which it has to annul or lose itself, as
being at the same time *its* essence, *its* substance, in which,
therefore, self-consciousness is inherently contained. It is this
unity, reconciliation, restoration of the subject and of its
self-consciousness, the positive feeling of possessing a share
in, of partaking in this absolute, and making unity with it
actually one's own—this abolition of the dualism, which
constitutes the sphere of worship. Worship comprises this
entire inward and outward action, which has this restoration
to unity as its object. The expression "worship" is usually
taken merely in the limited sense in which it is understood to
mean only outward public acts, and the inward action of the
heart does not get so much prominence. We, however, shall
conceive of worship as that action which includes both inwardness and outward manifestation, and which in fact produces restoration of unity with the absolute, and in so doing
is also essentially an inward conversion of the spirit and soul.
Thus Christian worship does not only include the sacraments
and the acts and duties pertaining to the Church, but it also
includes the so-called way of salvation as a matter of absolutely inward history, and as a series of actions on the part of
the inner life—in fact, a movement which goes forward in the
soul and has its right place there.

But we shall always find these two sides, that of self-consciousness—that is, of worship—and that of consciousness or of idea, corresponding with each other at every stage of religion. According as the content of the notion or conception of God or consciousness is determined, so too is the attitude of the subject to him; or to put it otherwise, so too is self-consciousness in worship determined. The one moment is always a reflection or copy of the other, the one points to the other. Both modes, of which the one holds fast to objective consciousness only, and the other to pure self-consciousness, are one-sided, and each brings about its own abrogation.

It was, therefore, a one-sided view if the natural theology of former times looked upon God as object of consciousness only. Such a mode of contemplating the Idea of God, although the words "spirit" or "person" might be made use of, could never in reality get beyond the idea of an essence. It was inconsistent, for if actually carried out it must have led to the other, the subjective side, that of self-consciousness.

It is just as one-sided to conceive of religion as something subjective only, thus in fact making the subjective aspect the only one. So regarded, worship is absolutely sterile and empty; its action is a movement which makes no advance, its attitude toward God a relation to a nullity, an aiming at nothing. But even this merely subjective action has inconsistency inherent in it, and must of necessity annul itself. For if the subjective side also is to be in any way determined or qualified, it is involved too in the very conception of spirit, that it is consciousness, and that its determinate character becomes object to it. The richer the feeling, the more fully determined or specialised it is, the richer must the object be for it too. And further, the absoluteness of that feeling, which is supposed to be substantial, would, in accordance with its very nature, require to set itself free from its subjectivity; for the substantial character which is supposed to belong to it is specially directed against the accidental element of opinion and of inclination, is in fact something permanent and fixed in and for itself, independent of our feeling or experience. It is the objective, what exists in and for itself. If this substantial element remains shut up in the heart only, it is not recognised as the something higher than ourselves, and God himself becomes something merely sub- jective, while the efforts of subjectivity remain at the most, as it were, a drawing of lines into empty space. For the recognition of a something higher than ourselves, which is capable too of being described, this recognition of One who is undefined, and these lines which are to be drawn in accordance with such recognition, possess no support, no connecting element, derived from what is objective, and are and remain merely *our* act, our lines, something subjective, and the finite never attains to a true real renunciation of itself; while spirit ought, on the contrary, in worship to liberate itself from its finiteness, and to feel and know itself in God.

In the absence of that which is self-existent and commands our obedience, all worship shrinks up into subjectivity. Wor- ship is essentially made up of dealings with and enjoyment of a something higher than ourselves, and includes assurances, evidences, and confirmation of the existence of this higher being; but such definite dealings, such actual enjoying and assurances can have no place if the objective, obligatory moment be wanting to them, and worship would, in fact, be annihilated if the subjective side were taken to be the whole. The possibility of getting out of the subjective heart into action would thus be as much precluded as the possibility of consciousness attaining to objective knowledge. The one is connected in the closest manner with the other. What a man believes he has to do in relation to God corresponds with the idea which he has formed of God. His consciousness of self answers to his consciousness, and conversely he cannot believe himself to have any definite duties toward God if he neither has nor supposes himself to have any definite idea of him as an object. Not until religion is really relation, and contains the distinction involved in consciousness, does wor- ship attain to a definite form as the lifting up into a higher unity of the severed elements and become a vital process. This movement of worship does not, however, confine itself to the inner life alone, in which consciousness frees itself from its finiteness, is the consciousness of its essence, and the subject as knowing itself in God has penetrated into the foundation of its life. But this its infinite life now develops towards what is outside too, for the worldly life which the subject leads has that substantial consciousness as its basis, and the way and manner in which the subject defines its ends depends on the consciousness of its essential truth. It is in connection with this side that religion reflects itself into worldly or secular life, and that knowledge of the world shows itself. This going out into the actual world is essential to religion, and in this transition religion appears as morality in relation to the state and to the entire life of the state. According as the religion of nations is constituted, so also is their morality and their government. The shape taken by these latter depends entirely on whether the conception of the freedom of spirit which a people has reached is a limited one, or on whether the nation has the true consciousness of freedom.

The more definite characteristics of worship will be seen to be the moment of presupposed unity, the sphere of separation, and the freedom which re-establishes itself in the separation.

a. Worship is thus, in fact, the eternal process by which the subject posits itself as identical with its essential being.

This process of the cancelling of the dualism seems to belong to the subjective side only, but it is posited in the object of consciousness, too. Through worship, unity is attained; what is not originally united, however, cannot be posited or made explicit as such. This unity, which appears as the act, the result of worship, must be recognised, too, as existing in and for itself. For what is object for consciousness is the absolute, and its essential characteristic is that it is unity of its absoluteness with particularity. This unity is therefore in the object itself; for example, in the Christian conception of the Incarnation of God.

This self-existent unity, or, put more definitely, the human form, God's becoming man, is in fact an essential moment of religion, and must necessarily appear in the definition of its object. In the Christian religion this characteristic is completely developed, but it occurs, too, in inferior religions, even if the only sign of it is that the infinite is seen in unity with the finite in such a way that it appears as this particular being, as a definite immediate existence in stars or animals. Further, too, it must be observed here that it is only momentarily that God assumes a human or other form of existence, that he becomes externally manifest, or inwardly reveals himself in a dream or as an inward voice.

This is the moment of presupposed or hypothetical unity, which is essentially involved in the conception of God, and in such a way that the object of consciousness (God) exhibits the entire conception of religion in its content, and is itself totality. The moments of the conception of religion thus present themselves here in the character of unification. Each of the aspects or sides of the true Idea is itself the same totality which the whole is. The specific characteristics of content in the two sides are consequently not different in themselves but only in their form. The absolute object therefore determines itself for consciousness as totality which is in unity with itself.

b. This totality now presents itself in the form of separation and of finiteness, which, as representing the other side, stands over against that totality which is in unity with itself. The moments of the content of the entire conception are here posited as separating themselves from one another, as differentiated, and consequently as abstract. The first moment of this side of differentiation is that of potentiality, the moment of being which is in identity with itself, of formlessness, of objectivity, in fact. This is matter as representing what is indifferent or undifferentiated, as existence of which all parts are of equal value. Form may be introduced into it, but it remains still in a condition of abstract being for self. We then call it the world, which in relation to God appears partly as his garment, vesture, form, or as something in contrast with himself.

Over against this moment of undifferentiated potential being there now stands being-for-self, the negative in general, form. This negative now appears, in its at first indeterminate form, as the negative element in the world, while the latter is the positive element, what subsists. The negativity which is opposed to this subsisting element, to this feeling of self, to this definite being, to this established existence, is evil. In contrast to God, to this reconciled unity of being-in-itself and being-for-itself, appears the element of distinction or difference. We have on the one hand the world as positively and independently existing, and on the other destruction and contradiction in the world; and here the questions suggest themselves, which pertain to all religions based on a more or less developed consciousness, as to how evil is to be reconciled with the absolute unity of God, and wherein lies the origin of evil.

This negative, in the first place, appears as the evil in the world, but it recalls itself into identity with itself, in which it is the being-for-self of self-consciousness—finite spirit.

This negative which recalls itself into itself is now once more a something positive, because it relates itself simply to itself. As evil, it appears as involved in positive existence. But the negativity which is present for itself and independently, and not in another which is regarded as having independent existence of its own, the negativity which reflects itself into itself, the inward, infinite negativity which is object to itself, is just the "ego." In this self-consciousness, and in its own inner movement, finiteness definitely appears, and self-contradiction is thus incident in it. Thus there is an element of disturbance in it, evil makes its appearance in it, and thus is evil of the will.

c. I, however, who am free can abstract from everything; it is this negativity and isolation which constitutes my essential being. Evil is not the whole of the subject. On the contrary, this latter has in it also unity with itself, which constitutes the positive side (goodness) and the absoluteness, the infinitude of consciousness of self. It is this ability to abstract from all that is immediate, from all that is external, which constitutes the essential moment of the isolation or seclusion of spirit. This isolation is exempted from the temporariness, change and vicissitude of this world, from evil and from disunion, and is represented as the absoluteness of consciousness of self in the thought of the immortality of the soul. At first the prominent element in this thought is continued existence in time; this exemption from the dominion and from the vicissitudes of change is represented, however, as essentially and originally belonging to spirit and not as being brought about secondarily by means of reconciliation. And thus advance is made to the further determination that the Spirit's consciousness of self is an eternal, absolute moment in that eternal life in which it is lifted up far above time, above this abstraction of change, and above the reality of change, above dualism, when it is taken up into the unity and reconciliation which is *presupposed* as originally present in the object of consciousness.

Of Judgment, or Definite Religion

If in the first part we have considered religion in its notion or conception, the simple conception of religion, the character of the content, the universal, it is now necessary to leave this sphere of universality and go on to treat of determinateness in religion.

The notion as such is not as yet unfolded; the determinate qualities, the moments are contained in it, but are not as yet openly displayed and have not received the right distinction or difference which belongs to them. It is only by means of the judgment (i.e. the act of differentiation) that they receive this. It is when God, the notion, performs the act of judgment, and the category of determinateness enters, that we first come to have existing religion, which is at the same time definitely existing religion.

The course followed in passing from the abstract to the

concrete is based upon our method, upon the notion, and not on the fact that much special content is present. There is a complete distinction between this and our point of view. Spirit, to which belongs being which is absolute and supreme, is, exists only as activity; that is to say, in so far as it posits itself, is actual or for itself, and produces itself. But in this its activity it has the power of *knowing*, and only as it thus knows is it that which it is. It is thus essential to religion not only to exist in its notion, but also to be the consciousness of that which the notion is, and the material in which the notion as the plan, so to speak, realises itself, which it makes its own, which it moulds in accordance with itself, is human consciousness. So too, Right, for example, only is when it exists in the spirit, when it takes possession of the wills of men, and they know of it as the determination of their wills. And it is in this way that the Idea first realises itself, having before only been posited as the form of the notion.

Spirit, in short, is not immediate; natural things are immediate and remain in this condition of immediate being. The being of spirit is not thus immediate, but is, exists only as producing itself, as making itself for itself by means of negation as subject; otherwise it would be substance only. And this coming to itself on the part of spirit is movement, activity, and mediation of itself with itself.

A stone is immediate, it is complete. Wherever there is life, however, this activity is already to be found. Thus the first form of the existence of plants is the feeble existence of the germ, and out of this it has to develop itself and to produce itself. Finally the plant epitomises itself when it has unfolded itself in the seed; this beginning of the plant is also its ultimate produce. In like manner man is at first a child, and as belonging to nature he describes this round in order to beget another.

In plants there are two kinds of individual forms: this germ which begins is different from the one which is the completion of its life, and in which this evolution reaches maturity. But it is the very nature of spirit, just because it is living, to be at first only potential, to be in its notion or conception, then to come forward into existence, to unfold, produce itself, become mature, bringing forth the notion of itself, that which it implicitly is, so that what it is in itself or implicitly may be its notion actually or for itself. The child is not as yet a reasonable person; it has capacities only, it is at first reason, spirit, potentially only. It is by means of education and development that it becomes spirit.

This, then, is what is called self-determination entering into existence, being "for other," bringing one's moments or factors into distinction, and unfolding oneself. These distinctions are no other than the characteristics which the notion itself implicitly contains.

The development of these distinctions, and the course of the tendencies which result from them, are the way by which spirit comes to itself; it is itself, however, the goal. The absolute end or goal, which is that spirit should know itself, comprehend itself, should become object to itself as it is in itself, arrive at perfect knowledge of itself, first appears as its true being. Now this process, followed by self-producing spirit, this path taken by it, includes distinct moments; but the path is not as yet the goal, and spirit does not reach the goal without having traversed the path; it is not originally at the goal; even what is most perfect must traverse the path to the goal in order to attain it. Spirit, in these halting places of its progress, is not as yet perfect; its knowledge, its consciousness regarding itself, is not what is true, and it is not as yet revealed to itself. Spirit being essentially this activity of self-production, it follows that there are stages of its consciousness, but its consciousness of itself is always in proportion only to the stage which has been reached. Now these stages supply us with definite religion; here religion is consciousness of the universal spirit, which is not as yet fully developed as absolute; this consciousness of spirit at each stage is definite consciousness of itself, it is the path of the education of spirit. We have therefore to consider the definite forms of religion. These, as being stages on the road followed by spirit, are imperfect.

The different forms or specific kinds of religion are, in one aspect, moments of religion in general, or of perfected religion. They have, however, an independent aspect too, for in them religion has developed itself in time, and historically.

Religion, insofar as it is definite, and has not as yet completed the circle of its determinateness—so far, that is, as it is finite religion, and exists as finite—is historical religion, or a particular form of religion. Its principal moments, and also the manner in which they exist historically, being exhibited in the progress of religion from stage to stage, and in its development, there thus arises a series of forms of religion, or a history of religion.

That which is determined by means of the notion must of necessity have existed, and the religions, as they have followed upon one another, have not arisen accidentally. It is spirit which rules inner life, and to see only chance here, after the fashion of the historical school, is absurd.

The essential moments of the notion or conception of religion show themselves and make their appearance at every stage in which religion exists at all. It is only because the moments are not as yet posited in the totality of the notion that any difference between it and its true form arises. These definite religions are not indeed *our* religion, yet they are included in ours as essential, although as subordinate moments, which cannot miss having in them absolute truth. Therefore in them we have not to do with what is foreign to us, but with what is our own, and the knowledge that such is the case is the reconciliation of the true religion with the false. Thus the moments of the notion or conception of religion appear on lower stages of development, though as yet in the shape of anticipations or presentiments, as natural flowers and creations of fancy which have, so to speak, blossomed forth by chance. What determines the characteristics of these stages, however, through their entire history, is the determinateness of the notion itself, which can at no stage be absent. The thought of the Incarnation, for example, pervades every religion. Such general conceptions make their presence felt, too, in other spheres of spirit. What is substantial in moral relations, as, for example, property, marriage, protection of the sovereign and of the state, and the ultimate decision which rests with subjectivity regarding that which is to be done for the whole, all this is to be found in an uneducated society as well as in the developed state; only the definite form of this substantial element differs according to the degree of culture which such a society has reached.

What is here of special importance, however, is that the notion should also become actually known in its totality, and in exact accordance with the degree in which this knowledge is present, is the stage at which the religious spirit is, higher or lower, richer or poorer. Spirit may have something in its possession without having a developed consciousness of it. It actually has the immediate, proper nature of spirit, has a physical, organic nature, but it does not know that nature in its essential character and truth, and has only an approximate, general idea of it. Men live in the state, they are themselves the life, activity, actuality of the state, but the positing, the becoming conscious of what the state is, does not on that account take place, and yet the perfected state just means that everything which is *potentially* in it, that is to say, in its notion or conception, should be developed, posited, and made into rights and duties, into law. In like manner the moments of the notion or conception are actually present in the definite religions, in mental pictures, feelings, or immediate imagery; but the *consciousness* of these moments is not as yet evolved, or, in other words, they have not as yet been elevated to the point at which they are the determination of the absolute object, and God is not as yet actually represented under these determinations of the totality of the conception of religion.

It is undoubtedly true that the definite religions of the various peoples often enough exhibit the most distorted, confused, and abortive ideas of the Divine Being, and likewise of duties and ways of conduct as expressed in worship. But we must not treat the matter so lightly and conceive of it in so superficial a manner as to reject these ideas and these rites as superstition, error, and deceit, or only trace back their origin to pious feeling, and thus value them as merely representing some sort of religious feeling, without caring how they may chance to be constituted. The mere collection and elaboration of the external and visible elements cannot satisfy us either. On the contrary, something higher is necessary, namely, to recognise the meaning, the truth, and the connection with truth; in short, to get to know what is *rational* in them. They are human beings who have hit upon such religions, therefore there must be *reason* in them, and amidst all that is accidental in them a higher necessity. We must do them this justice, for what is human, rational in them, is *our own*, too, although it exists in our higher consciousness as a moment only. To get a grasp of the history of religions in this sense means to reconcile ourselves even with what is horrible, dreadful, or absurd in them, and to justify it. We are on no account to regard it as right or true, as it presents itself in its purely immediate form—there is no question of doing this—but we are at least to recognise its beginning, the source from which it has originated as being in human nature. Such is the reconciliation with this entire sphere, the reconciliation which completes itself in the notion. Religions, as they follow upon one another, are determined by means of the notion. Their nature and succession are not determined from without; on the contrary, they are determined by the nature of spirit, which has entered into the world to bring itself to consciousness of itself. Since we look at these definite religions in accordance with the notion, this is a purely philosophical study of what actually is or exists. Philosophy indeed treats of nothing which is not and does not concern itself with what is so powerless as not even to have the energy to force itself into existence.

Now in development as such, insofar as it has not as yet

reached its goal, the moments of the notion are still in a state of separation or mutual exclusion, so that the reality has not as yet come to be equal to the notion or conception. The finite religions are the appearance in history of these moments. In order to grasp these in their truth, it is necessary to consider them under two aspects; on the one hand, we have to consider how God is known, how he is characterised; and on the other, how the subject at the same time knows itself. For the two aspects the objective and subjective have but one foundation for their further determination, and but one specific character pervades them both. The idea which a man has of God corresponds with that which he has of himself, of his freedom. Knowing himself in God, he at the same time knows his imperishable life in God; he knows of the truth of his being, and therefore the idea of the *immortality of the soul* here enters as an essential moment into the history of religion. The ideas of God and of immortality have a necessary relation to each other; when a man knows truly about God, he knows truly about himself, too: the two sides correspond to each other. At first God is something quite undetermined; but in the course of the development of the human mind, the consciousness of that which God is gradually forms and matures itself, losing more and more of its initial indefiniteness, and with this the development of true *self*-consciousness advances also. The proofs of the existence of God are included also within the sphere of this progressive development, it being their aim to set forth the necessary elevation of the spirit to God. For the diversity of the characteristics which in this process of elevation are attributed to God is fixed by the diversity of the points of departure, and this diversity again has its foundation in the nature of the historical stage of actual self-consciousness which has been reached. The different forms which this elevation of the spirit takes will always indicate the metaphysical spirit of the period in question, for this corresponds to the prevalent idea of God and the sphere of worship.

If we now attempt to indicate in a more precise way the

divisions of this stage of definite religion, we find that what is
of primary importance here is the manner of the divine
manifestation. God is manifestation, not in a general sense
merely, but as being spirit he determines himself as appearing
to himself; that is to say, he is not object in the general sense,
but is object to himself.

1. As for manifestation generally, or abstract manifestation, it is What is Natural in general. Manifestation is being
for other, an externalisation of things mutually distinct, and
one, in fact, which is immediate and not yet reflected into
itself. This logical determination is taken here in its concrete
sense as the natural world. What is for an "Other" exists for
this very reason in a sensuous form. The thought, which is for
another thought, which, as having being, is to be posited as
distinct, that is to say, as something which exists as an
independent subject in reference to the other, is only capable
of being communicated by the one to the other through the
sensuous medium of sign or speech, in fact, by bodily means.

But since God exists essentially only as appearing to himself, that abstract attitude of man to nature does not belong
to religion; on the contrary, in religion nature is only a
moment of the divine, and therefore must, as it exists for the
religious consciousness, have also the characteristic note of
the spiritual mode of existence in it. It thus does not remain
in its pure, natural element, but receives the characteristic
quality of the divine which dwells in it. It cannot be said of
any religion that in it men have worshipped the sun, the sea,
or nature; when they worship these objects, the latter no
longer have for the worshippers the prosaic character which
they have for ourselves. Even while these objects are for them
divine, they still, it is true, remain natural; but when they
become objects of religion, they at once assume a spiritual
aspect. The contemplation of the sun, the stars, etc., as
individual natural phenomena, is outside the sphere of religion. The so-called prosaic manner of looking at nature, as
the latter exists for consciousness when regarding it through
the understanding, betokens a separation which comes later;

its presence is consequent on much deeper and more thoroughgoing reflection. Not till the spirit or mind has posited itself independently for itself, and as free from nature, does the latter appear to it as an Other, as something external.

The first mode of manifestation then, in the form of nature namely, has the subjectivity, the spiritual nature of God as its centre in a general sense only, and consequently these two determinations have not as yet come into relation through reflection. When this takes place, it constitutes the second mode of manifestation.

2. In himself or potentially God is Spirit; this is our notion or conception of him. But for this very reason He must be posited too as spirit, and this means that the manner of his manifestation must be itself a *spiritual* one, and consequently the negation of the natural. And for this it is necessary that his determinateness, the Idea on the side of reality, be equal to the conception; and the relation of reality to the divine conception is complete when spirit exists as spirit; that is to say, when both the conception and reality exist as this spirit. To begin with, however, we see that the form of nature constitutes that determinateness of the conception of God, or the aspect of reality belonging to the Idea. The emergence of the spiritual element of subjectivity out of nature accordingly appears at first merely as a conflict between the two sides, which are still entangled with one another in that conflict. Therefore this stage of definite religion, too, remains in the sphere of what is natural, and in fact constitutes, in common with the preceding one, the stage of the religion of nature.

3. It is actually within the definite religions as they succeed each other that spirit in its movement attempts to make the determinateness correspond with the notion or conception, but this determinateness appears here as still abstract, or, to put it otherwise, the notion appears as still the finite notion. These attempts, in which the principle of the preceding stages, namely, essence, or essential being, strives to comprehend itself as infinite inwardness are: (1) the Jewish

religion; (2) the Greek; (3) the Roman. The God of the Jews
is oneness or soleness, which as such continues to be abstract
unity, and is not as yet concrete in itself. This God is indeed
God in the spirit, but does not exist as yet *as* spirit. He is
something not presented to sense, an abstraction of thought,
which has not as yet that fulness in itself which constitutes it
spirit. The freedom which the notion seeks to reach through
self-development in the Greek religion, still lives under the
sway of the sceptre of necessity of essence; and the notion as
it appears in and seeks to win its independence in the Roman
religion is still limited, since it is related to an external world
which stands opposite to it, in which it is only to be objective, and is, therefore, external adaptation to an end, or
external purposiveness.

These are the principal specific forms which here present
themselves as the modes of the reality of spirit. As *determinate* they are inadequate to the notion or conception of
spirit, and are finite in character, and this infinitude, namely,
that there is one God, this abstract affirmation, is finite also.
This determination of the manifestation of God in consciousness as pure ideality of the one, as abolition of the manifold
character of external manifestation, might perhaps be contrasted with the religion of nature as being that which is true,
but it is really only *one* form of determinateness as against
the totality of the notion of spirit. It corresponds with this
totality just as little as its opposite does. These definite religions are not in fact as yet the true religion; and in them God
is not as yet known in his true nature, since there is wanting
to them the absolute content of spirit.

Revealed Religion

Manifestation, development, and determination or specification do not go on *ad infinitum* and do not cease *accidentally*. True progress consists rather in this: that this re-
flexion of the notion into itself stops short, inasmuch as it
really returns into itself. Thus manifestation is itself infinite

in nature; the content is in accordance with the conception of spirit, and the manifestation is, like spirit, in and for itself. The notion or conception of religion has in religion become objective to itself. Spirit, which is in and for itself, has now no longer individual forms, determinations of itself, before it, as it unfolds itself. It knows itself no longer as spirit in any definite form or limitation but has now overcome those limitations, this finiteness, and is actually what it is potentially. This knowledge of spirit for itself or actually, as it is in itself or potentially, is the being in-and-for-itself of spirit as exercising knowledge, the perfected, absolute religion, in which it is revealed what spirit, what God is; this is the Christian religion.

That spirit, as it does in all else, must in religion also run through its natural course, is necessarily bound up with the conception of spirit. Spirit is only spirit when it exists for itself as the negation of all finite forms, as this absolute ideality.

I form ideas, I have perceptions, and here there is a certain definite content, as, for instance, this house, and so on. They are my perceptions, they present themselves to me; I could not, however, present them to myself if I did not grasp this particular content in myself, and if I had not posited it in a simple, ideal manner in myself. Ideality means that this definite external existence, these conditions of space, of time, and matter, this separateness of parts, is done away with in something higher, in that I know this external existence, these forms of it are not ideas which are mutually exclusive, but are comprehended, grasped together in me in a simple manner.

Spirit is knowledge; but in order that knowledge should exist, it is necessary that the content of that which it knows should have attained to this ideal form, and should in this way have been negated. What spirit is must in that way have become its own, it must have described this circle; and these forms, differences, determinations, finite qualities, must have existed in order that it should make them its own.

This represents both the way and the goal—that spirit should have attained to its own notion or conception, to that which it implicitly is, and in this way only, the way which has been indicated in its abstract moments, does it attain it. Revealed religion is manifested religion, because in it God has become wholly manifest. Here all is proportionate to the notion; there is no longer anything secret in God. Here, then, is the consciousness of the developed conception of spirit, of reconciliation, not in beauty, in joyousness, but *in the spirit*. Revealed religion, which was hitherto still veiled, and did not exist in its truth, came at its own time. This was not a chance time, dependent on someone's liking or caprice, but determined on in the essential, eternal counsel of God; that is, in the eternal reason, wisdom of God; it is the notion of the reality or fact itself, the divine notion, the notion of God Himself, which determines itself to enter on this development, and has set its goal before it.

This course thus followed by religion is the true theodicy; it exhibits all products of spirit, every form of its self-knowledge, as necessary, because spirit is something living, working, and its impulse is to press on through the series of its manifestations towards the consciousness of itself as embracing all truth.

On Philosophy

The work that follows is a translation of G. W. F. Hegel's *(Vorlesungen über die Geschichte der Philosophie,* Erster Band). The version here was translated from the German by E. S. Haldane. It is the Introduction from *Hegel's Lectures on the History of Philosophy* (London: Routledge & Kegan Paul, Ltd., 1892), pp. 1-116. J. Glenn Gray has emended the translation slightly for this edition (1969).

In the history of philosophy the observation is immediately forced upon us that it certainly presents great interest if its subject is regarded from a favourable point of view, but that it would still possess interest even if its end were regarded as opposite to what it is. Indeed, this interest may seem to increase in the degree to which the ordinary conception of philosophy, and of the end which its history serves, is reversed; for from the history of philosophy a proof of the futility of the science is mainly derived.

The demand that a history, whatever the subject may be, should state the facts without prejudice and without any particular object or end to be gained by its means, must be regarded as a fair one. But with a commonplace demand like this, we do not get far; for the history of a subject is necessarily intimately connected with the ordinary conception[1] which is formed of it. In accordance with this what is important in it is determined, and the relation of the events to the end regulates the selection of facts to be recorded, the mode of comprehending them, and the point of view under which they are regarded. It may happen from the ideas formed of what a state really is, that a reader of the political

1. *Vorstellung.*

history of a country may find therein nothing of what he looks for. Still more may this be the case in the history of philosophy, and representations of this history may be instanced in which everything, excepting what was supposed to be philosophy, appears to be found.

In other histories we have a clear conception of their subjects, at least so far as their principal points are concerned; we know whether they concern a particular land, people or race, or whether their subject is the science of mathematics, physics, etc., or an art, such as painting. The science of philosophy has, however, this distinguishing feature, and, if you will, this disadvantage as compared with other sciences: that we find the most varied points of view as regards its notion[2], and regarding that which it ought to and can accomplish. If this first assumption, the conception of the subject of the history, is not established, the history itself is necessarily made vacillating, and it only obtains consistency when it sets forth a definite conception: but then in view of the various ways of regarding its subject, it easily draws upon itself the reproach of one-sidedness.

That drawback relates, however, only to an external consideration of this narrative; there is another and greater disadvantage allied to it. If there are different notions of the science of philosophy, it is the true notion alone that puts us in a position to understand the writings of philosophers who have worked in the knowledge of it. For in thought, and particularly in speculative thought, comprehension means something quite different from understanding the grammatical sense of the words alone, and also from understanding them in the region of ordinary conception only. Hence we may possess a knowledge of the assertions, propositions, or of the opinions of philosophers; we may have occupied ourselves largely with the grounds of and deductions from these opinions, and the main point in all that we have done may be wanting—the comprehension of the propositions. There is hence no lack of voluminous and even learned

2. *Begriff.*

histories of philosophy in which the knowledge of the matter itself, about which so much ado has been made, is absent. The authors of such histories may be compared to animals which have listened to all the tones in some music, but to whose senses the unison, the harmony of their tones, has not penetrated.

The circumstance mentioned makes it in no science so necessary as in the history of philosophy to commence with an Introduction, and in it correctly to define, in the first place, the subject of the history about to be related. For it may be said, How should we begin to treat a subject, the name of which is certainly mentioned often enough, but of whose nature we as yet know nothing? In treating the history of philosophy thus, we could have no other guidance than that of seeking out and taking up whatever has received the name of philosophy, anywhere or any time. But in fact, when the notion of philosophy is established, not arbitrarily but in a scientific way, such treatment becomes the science of philosophy itself. For in this science the peculiar characteristic is that its notion forms the beginning in appearance merely, and it is only the whole treatment of the science that is the proof, and indeed we may say the finding of its notion; and this is really a result of that treatment.

In this Introduction the notion of the science of philosophy, of the subject matter of its history, has thus likewise to be assumed. At the same time, though this Introduction professes to relate to the history of philosophy only, what has just been said of philosophy on the whole also holds good. What can be said in this Introduction is not so much something which may be stated beforehand, as what can be justified or proved in the treatment of the history. These preparatory explanations are, for this reason only, not to be placed in the category of arbitrary assumptions. But to begin with stating what in their justification are really results can only have the interest which may be possessed by a summary, given in advance, of the most general contents of a science. It must serve to set aside many questions and demands which might, from our ordinary prejudices, arise in such a history.

There are various aspects under which the history of philosophy may possess interest. We shall find the central point of
this interest in the essential connection existing between
what is apparently past and the present stage reached by
philosophy. That this connection is not one of the external
considerations which may be taken into account in the
history of philosophy, but really express its inner character;
that the events of this history, while they perpetuate themselves in their effects like all other events, yet produce their
results in a special way—this it is which is here to be more
clearly expounded.

What the history of philosophy shows us is a succession of
noble minds, a gallery of heroes of thought, who, by the
power of reason, have penetrated into the being of things, of
nature and of spirit, into the being of God, and have won for
us by their labours the highest treasure, the treasure of
reasoned knowledge.

The events and actions of this history are therefore such
that personality and individual character do not enter to any
large degree into its content and matter. In this respect the
history of philosophy contrasts with political history, in
which the individual, according to the peculiarity of his
disposition, talents, affections, the strength or weakness of
his character, and in general, according to that through which
he is this individual, is the subject of actions and events. In
philosophy, the less deserts and merits are accorded to the
particular individual, the better is the history; and the more it
deals with thought as free, with the universal character of
man as man, the more this thought, which is devoid of special characteristic, is itself shown to be the producing subject.

The acts of thought appear at first to be a matter of
history, and, therefore, things of the past, and outside our
real existence. But in reality we are what we are through
history: or, more accurately, as in the history of thought,
what has passed away is only one side, so in the present, what
we have as a permanent possession is essentially bound up

with our place in history. The possession of self-conscious reason, which belongs to us of the present world, did not arise suddenly, nor did it grow only from the soil of the present. This possession must be regarded as previously present, as an inheritance, and as the result of labour—the labour of all past generations of men. Just as the arts of outward life, the accumulated skill and invention, the customs and arrangements of social and political life, are the result of the thought, care, and needs, of the want and the misery, of the ingenuity, the plans and achievements of those who preceded us in history, so, likewise, in science, and especially in philosophy, do we owe what we are to the tradition which, as Herder has put it,[3] like a holy chain, runs through all that was transient, and has therefore passed away. Thus has been preserved and transmitted to us what antiquity produced.

But this tradition is not only a stewardess who simply guards faithfully that which she has received, and thus delivers it unchanged to posterity, just as the course of nature in the infinite change and activity of its forms ever remains constant to its original laws and makes no step in advance. Such tradition is no motionless statue, but is alive, and swells like a mighty river, which increases in size the further it advances from its source.

The content of this tradition is that which the intellectual world has brought forth, and the universal mind[4] does not remain stationary. But it is just the universal mind with which we have to do. It may certainly be the case with a single nation that its culture, art, science—its intellectual activities as a whole—are at a standstill. This appears, perhaps, to be the case with the Chinese, for example, who may have been as far advanced in every respect two thousand years ago as now. But the world spirit does not sink into this rest of indifference; this follows from its very nature, for its activity

3. *Zur Philosophie und Geschichte,* 5, pp 184-86. (Edition of 1828, in 12 vols.).
4. *Geist.* The other translators in this volume frequently render this crucial word as "spirit." Ed.

is its life. This activity presupposes a material already present, on which it acts, and which it does not merely augment by the addition of new matter, but completely fashions and transforms. Thus that which each generation has produced in science and in intellectual activity is an heirloom to which all the past generations have added their savings, a temple in which all races of men thankfully and cheerfully deposit that which rendered aid to them through life, and which they had won from the depths of nature and of mind. To receive this inheritance is also to enter upon its use. It constitutes the soul of each successive generation, the intellectual substance of the time, its principles, prejudices, and possessions; and this legacy is reduced to a material which becomes metamorphosed by mind. In this manner that which is received is changed, and the material worked upon is both enriched and preserved at the same time.

This is the function of our own and of every age: to grasp the knowledge which is already existing, to make it our own, and in so doing to develop it still further and to raise it to a higher level. In thus appropriating it to ourselves we make it into something different from what it was before. On the presupposition of an already existing intellectual world which is transformed in our appropriation of it, depends the fact that philosophy can only arise in connection with previous philosophy, from which of necessity it has arisen. The course of history does not show us the becoming of things foreign to us, but the becoming of ourselves and of our own knowledge.

The ideas and questions which may be present to our mind regarding the character and ends of the history of philosophy, depend on the nature of the relationship here given. In this lies the explanation of the fact that the study of the history of philosophy, is an introduction to philosophy itself. The guiding principles for the formation of this history are given in this fact, the further discussion of which must thus be the main object of this introduction. We must also, however, keep in mind as being of fundamental importance, the conception of the aim of philosophy. And since, as already mentioned, the systematic exposition of this conception cannot here find a place, such discussion as we can now undertake can only propose to deal with the subject provisionally and not to give a thorough and conclusive account of the nature of the becoming of philosophy.

The becoming is not merely a passive movement, as we suppose movements such as those of the sun and moon to be. It is no mere movement in the unresisting medium of space and time. What we must represent to ourselves is the activity of free thought; we have to present the history of the world of thought as it has arisen and produced itself.

There is an old prejudice that it is the faculty of thought which separates men from beasts; and to this prejudice we shall adhere. In accordance with this, what man has, as being nobler than a beast, he has through thinking. Everything which is human, however it may appear, is so only because the thought contained in it works and has worked. But thought, although it is thus the essential, substantial, and effectual, has many other elements. We must, however, consider it best when thought does not pursue anything else, but is occupied only with itself—with what is noblest—when it has sought and found itself. The history which we have before us is the history of thought finding itself, and it is the case with thought that it only finds itself in producing itself; indeed, that it only exists and is actual in finding itself. These productions are the philosophic systems; and the series of discoveries on which thought sets out in order to discover itself forms a work which has lasted twenty-five hundred years.

If the thought which is essentially thought is in and for itself and eternal, and that which is true is contained in thought alone, how, then, does this intellectual world come to have a history? In history what appears is transient, has disappeared in the night of the past and is no more. But true, necessary thought—and it is only with such that we have to do—is capable of no change. The question here raised constitutes one of those matters first to be brought under our consideration. But in the second place, there are also many most important things outside of philosophy, which are yet the work of thought, and which are left unconsidered. Such are religion, political history, forms of government, and the arts and sciences. The question arises as to how these works differ from the subject of consideration, and how they are related in history. As regards these two points of view, it is desirable to show in what sense the history of philosophy is here taken, in order to see clearly what we are about. Moreover, in the third place, we must first take a general survey before we descend to particulars, else the whole is not seen for the mere details—the wood is not seen for the trees, nor philosophy for mere philosophies. We require to have a general idea of the nature and aim of the whole in order to know what to look for. Just as we first desire to obtain a general idea of a country, which we should no longer see in going into detail, so we desire to see the relation which single philosophies bear to the whole; for in reality, the high value of the detail lies in its relation to the whole. This is nowhere more the case than with philosophy, and also with its history. In the case of a history, indeed, the establishment of the universal seems to be less needful than in that of one of the sciences proper. For history seems at first to be a succession of chance events, in which each fact stands isolated by itself, which has time alone as a connecting link. But even in political history we are not satisfied with this. We see, or at least divine in it, that essential connection in which the individual events have their place and relation to an end or aim, and in this way obtain significance. For the significant in history is such only through its relation to and connection with a universal. To perceive this universal is thus to apprehend the significance.

There are, therefore, the following points with which I wish to deal in this introduction.

The first of these will be to investigate the character of the history of philosophy, its significance, its nature, and its aim, from which will follow inferences as to its treatment. In particular, we shall get an insight into the relation of the history of philosophy to the science of philosophy, and this will be the most interesting point of all. That is to say, this history not merely represents the external, accidental events contained within it, but shows how the content, or that which appears to belong to mere history, really belongs to the science of philosophy. The history of philosophy is itself scientific, and thus essentially becomes the science of philosophy.

In the second place, the notion of philosophy must be more adequately determined, and from it must be deduced what should be excluded from the history of philosophy out of the infinite material and the manifold aspects of the intellectual culture of the nations. Religion, certainly, and the thoughts contained in and regarding it, particularly when these are in the form of mythology, are, on account of their subject matter, and the sciences with their ideas on the state, duties, and laws, on account of their form, so near philosophy that the history of the science of philosophy threatens to become quite indefinite in extent. It might be supposed that the history of philosophy should take account of all these ideas. Has not everything been called philosophy and philosophizing? On the one hand, the close connection has to be further considered in which philosophy stands with its allied subjects, religion, art, the other sciences, and likewise with political history. On the other hand, when the province of philosophy has been correctly defined, we reach, with the determination of what philosophy is and what pertains to it, the starting point of history, which must be distinguished from the commencements of religious ideas and mere thoughtful conjectures.

From the idea of the subject which is contained in these first two points of view, it is necessary to pass on to the consideration of the third point, to the general review of this history and to the division of its progress into natural periods—such an arrangement to exhibit it as an organic, progressive whole, as a rational connection through which this history attains the dignity of a science. And I will not occupy further space with reflections on the use of the history of philosophy and other methods of treating it. The use is evident. But, in conclusion, I wish to consider the sources of the history of philosophy, for this is customary.

THE NOTION OF THE HISTORY OF PHILOSOPHY

The thought which may first occur to us in the history of philosophy is that the subject itself contains an inner contradiction. For philosophy aims at understanding what is unchangeable, eternal, in and for itself: its end is truth. But history tells us of that which has at one time existed, at another time has vanished, having been expelled by something else. Truth is eternal; it does not fall within the sphere of the transient and has no history. But if it has a history, and as this history is only the representation of a succession of past forms of knowledge, the truth is not to be found in it, for the truth cannot be what has passed away.

It might be said that this argument would affect not only the other sciences, but in like degree the Christian religion, and it might be found inconsistent that a history of this religion and of the other sciences should exist. But it would be superfluous further to examine this argument, for it is immediately contradicted by the very fact that there are such histories. But in order to get a better understanding of this apparent contradiction, we must distinguish between the outward history of a religion or a science and the history of the subject itself. And then we must take into account that the history of philosophy, because of the special nature of its subject-matter, is different from other histories. It is at once evident that the contradiction in question could not refer to the outward history, but merely to the inward, or that of the content itself. There is a history of the spread of Christianity and of the lives of those who have avowed it, and its existence has formed itself into that of a church. This in itself constitutes an external existence such that, being brought into contact with temporal affairs of the most diverse kind, its lot is a varied one and it essentially possesses a history. And of the Christian doctrine it is true that it, too, has its history, but it necessarily soon reached its full development and attained to its appointed powers. And this old creed has been an acknowledged influence to every age, and will still be acknowledged unchanged as the truth, even though this acknowledgment were become no more than a pretence, and the words an empty form. But the history of this doctrine in its wider sense includes two elements: first the various additions to and deviations from the truth formerly established, and secondly the combating of these errors, the purification of the principles that remain from such additions, and a consequent return to their first simplicity.

The other sciences, including philosophy, have also an external history like religion. Philosophy has a history of its origin, diffusion, maturity, decay, revival; a history of its teachers, promoters, and of its opponents—often, too, of an outward relation to religion and occasionally to the state. This side of its history likewise gives occasion to interesting questions. Amongst other such, it is asked why philosophy, the doctrine of absolute truth, seems to have revealed itself on the whole to a small number of individuals, to special nations, and how it has limited itself to particular periods of time. Similarly with respect to Christianity, to the truth in a much more universal form than the philosophical, a difficulty has been encountered in respect to the question whether there is a contradiction in the fact that this religion should have appeared so late in time, and that it should have remained so long and should still remain limited to special races of men. But these and other similar questions are too much a matter of detail to depend merely on the general conflict referred to, and when we have further touched upon the peculiar character of philosophic knowledge, we may go more specially into the aspects which relate to the external existence and external history of philosophy.

But as regards the comparison between the history of religion and that of philosophy as to inner content, there is

not in the latter as there is in religion a fixed and fundamental truth which, as unchangeable, is apart from history.
The content of Christianity, which is truth, has, however,
remained unaltered as such, and has therefore little history or
as good as none.[5] Hence in religion, on account of its very
nature as Christianity, the conflict referred to disappears. The
errors and additions constitute no difficulty. They are transitory and altogether historical in character.

The other sciences, indeed, have also according to their
content a history, a part of which relates to alterations and
the renunciation of tenets which were formerly current. But
a great, perhaps the greater, part of the history relates to
what has proved permanent, so that what was new, was not
an alteration on earlier acquisitions, but an addition to them.
These sciences progress through a process of juxtaposition. It
is true that in botany, mineralogy, and so on much is dependent on what was previously known, but by far the greatest
part remains stationary and by means of fresh matter is
merely added to without itself being affected by the addition. With a science like mathematics, history has, in the
main, only the pleasing task of recording further additions.
Thus to take an example, elementary geometry, in so far as it
was created by Euclid, may from his time on be regarded as
having no further history.

The history of philosophy, on the other hand, shows
neither the motionlessness of a complete, simple content, nor
altogether the onward movement of a peaceful addition of
new treasures to those already acquired. It seems merely to
afford the spectacle of ever-recurring changes in the whole,
such as finally are no longer even connected by a common
aim. Rather it is the abstract subject itself, rational knowledge, which disappears; and in the end the structure of the
science must share that empty place with pretension and the
reputation of philosophy becomes vacuous.

5. S. Marheineke *Lehrbuch des Christlichen Glaubens und Lebens* (Berlin,
1823), § 133, 134.

Common Ideas Regarding The History Of Philosophy

At this point appear these ordinary superficial ideas regarding the history of philosophy which have to be referred to and corrected. As regards these very current views, which are doubtless known to you, gentlemen, for indeed they are the reflections most likely to occur in one's first crude thoughts on a history of philosophy, I will shortly explain what requires explanation, and the explanation of the differences in philosophies will lead us further into the matter itself.

The History of Philosophy as an Accumulation of Opinions

History, at the first glance, includes in its aim the narration of the accidental circumstances of times, of peoples, and of individuals, treated impartially partly as regards their relation in time, and partly as to their content. The appearance of contingency in temporal succession is to be dealt with later on. It is contingency of content which is the idea with which we have first to deal—the idea of contingent actions. But thoughts and not external actions, or griefs, or joys, form the content of philosophy. Contingent thoughts, however, are nothing but opinions, and philosophical opinions are opinions relating to the more special content of philosophy, regarding God, nature, and spirit.

Thus we now meet the view very usually taken of the history of philosophy which ascribes to it the narration of a number of philosophical opinions as they have arisen and manifested themselves in time. This kind of matter is in courtesy called opinions; those who think themselves more capable of judging rightly, call such a history a display of senseless follies, or at least of errors made by men engrossed in thought and in mere ideas. This view is not only held by those who recognise their ignorance of philosophy. Those who do this acknowledge it, because that ignorance is, in common estimation, held to be no obstacle to giving judgment upon what has to do with the subject; for it is thought that anybody can form a judgment on its character and value without any comprehension of it whatever. But the same view is even held by those who write or have written on the history of philosophy. This history, considered only as the enumeration of various opinions, thus becomes an idle tale, or, if you will, an erudite investigation. For erudition is, in the main, acquaintance with a number of useless things, that is to say, with that which has no intrinsic interest or value further than being known. Yet it is thought that profit is to be derived from learning the various opinions and reflections of other men. It stimulates the powers of thought and also leads to many excellent reflections; this signifies that now and then it occasions an idea, and its art thus consists in the spinning of one opinion out of the other.

If the history of philosophy merely represented various opinions in array, whether they be of God or of natural and spiritual things existent, it would be a most superfluous and tiresome science, no matter what advantage might be brought forward as derived from such thought activity and learning. What can be more useless than to learn a string of bald opinions, and what more unimportant? Literary works, being histories of philosophy in the sense that they produce and treat the ideas of philosophy as if they were opinions, need be only superficially glanced at to find how dry and destitute of interest everything about them is.

An opinion is a subjective conception, an uncontrolled thought, an idea which may occur to me in one direction or in another: an opinion is mine,[6] it is not in itself a universal thought which is existent in and for itself. But philosophy possesses no opinions, for there is no such thing as philosophical opinions. When we hear a man speaking of philosophical opinions, even though he be a historian of philosophy itself, we detect at once this want of fundamental education. Philosophy is the objective science of truth, it is science of necessity, conceiving knowledge, and neither opinion nor the spinning out of opinions.

The more precise significance of this idea is that we get to know opinions only, thus laying emphasis upon the word opinion. Now the direct opposite of opinion is the truth; it is truth before which mere opinion pales. Those who in the history of philosophy seek mere opinions, or who suppose that on the whole only such are to be found within it, also turn aside when that word truth confronts them. Philosophy here encounters opposition from two different sides. On the one hand, piety openly declares reason or thought to be incapable of apprehending what is true, and to lead only to the abyss of doubt; it declares that independent thought must be renounced, and reason held in bounds by faith in blind authority, if truth is to be reached. Of the relation existing between religion and philosophy and of its history, we shall deal later on. On the other hand, it is known just as well, that so-called reason has maintained its rights, abandoning faith in mere authority, and has endeavoured to make Christianity rational, so that throughout it is only my personal insight and conviction which obliges me to esteem something. But this affirmation of the right of reason is turned round in an astonishing manner, so that it results in making knowledge of the truth through reason an impossibility. This so-called reason on the one hand has combated religious faith in the name and power of thinking reason, and at the same time it has itself turned against reason and is true reason's adversary. Instinct and feeling are maintained by it against the true reason, thus making the measure of true value the merely subjective—that is a particular conviction such as each can form in and for himself in his subjective capacity. A personal conviction such as this is no more than the particular opinion that has become final for men.

If we begin with what meets us in our very first conceptions, we cannot neglect to make mention of this view in the history of philosophy. In its results it permeates culture generally, being at once the misconception and true sign of our times. It is the principle through which men mutually understand and know each other; a hypothesis whose value is established and which is the ground of all the other sciences.

In theology it is not so much the creed of the church that passes for Christianity, as that every one to a greater or less degree makes a Christianity of his own to tally with his conviction. And in history we often see theology driven into acquiring the knowledge of various opinions in order that an interest may thus be furnished to the science, and one of the first results of the attention paid them is the honour awarded to all convictions, and the esteem vouchsafed to what has been constituted merely by the individual. The endeavour to know the truth is then of course relinquished.

It is true that personal conviction is the ultimate and absolute essential which reason and its philosophy, from a subjective point of view, demand in knowledge. But there is a distinction between conviction when it rests on subjective grounds such as feelings, speculations and perceptions, or speaking generally, on the particular nature of the subject, and when it rests on thought proceeding from acquaintance with the notion and the nature of things. In the former case conviction is opinion.

This opposition between mere opinion and truth now sharply defined, we already recognize in the culture of the period of Socrates and Plato—a period of corruption in Greek life—as the Platonic opposition between opinion ($\delta\acute{o}\xi a$) and science ($\dot{\epsilon}\pi\iota\sigma\tau\acute{\eta}\mu\eta$). It is the same opposition as that which existed in the decadence of Roman public and political life under Augustus, and subsequently when Epicureanism and indifference set themselves up against philosophy. Under this influence, when Christ said, "I came into the world that I should bear witness unto the Truth," Pilate answered, "What is Truth?" That was said in a superior way, and signifies that this idea of truth is an expedient which is obsolete: we have got further, we know that there is no longer any question about knowing the truth, seeing that we have gone beyond it. Who makes this statement has gone beyond it indeed.

If this is made our starting point in the history of philosophy, its whole significance will consist in finding out the particular ideas of others, each one of which is different from the other: these individual points of view are thus foreign to me: my thinking reason is not free, nor is it present in them. For me they are but extraneous, dead historic matter, or so much empty content, and to satisfy oneself with empty vanity is mere subjective vanity itself.

To the impartial man, truth has always been a heart-stirring word and one of great import. As to the assertion that the truth cannot be known, we shall consider it more closely in the history of philosophy itself where it appears. The only thing to be here remarked is that if this assumption be allowed, as was the case with Tennemann, it is beyond conception why anyone should still trouble about philosophy, since each opinion asserts falsely in its turn that it has found the truth. This immediately recalls to me the old belief that truth consists in knowledge, but that an individual only knows the truth insofar as he reflects and not just as he is; and that the truth cannot be known in immediate apprehension and perception, whether it be external and sensuous, or whether it be intellectual perception (for every perception as a perception is sensuous) but only through the labour of thought.

Proof of the Futility of Philosophical Knowledge Obtained Through the History of Philosophy Itself

From another point of view another consequence ensues from the above conception of the history of philosophy which may at will be looked at as an evil or a benefit. In view of such manifold opinions and philosophical systems so numerous, one is perplexed to know which one ought to be accepted. In regard to the great matters to which man is attracted and a knowledge of which philosophy would bestow, it is evident that the greatest minds have erred, because they have been contradicted by others. "Since this has been so with minds so great, how then can *ego homuncio* attempt to form a judgment? This consequence, which ensues from the diversity in philosophical systems, is, as may be supposed, the evil in the matter, while at the same time it is a subjective good. For this diversity is the usual plea urged by those who, with an air of knowledge, wish to make a show of interest in philosophy, to explain the fact that they, with this pretence of good will, and, indeed, with added motive for working at the science, do in fact utterly neglect it. But this diversity in philosophical systems is far from being merely an evasive plea. It has far more weight as a genuine serious ground of argument against the zeal which philosophy requires. It justifies its neglect and demonstrates conclusively the powerlessness of the endeavour to attain to philosophic knowledge of the truth. When it is admitted that philosophy ought to be a real science, and one philosophy must certainly be the true, the question arises as to which philosophy it is, and when it can be known. Each one asserts its genuineness, each even gives different signs and criteria by which the truth can be discovered; sober reflective thought must therefore hesitate to give its judgment.

This, then, is the wider interest which the history of philosophy is said to afford. Cicero (*De natura Deorum* I. 8 seq.) gives us from this point of view a most slovenly history of philosophic thought on God. He puts it in the mouth of an Epicurean, but he himself knew of nothing more favourable to say, and it is thus his own view. The Epicurean says that no certain knowledge has been arrived at. The proof that the efforts of philosophy are futile is derived directly from the usual superficial view taken of its history; the results attendant on that history make it appear to be a process in which the most various thoughts arise in numerous philosophies, each of which opposes, contradicts, and refutes the others. This fact, which cannot be denied, seems to contain the justification, indeed the necessity for applying to philosophy the words of Christ, "Let the dead bury their dead; arise, and follow Me." The whole of the history of philosophy becomes a battlefield covered with the bones of the dead; it is a kingdom not merely formed of dead and lifeless individuals, but of refuted and spiritually dead systems, since each has killed and buried the other. Instead of "Follow thou

Me," here then it must indeed be said, "Follow thine own self"—that is, hold by thine own convictions, remain steadfast to thine own opinion, why adopt another?

It certainly happens that a new philosophy makes its appearance, which maintains the others to be valueless; and indeed each one in turn comes forth at first with the pretext that by its means all previous philosophies not only are refuted, but what in them is wanting is supplied, and now at length the right one is discovered. But following upon what has gone before, it would rather seem that other words of Scripture are just as applicable to such a philosophy—the words which the Apostle Peter spoke to Ananias, "Behold the feet of them that shall carry thee out are at the door." Behold the philosophy by which thine own will be refuted and displaced shall not tarry long as it has not tarried before.

Explanatory Remarks on the Diversity in Philosophies

Certainly the fact is sufficiently well established that there are and have been different philosophies. The truth is, however, one; and the instinct of reason maintains this ineradicable intuition or belief. It is said that only one philosophy can be true, and, because philosophies are different, it is concluded that all others must be erroneous. But, in fact, each one in turn gives every assurance, evidence, and proof of being the one and true philosophy. This is a common mode of reasoning and is what seems in truth to be the view of sober thought. As regards the sober nature of the word at issue—thought—we can tell from everyday experience that if we fast we feel hunger either at once or very soon. But sober thought always has the fortunate power of not resulting in hunger and desire, but of being and remaining as it is, content. Hence the thought expressed in such an utterance reveals the fact that it is dead understanding; for it is only death which fasts and yet rests satisfied. But neither physical nor intellectual life remains content with mere abstention; as desire it presses on through hunger and through thirst towards truth, towards knowledge itself. It presses on to satisfy this desire and does not allow itself to feast and find sufficiency in a reflection such as this.

As to this reflection, the next thing to be said of it is that however different the philosophies have been, they had a common bond in that they were philosophy. Thus whoever may have studied or become acquainted with a philosophy, of whatever kind, provided only that it is such, has thereby become acquainted with philosophy. That delusive mode of reasoning which regards diversity alone, and from doubt of or aversion to the particular form in which a universal finds its actuality, will not grasp or even allow this universal nature, I have elsewhere[7] likened to an invalid recommended by the doctor to eat fruit, and who has cherries, plums, or grapes, before him, but who pedantically refuses to take anything because no part of what is offered him is fruit, some of it being cherries, and the rest plums or grapes.

But it is really important to have a deeper insight into the bearings of this diversity in the systems of philosophy. Truth and philosophy known philosophically, make such diversity appear in another light from that of abstract opposition between truth and error. The explanation of how this comes about will reveal to us the significance of the whole history of philosophy. We must make the fact conceivable, that the diversity and number of philosophies not only does not prejudice philosophy itself, that is to say the possibility of Philosophy, but that such diversity is, and has been, absolutely necessary to the existence of a science of philosophy and that it is essential to it.

This makes it possible for us to comprehend the aim of philosophy, which is in thought and in conception to grasp the truth, and not merely to discover that nothing can be known, or that at least temporal, finite truth, which also is an untruth, can alone be known and not the truth indeed. Further we find that in the history of philosophy we have to deal with philosophy itself. The facts within that history are

7. Cf. Hegel's *Werke,* vol. VI. § 13, pp. 21, 22.

not adventures and contain no more romance than does the history of the world. They are not a mere collection of chance events, of expeditions of wandering knights, each going about fighting, struggling purposelessly, leaving no results to show for all his efforts. Nor is it so that one thing has been thought out here, another there, at will; in the activity of thinking mind there is real connection, and what there takes place is rational. It is with this belief in the spirit of the world that we must proceed to history, and in particular to the history of philosophy.

Explanatory Remarks upon the Definition of the History of Philosophy

The above statement, that the truth is only one, is still abstract and formal. In the deeper sense it is our starting point. But the aim of philosophy is to know this one truth as the immediate source from which all else proceeds, both all the laws of nature and all the manifestations of life and consciousness of which they are mere reflections, or to lead these laws and manifestations in ways apparently contrary, back to that single source, and from that source to comprehend them, which is to understand their derivation. Thus what is most essential is to know that the single truth is not merely a solitary, empty thought, but one determined within itself.

To obtain this knowledge we must enter into some abstract notions which, as such, are quite general and dry, and which are the two principles of *development* and of the *concrete*. We could, indeed, embrace the whole in the single principle of development; if this were clear, all else would result and follow of its own accord. The product of thinking is the thought; thought is, however, still formal; somewhat more defined it becomes notion, and finally Idea is thought in its totality, implicitly and explicitly determined. Thus the Idea, and it alone, is truth. Now it is essentially in the nature of the Idea to develop, and only through development to arrive at comprehension of itself, or to become what it is.

That the Idea should have to make itself what it is, seems like a contradiction; it may be said that it is what it is.

The Notion of Development

The idea of development is well known, but it is the special characteristic of philosophy to investigate such matters as were formerly held as known. What is dealt with or made use of without consideration as an aid to daily life is certainly the unknown to man unless he be informed in philosophy. The further discussion of this idea belongs to the science of logic.

In order to comprehend what development is, what may be called two different states must be distinguished. The first is what is known as capacity, power, what I call being-in-itself (*potentia*, δύναμις); the second principle is that of being--for-itself, actuality (*actus*, ἐνέργεια). If we say, for example, that man is by nature rational, we would mean that he has reason only inherently or in embryo. In this sense, reason, understanding, imagination, will are possessed from birth or even from the mother's womb. But while the child only has capacities or the actual possibility of reason, it is just the same as if he had no reason; reason does not yet exist in him since he cannot yet do anything rational, and has no rational consciousness. Thus what man is at first implicitly becomes explicit, and it is the same with reason. If, then, man has actuality on whatever side, he is actually rational; and now we come to reason.

What is the real meaning of this word? That which is *in* itself must become an object to mankind, must arrive at consciousness, thus becoming *for* man. What has become an object to him is the same as what he is in himself; through the becoming objective of this implicit being, man first becomes for himself; he is made double, is preserved and not changed into another. For example, man is thinking, and thus he thinks out thoughts. In this way it is in thought alone that thought is object; reason produces what is rational: reason is its own object. The fact that thought may also descend to what is destitute of reason is a consideration involving wider issues, which do not concern us here. But even though man, who in himself is rational, does not at first seem to have got further on since he became rational for himself—what is implicit having preserved itself—the difference is quite enormous. No new content has been produced, and yet this form of being-for-self makes all the difference. The whole variation in the development of the world in history is founded on this difference. This alone explains how since all mankind is naturally rational, and freedom is the hypothesis on which this reason rests, slavery yet has been, and in part still is, maintained by many peoples, and men have remained contented under it. The only distinction between the Africans and the Asiatics on the one hand, and the Greeks, Romans, and moderns on the other, is that the latter know and it is explicit for them, that they are free, but the others are so without knowing that they are, and thus without existing as being free. This constitutes the enormous difference in their condition. All knowledge, and learning, science, and even action have no other object than to draw out what is inward or implicit and thus to become objective.

To enter into existence is to undergo change, yet still to remain one and the same thing. Potentiality governs the process. The plant, for example, does not lose itself in mere indefinite change. From the germ much is produced when at first nothing was to be seen; but the whole of what is brought forth, if not developed, is yet hidden and ideally contained within itself. The principle of this projection into existence is that the germ cannot remain merely implicit, but is impelled towards development, since it presents the contradiction of being only implicit and yet not desiring so to be. But this coming without itself has an end in view; its completion fully reached, and its previously determined end is the fruit or produce of the germ, which causes a return to the first condition. The germ will produce itself alone and manifest what is contained in it, so that it then may return to itself once more thus to renew the unity from which it started.

With nature it certainly is true that the subject which commenced and the matter which forms the end are two separate units, as in the case of seed and fruit. The doubling process has apparently the effect of separating into two things that which in content is the same. Thus in animal life the parent and the young are different individuals although their nature is the same.

In mind it is otherwise: it is consciousness and therefore it is free, uniting in itself the beginning and the end. As with the germ in nature, mind indeed resolves itself back into unity after constituting itself another. But what is *in* itself becomes *for* mind and thus arrives at being-for-itself. The fruit and seed newly contained within it on the other hand, do not become for the original germ, but for us alone; in the case of mind both factors not only are implicitly the same in character, but there is a being for the other and at the same time a being-for-self. That for which the "other" is, is the same as that "other"; and thus alone mind is at home with itself in its "other." The development of mind lies in the fact that its going forth and separation constitutes its coming to itself.

This being-at-home-with-self, or coming-to-self of mind may be described as its complete and highest end: it is this alone that it desires and nothing else. Everything that from eternity has happened in heaven and earth, the life of God, and all the deeds of time simply are the struggles for mind to know itself, to make itself objective to itself, to find itself, be for itself, and finally unite itself to itself: It is alienated and divided, but only so as to be able thus to find itself and return to itself. Only in this manner does mind attain its freedom, for that is free which is not referred to or dependent on another. True self-possession and satisfaction are only to be found in this, and in nothing else but thought does mind attain this freedom. In sense perception, for instance, and in feeling, I find myself confined and am not free; but I am free when I have a consciousness of this my feeling. Man has particular ends and interests even in will; I am free indeed when this is mine. Such ends, however, always contain "another," or something which constitutes for me "another," such as desire and impulse. It is in thought alone that all foreign matter disappears from view and that mind is absolutely free. All interest which is contained in the Idea and in philosophy is expressed in it.

The Notion of the Concrete

As to development, it may be asked, what does develop and what forms the absolute content? Development is considered in the light of a formal process in action and as destitute of content. But the act has no other end but activity, and through this activity the general character of the content is already fixed. For being-in-self and being-for-self are the moments present in action; but the act is the retention of these diverse elements within itself. The act thus is really one, and it is just this unity of differences which is the concrete. Not only is the act concrete, but also the potential, which stands to action in the relation of subject which begins, and finally the product is just as concrete as the action or as the subject which begins. Development in process likewise forms the content, the Idea itself; for this we must have the one element and then the other: both combined will form a unity as third, because the one in the other is at home with, and not without, itself. Thus the Idea is in its content concrete within itself, and this in two ways: first it is concrete potentially, and then it is its interest that what is in itself should be there for it.

It is a common prejudice that the science of philosophy deals only with abstractions and empty generalities, and that sense perception, our empirical self-consciousness, natural instinct, and the feelings of everyday life, lie, on the contrary, in the region of the concrete and the self-determined. As a matter of fact, philosophy is in the region of thought, and has therefore to deal with universals; its content is abstract, but only as to form and element. In itself the Idea is

really concrete, for it is the union of the different determinations. It is here that reasoned knowledge differs from
mere knowledge of the understanding, and it is the business
of philosophy, as opposed to understanding, to show that the
truth or the Idea does not consist in empty generalities, but
in a universal; and that is in itself the particular and the
determined. If the truth is abstract it must be untrue.
Healthy human reason goes out towards what is concrete; the
reflection of the understanding comes first as abstract and
untrue; correct in theory only, and amongst other things
unpractical. Philosophy is what is most antagonistic to
abstraction, and it leads back to the concrete.

If we unite the notion of the concrete with that of
development we have the motion of the concrete. Since the
implicit is already concrete within itself, and we only set
forth what is implicitly there, the new form which now looks
different and which was formerly shut up in the original
unity, is simply distinguished. The concrete must become for
itself or explicit; as implicit or potential it is only differentiated within itself, not as yet explicitly set forth, but still
in a state of unity. The concrete is thus simple, and yet at the
same time differentiated. This, its inward contradiction,
which is indeed the impelling force in development, brings
distinction into being. But thus, too, its right to be taken
back and reinstated extends beyond the difference; for its
truth is only to be found in unity. Life, both that which is in
nature and that which is of the Idea, of mind within itself, is
thus manifested. Were the Idea abstract, it would simply be
the highest conceivable existence, and that would be all that
could be said of it; but such a God is the product of the
understanding of modern times. What is true is rather found
in motion, in a process, however, in which there is rest;
difference, while it lasts, is but a temporary condition,
through which comes unity, full and concrete.

We may now proceed to give examples of sensuous things,
which will help us further to explain this notion of the

concrete. Although the flower has many qualities, such as smell, taste, form, colour, etc., yet it is one. None of these qualities could be absent in the particular leaf or flower: each individual part of the leaf shares alike all the qualities of the leaf entire. Gold, similarly, contains in every particle all its qualities unseparated and entire. It is frequently allowed with sensuous things that such varied elements may be joined together, but, in the spiritual, differentiation is supposed to involve opposition. We do not controvert the fact, or think it contradictory, that the smell and taste of the flower, although otherwise opposed, are yet clearly in one subject; nor do we place the one against the other. But the understanding and understanding thought find everything of a different kind, placed in conjunction, to be incompatible. Matter, for example, is complex and coherent, or space is continuous and uninterrupted. Likewise we may take separate points in space and break up matter dividing it ever further into infinity. It then is said that matter consists of atoms and points, and hence is not continuous. Therefore we have here the two determinations of continuity and of definite points, which understanding regards as mutually exclusive, combined in one. It is said that matter must be clearly either continuous or divisible into points, but in reality it has both these qualities.

Or when we say of the mind of man that it has freedom, the understanding at once brings up the other quality, which in this case is necessity, saying, that if mind is free it is not in subjection to necessity, and, inversely, if its will and thought are determined through necessity, it is not free—the one, they say, excludes the other. The distinctions here are regarded as exclusive, and not as forming something concrete. But that which is true, the mind, is concrete, and its attributes are freedom and necessity. Similarly the higher point of view is that mind is free in its necessity, and finds its freedom in it alone, since its necessity rests on its freedom. But it is more difficult for us to show the unity here than in the case of natural objects. Freedom can, however, be also abstract freedom without necessity, which false freedom is self-will, and for that reason it is self-opposed, unconsciously limited, an imaginary freedom which is free in form alone.

The fruit of development, which comes third, is a result of motion, but inasmuch as it is merely the result of one stage in development, as being last in this stage, it is both the starting point and the first in order in another such stage. Goethe somewhere truly says, "That which is formed ever resolves itself back into its elements." Matter—which as developed has form—constitutes once more the material for a new form. Mind again takes as its object and applies its activity to the notion in which in going within itself, it has comprehended itself, which it is in form and being, and which has just been separated from it anew. The application of thought to this, supplies it with the form and determination of thought. This action thus further forms the previously formed, gives it additional determinations, and makes it more determinate in itself, further developed, and more profound. As concrete, this activity is a succession of processes in development which must be represented not as a straight line drawn out into vague infinity, but as a circle returning within itself, which, as periphery, has very many circles, and whose whole is a large number of processes in development turning back within themselves.

Philosophy as the Apprehension of the Development of the Concrete

Having thus generally explained the nature of the concrete, I now add as regards its import that the truth thus determined within itself is impelled towards development. It is only the living and spiritual which internally bestirs and develops itself. Thus the Idea as concrete in itself, and self-developing, is an organic system and a totality which contains a multitude of stages and of moments in development. Philosophy has now become for itself the apprehension of this development, and as conceiving thought, is itself this development in thought. The more progress made in this development, the more perfect is philosophy.

This development goes no further out than into externality, but the going without itself of development also is a going inwards. That is to say, the universal Idea continues to remain at the foundation and still is the all-embracing and unchangeable.

While in philosophy the going out of the Idea in course of its development is not a change, a becoming "another," but really is a going within itself, a self-immersion, the progress forward makes the Idea, which was previously general and undetermined, determined within itself. Further development of the Idea or its further determination is the same thing exactly. Depth seems to signify intensiveness, but in this case the most extensive is also the most intensive. The more intensive is the mind, the more extensive is it, hence the larger is its embrace. Extension as development, is not dispersion or falling asunder, but a uniting bond which is the more powerful and intense as the expanse of that embraced is greater in extent and richer. In such a case what is greater is the strength of opposition and of separation; and the greater power overcomes the greater separation.

These are the abstract propositions regarding the nature of the Idea and of its development, and thus within it philosophy in its developed state is constituted: it is one Idea in its totality and in all its individual parts, like one life in a living being, one pulse throbs throughout all its members. All the parts represented in it, and their systematization, emanate from the one Idea; all these particulars are but the mirrors and copies of this one life, and have their actuality only in this unity. Their differences and their various qualities are only the expression of the Idea and the form contained within it. Thus the Idea is the central point, which is also the periphery, the source of light, which in all its expansion does not come without itself, but remains present and immanent within itself. Thus it is both the system of necessity and its own necessity, which also constitutes its freedom.

Results Obtained with Respect to the Notion of the History of Philosophy

Thus we see that philosophy is system in development; the history of philosophy is the same; and this is the main point to be noted and the first principle to be dealt with in this treatise on that history.

In order to make this evident, the difference in respect to the possible modes of manifestation must first be pointed out. That is to say, the progression of the various stages in the advance of thought may occur with the consciousness of necessity, in which case each in succession deduces itself, and this form and this determination can alone emerge. Or else it may come about without this consciousness as does a natural and apparently accidental process, so that while inwardly, indeed, the notion brings about its result consistently, this consistency is not made manifest. This is so in nature; in the various stages of the development of twigs, leaves, blossom and fruit, each proceeds for itself, but the inward Idea is the directing and determining force which governs the progression. This is also so with the child whose bodily powers, and above all whose intellectual activities, make their appearance one after the other, simply and naturally, so that those parents who form such an experience for the first time, marvel whence all that is now showing itself from within comes; for the whole of these manifestations merely have the form of a succession in time.

The one kind of progression which represents the deduction of the forms, the necessity thought out and recognised, of the determinations, is the task and the business of philosophy; and because it is the pure Idea which is in question and not yet its mere particularized form as nature and as mind, that representation is, in the main, the task of logical philosophy. But the other method, which represents the part played by the history of philosophy, shows the different stages and moments in development in time, in manner of occurrence, in particular places, in particular people or political circumstances, the complications arising thus, and, in short, it shows us the empirical form. This point of view is the only one worthy of this science. From the very nature of the subject it is inherently the true one, and through the study of this history it will be made manifest that it actually shows and proves itself so.

Now in reference to this Idea, I maintain that the sequence in the systems of philosophy in history is similar to the sequence in the logical deduction of the conceptual determinations in the Idea. I maintain that if the fundamental conceptions of the systems appearing in the history of philosophy be entirely divested of what regards their outward form, their relation to the particular, and the like, the various stages in the determination of the Idea are found in their logical notion. Conversely in the logical progression taken for itself, there is, so far as its principal elements are concerned, the progression of historical manifestations. But it is necessary to have these pure notions in order to know what the historical form contains. It may be thought that philosophy must have another order as to the stages in the Idea than that in which these notions have gone forth in time; but in the main the order is the same. This succession undoubtedly separates itself, on the one hand, into the sequence in time of history, and on the other into succession in the order of ideas. But to treat more fully of this last would divert us too far from our aim.

I would only remark this, that what has been said reveals that the study of the history of philosophy is the study of philosophy itself, for, indeed, it can be nothing else. Whoever studies the history of sciences such as physics and mathematics makes himself acquainted with physics and mathematics themselves. But in order to obtain a knowledge of its progress as the development of the Idea in the empirical, external form in which philosophy appears in history, a corresponding knowledge of the Idea is absolutely essential, just as in judging of human affairs one must have a conception of that which is right and fitting. Else, indeed, as in so many histories of philosophy, there is presented to the vision devoid of idea only a disarranged collection of opinions. To make you acquainted with this Idea, and consequently to explain the manifestations, is the business of the history of philosophy, and to do this is my object in undertaking to lecture on the subject. Since the observer must bring with him the notion of the subject in order to see it in its phenomenal aspect and in order to expose the object faithfully to view, we need not wonder at there being so many dull histories of philosophy in which the succession of its systems are represented simply as a number of opinions, errors, and freaks of thought. They are freaks of thought which, indeed, have been devised with a great pretension of acuteness and of mental exertion, and with everything else which can be said in admiration of what is merely formal. considering the absence of philosophic mind in such historians as these, how should they be able to comprehend and represent the content, which is reasoned thought?

It is shown from what has been said regarding the formal nature of the Idea that only a history of philosophy thus regarded as a system of development in Idea is entitled to the name of science: a collection of facts constitutes no science. Only thus as a succession of phenomena established through reason, and having as content just what is reason and revealing it, does this history show that it is rational: it shows that the events recorded are in reason. How should the whole of what has taken place in reason not itself be rational? That faith must surely be the more reasonable in which chance is not made ruler over human affairs, and it is the task of philosophy to recognise that however much its own manifestations may be history, it is yet determined through the Idea alone.

Through these general preliminary conceptions the categories are now determined, and more immediate application of which to the history of philosophy we have now to consider. This application will bring before us the most significant aspects in this history.

The Development in Time of the Various Philosophies

The first question which may be asked in reference to this history concerns that distinction in regard to the manifestation of the Idea which has just been noticed: It is the question as to how it happens that philosophy appears to be a development in time and has a history. The answer to this question encroaches on the metaphysics of time, and it would be a digression from our object to give here more than the elements on which the answer rests.

It has been shown above in reference to the existence of mind, that its being is its activity. Nature, on the contrary, is as it is; its changes are thus only repetitions, and its movements take the form of a circle merely. To express this better, the activity of mind is to know itself. I am, immediately, but this I am only as a living organism; as mind I am only in so far as I know myself. Γνῶθι σεαυτόν, Know thyself, the inscription over the temple of the oracle at Delphi, is the absolute command which is expressed by mind in its essential character. But consciousness really implies that for myself, I am object to myself. In forming this absolute division between what is mine and myself, mind constitutes its existence and establishes itself as external to itself. It postulates itself in the externality which is just the universal and the distinctive form of existence in nature. But one of the forms of externality is time, and this form requires to be further examined both in the philosophy of nature and the finite mind.

This being in existence and therefore being in time is a moment not only of the individual consciousness, which as such is essentially finite, but also of the development of the philosophical Idea in the element of thought. For the Idea, thought of as being at rest, is, indeed, not in time. To think of it as at rest and to preserve it in the form of immediacy is equivalent to its inward perception. But the Idea as concrete, is, as has been shown, the unity of differences; it is not really at rest, and its existence is not really sense perception, but as differentiation within itself and therefore as development, it comes into existent being and into externality in the element of thought, and thus pure philosophy appears in thought as a progressive existence in time. But this element of thought is itself abstract and is the activity of a single consciousness. Mind is, however, not only to be considered as individual, finite consciousness, but as that mind which is universal and concrete within itself; this concrete universality, however, comprehends all the various sides and modes evolved in which it is and becomes object to the Idea. Thus mind's thinking comprehension of self is at the same time the progression of the total actuality evolved. This progression is not one which takes its course through the thought of an individual and exhibits itself in a single consciousness, for it shows itself to be universal mind presenting itself in the history of the world in all the richness of its form. The result of this development is that one form, one stage in the Idea comes to consciousness in one particular so that this people and this time expresses only this particular form, within which it constructs its universe and works out its conditions. The higher stage, on the other hand, centuries later reveals itself in another race of people.

Now if we thus grasp the principles of the concrete and of development, the nature of the manifold obtains quite another signification, and what is said of the diversity in philosophies, as if the manifold were fixed and stationary and composed of what is mutually exclusive, is at once refuted and relegated to its proper place. Such talk is that in which those who despise philosophy think they possess an invincible weapon against it, and in their truly beggarly pride in their pitiful representations of it, they are in perfect ignorance even of what they have and what they have to know in any meagre ideas attained, such as in that of the manifold and diverse. Yet this category is one which anybody can understand; no difficulty is made in regard to it, for it is thoroughly known, and those who use it think they can do so as being entirely comprehensible—as a matter of course they understand what it is. But those who believe the principle of diversity to be one absolutely fixed do not know its nature, or its dialectic. The manifold or diverse is in a state of flux; it must really be conceived of as in the process of development, and as but a passing moment. Philosophy in its concrete Idea is the activity of development in revealing the differences which it contains within itself. These differences are thoughts, for we are now speaking of development in thought. In the first place the differences which rest in the Idea are manifested as thoughts. Secondly, these distinctions must come into existence, one here and the other there. In order that they may do this, they must be complete, that is, they must contain within themselves the Idea in its totality. The concrete alone as including and supporting the distinctions is the actual; it is thus, and thus alone, that the differences are in their form entire.

A complete form of thought such as is here presented is a philosophy. But the Idea contains the distinctions in a peculiar form. It may be said that the form is indifferent, and that the content, the Idea, is the main consideration. People think themselves quite moderate and reasonable when they state that the different philosophies all contain the Idea, though in different forms, understanding by this that these forms are contingent. But everything hangs on this: these forms are nothing else than the original distinctions in the Idea itself, which is what it is only in them. They are in this way essential to, and constitute the content of the Idea, which in thus sundering itself attains to form. The manifold character of the principles which appear is, however, not accidental but necessary: the different forms constitute an integral part of the whole form. They are the determinations of the original Idea, which together constitute the whole. But as being outside of one another, their union does not take place in them, but in us, the observers.

Each system is determined as one, but it is not a permanent condition that the differences are thus mutually exclusive. The inevitable fate of these determinations must follow, and that is that they shall be drawn together and reduced to elements or moments. The independent attitude taken up by each moment is again laid aside. After expansion, contraction follows—the unity out of which they first emerged. This third may itself be but the beginning of a further development. It may seem as if this progression were to go on into infinitude, but it has an absolute end in view, which we shall know better later on; many turnings are necessary, however, before mind frees itself in coming to consciousness.

The temple of self-conscious reason is to be considered from this the point of view alone worthy of the history of philosophy. It is hence rationally built by an inward master worker, and not in Solomon's method, as freemasons build. The great assumption that what has taken place on this side, in the world, has also done so in conformity with reason— which is what first gives the history of philosophy its true interest—is nothing else than trust in Providence, only in another form. As the best of what is in the world is that which thought produces, it is unreasonable to believe that reason only is in nature, and not in mind. That man who believes that what, like the philosophies, belongs to the region of mind must be merely contingent is insincere in his belief in divine rule, and what he says of it is but empty talk.

A long time is undoubtedly required by mind in working out philosophy, and when one first reflects on it, the length of the time may seem astonishing, like the immensity of the space spoken of in astronomy. But it must be considered in regard to the slow progress of the world spirit that there is no need for it to hasten: "A thousand years are in Thy sight as one day." It has time enough just because it is itself outside of time, because it is eternal. The fleeting events of the day pass so quickly that there is not time enough for all that has to be done. Who is there who does not die before he has achieved his aims? The world spirit has time enough, but that is not all. It is not time alone which has to be made use of in the acquisition of a conception; much else is required. The fact that so many races and generations are devoted to these operations of its consciousness by mind, and that the appearance is so perpetually presented of rising up and passing away, concern it not at all. It is rich enough for such displays, it pursues its work on the largest possible scale, and has nations and individuals enough and to spare. The saying that nature arrives at its end in the shortest possible way, and that this is right, is a trivial one. The way shown by mind is indirect, and accommodates itself to circumstances. Considerations of finite life, such as time, trouble, and cost, have no place here. We ought, too, to feel no disappointment that particular kinds of knowledge cannot yet be attained, or that this or that is still absent. In the history of the world progression is slow.

The Application of the Foregoing to the Treatment of Philosophy

The first result which follows from what has been said is that the whole of the history of philosophy is a progression impelled by an inherent necessity, and one which is implicitly rational and *a priori* determined through its Idea. This the history of philosophy has to exemplify. Contingency must vanish on the appearance of philosophy. Its history is just as absolutely determined as the development of notions, and the impelling force is the inner dialectic of the forms. The finite is not true, nor is it what it is to be—its determinate nature is bound up with its existence. But the inward Idea abolishes these finite forms: a philosophy which has not the absolute form identical with the content must pass away because its form is not that of truth.

What follows secondly from what we have said is that every philosophy has been and still is necessary. Thus none have passed away, but all are affirmatively contained as elements in a whole. But we must distinguish between the particular principle of these philosophies as particular, and the realisation of this principle throughout the whole compass of the world. The principles are retained, the most recent philosophy being the result of all preceding, and hence no philosophy has ever been refuted. What has been refuted is not the principle of this philosophy, but merely the fact that this principle should be considered final and absolute in character. The atomic philosophy, for example, has arrived at the affirmation that the atom is the absolute, that it is the indivisible unit which is also the individual or subjèct; seeing, then, that the bare unit also is the abstract being-for-self, the absolute would be grasped as infinitely many units. The atomic theory has been refuted, and we are atomists no longer. Mind is certainly explicitly existent as a unit or atom, but that is to attribute to it a barren character and qualities incapable of expressing anything of its depth. The principle is indeed retained, although it is not the absolute in its entirety. This same contradiction appears in all development. The development of the tree is the negation of the germ, and the blossom that of the leaves, in so far as that they show that these do not form the highest and truest existence of the tree. Last of all, the blossom finds its negation in the fruit. Yet none of them can come into actual existence excepting as preceded by all the earlier stages. Our attitude to a philosophy must thus contain an affirmative side and a negative; when we take both of these into consideration, we do justice to a philosophy for the first time. We get to know the affirmative side later on both in life and in science; thus we find it easier to refute than to justify.

In the third place, we shall limit ourselves to the particular consideration of the principle itself. Each principle has reigned for a certain time, and when the whole system of the world has been explained from this special form, it is called a philosophical system. Its whole theory has certainly to be learned, but as long as the principle is abstract it is not sufficient to embrace the forms belonging to our conception of the world. The Cartesian principles, for instance, are very suitable for application to mechanism, but for nothing further; their representation of other manifestations in the world, such as those of vegetable and animal nature, are insufficent, and hence uninteresting. Therefore we take into consideration the principles of these philosophies only, but in dealing with concrete philosophies we must also regard the chief forms of their development and their applications. The subordinate philosophies are inconsistent; they have had bright glimpses of the truth, which are, however, independent of their principles. This is exemplified in the Timaeus of Plato, a philosophy of nature, the working out of which is empirically very barren because its principle does not as yet extend far enough, and it is not to its principle that we owe the deep gleams of thought there contained.

In the fourth place it follows that we must not regard the history of philosophy as dealing with the past, even though it is history. The scientific products of reason form the content of this history, and these are not past. What is obtained in this field of labour is the true, and, as such, the eternal; it is not what exists now, and not then; it is true not only today or tomorrow, but beyond all time, and in as far as it is in time, it is true always and for every time. The bodily forms of those great minds who are the heroes of this history, the temporal existence and outward lives of the philosophers, are, indeed, no more, but their works and thoughts have not followed suit, for they neither conceived nor dreamt of the rational import of their works. Philosophy is not somnambulism, but is developed consciousness; and what these heroes have done is to bring that which is implicitly rational out of the depths of mind, where it is found at first as substance only, or as inwardly existent, into the light of day, and to advance it into consciousness and knowledge. This forms a continuous awakening. Such work is not only deposited in the temple of memory as forms of times gone by but is just as present and as living now as at the time of its production. The effects produced and work performed are not again destroyed or interrupted by what succeeds, for they are such that we must ourselves be present in them. They have as medium neither canvas, paper, marble, nor representation or memorial to preserve them. These mediums are themselves transient, or else form a basis for what is such. But they do have thought, notion, and the eternal being of mind, which moths cannot corrupt, nor thieves break through and steal. The conquests made by thought when constituted into thought form the very being of mind. Such knowledge is thus not learning merely, or a knowledge of what is dead, buried, and corrupt. The history of philosophy has to do not with what is gone, but with the living present.

Further Comparison Between the History of Philosophy and Philosophy Itself

We may appropriate to ourselves the whole of the riches apportioned out in time: it must be shown from the succession in philosophies how that succession is the systematization of the science of philosophy itself. But a distinction is to be noted here: that which first commences is implicit, immediate, abstract, general—it is what has not yet advanced. The more concrete and richer comes later, and the first is poorer in determinations. This may appear contrary to one's first impressions, but philosophic ideas are often enough directly opposed to ordinary ideas, and what is generally supposed is not found to be the case. It may be thought that what comes first must be the concrete. The child, for instance, as still in the original totality of his nature, is thought to be more concrete than the man, hence we imagine the latter to be more limited, no longer forming a totality, but living an abstract life. Certainly the man acts in accordance with definite ends, not bringing his whole soul and mind into a subject, but splitting his life into a number of abstract unities. The child and the youth, on the contrary, act straight from the fulness of the heart. Feeling and sense perception come first, thought last, and thus feeling appears to us to be more concrete than thought, or the activity of abstraction and of the universal. In reality, it is just the other way. The sensuous consciousness is certainly the more concrete, and if poorer in thought, at least richer in content. We must thus distinguish the naturally concrete from the concrete of thought, which on its side, again, is wanting in sensuous matter. The child is also the most abstract and the poorest in thought: as to what pertains to nature, the man is abstract, but in thought he is more concrete than the child. Man's ends and objects are undoubtedly abstract in general affairs, such as in maintaining his family or performing his business duties, but he contributes to a great objective organic whole, whose progress he advances and directs. In the acts of a child, on the other hand, only a childish and, indeed, momentary "I" and in those of the youth his subjective training or the random aim form the principle of action. It is in this way that science is more concrete than sense perception.

In applying this to the different forms of philosophy, it follows in the first place, that the earliest philosophies are the poorest and the most abstract. In them the Idea is least determined; they keep merely to generalities not yet realized. This must be known in order that we may not seek behind the old philosophies for more than we are entitled to find; thus we need not require from them determinations proceeding from a deeper consciousness. For instance, it has been asked whether the philosophy of Thales is, properly speaking, theism or atheism,[8] whether he asserted a personal God or merely an impersonal, universal being. The question here regards the attribution of subjectivity to the highest Idea, the conception of the personality of God. Such subjectivity as we comprehend it is a much richer, more concentrated, and therefore much later conception, which need not be sought for in distant ages. The Greek gods had, indeed, personality in imagination and idea like the one God of the Jewish religion, but to know what is the mere picture of fancy, and what the insight of pure thought and notion, is quite another thing. If we take as basis our own ideas judged by these deeper conceptions, an ancient philosophy may

8. Flatt, *De Theismo Thaleti Milesio abjudicando* (Tübingen, 1785), p. 4.

undoubtedly be spoken of as atheism. But this expression would at the same time be false, for the thoughts as thoughts in beginning could not have arrived at the development which we have reached.

From this it follows—since the progress of development is equivalent to further determination, and this means further immersion in and a fuller grasp of the Idea itself—that the latest, most modern and newest philosophy is the most developed, richest and deepest. In that philosophy everything which at first seems to be past and gone must be preserved and retained, and it must itself be a mirror of the whole history. The original philosophy is the most abstract, because it is the original and has not as yet made any movement forward; the last, which proceeds from this forward and impelling influence, is the most concrete. This, as may at once be remarked, is no mere pride in the philosophy of our time, because it is in the nature of the whole process that the more developed philosophy of a later time is really the result of the previous operations of the thinking mind; and that it, pressed forwards and onwards from the earlier standpoints, has not grown up on its own account or in a state of isolation.

It must also be recollected that we must not hesitate to say what is naturally implied: that the Idea, as comprehended and shown forth in the latest and newest philosophy, is the most developed, the richest, and deepest. I call this to remembrance because the designation, new or newest of all in reference to philosophy, has become a very common by-word. Those who think they express anything by using such terms might quite easily render thanks respecting any number of philosophies just as fast as their inclination directs. They regard either every shooting star and even every candle gleam in the light of a sun, or else call every popular cry a philosophy, and adduce as proof that at any rate there are so many philosophies that every day one displaces another. Thus they have the category in which they can place any apparently significant philosophy, and through which they may at the same time set it aside; this they call a fashion philosophy.

Scoffer, thou call'st this but a fleeting phase
When the Spirit of man once again and anew,
Strives earnestly on towards forms that are higher.

A second consequence has regard to the treatment of the older philosophies. Such insight also prevents us from ascribing any blame to the philosophies when we miss determinations in them which were not yet present to their culture, and similarly it prevents our burdening them with deductions and assertions which were neither made nor thought of by them, though they might correctly enough allow themselves to be derived from the thought of such a philosophy. It is necessary to set to work on an historical basis, and to ascribe to philosophy what is immediately given to us, and that alone. Errors crop up here in most histories of philosophy, since we may see in them a number of metaphysical propositions ascribed to a philosopher and given out as an historical statement of the views which he has propounded, of which he neither thought nor knew a word, and of which there is not the slightest trace found in history. Thus in Brucker's extensive *History of Philosophy* (pt 1, pp. 465-78 seq.) a list of thirty, forty, or a hundred theorems are quoted from Thales and others, no idea of which can be traced in history as having been present to these philosophers. There are also propositions in support of them and citations taken from discussions of a similar kind with which we may occupy ourselves long enough. Brucker's method is to endow the single theorem of an ancient philosopher with all the consequences and premises which must, according to the idea of the Wolffian metaphysics, be the premises and conclusions of that theorem, and thus easily to produce a simple, naked fiction as if it were an actual historical fact. Thus, according to Brucker, Thales said, *Ex nihilo fit nihil,* since he said that water was eternal. Thus, too, he was to be counted amongst the philosophers who deny creation out of nothing; and of this, historically at least, Thales was ignorant. Professor Ritter, too, whose history of Ionic philosophy is carefully written, and who on the whole is cautious not to introduce foreign matter, has very possibly ascribed to Thales more than is found in history. He says (pp. 12,13), "Hence we must regard the view of nature which we find in Thales as dynamic in principle. He regarded the world as the all-embracing, living animal which has developed from a germ like every other animal, and this germ, like that of all other animals, is either damp or water. Thus the fundamental idea of Thales is that the world is a living whole which has developed from a germ and carries on its life as does an animal, by means of nourishment suitable to its nature" (cf. p. 16). This is quite a different account from that of Aristotle, and none of it is communicated by the ancients regarding Thales. The sequence of thought is evident, but historically it is not justified. We ought not by such deductions to make an ancient philosophy into something quite different from what it originally was.

We are too apt to mould the ancient philosophers into our own forms of thought, but this is just to constitute the progress of development; the difference in times, in culture, and in philosophies depends on whether certain reflections, certain thought determinations, and certain stages in the notion have come to consciousness, whether a consciousness has been developed to a particular point or not. The history of philosophy has simply to deal with this development and bringing forth of thought. The determinations involved certainly follow from a proposition, but whether they are put forth as yet or not is quite another thing, and the bringing forth of the inner content is the only matter of importance. We must therefore only make use of the words which are actually literal, for to use further thought determinations which do not yet belong to the consciousness of the philosopher in question is to anticipate development. Thus Aristotle states that Thales has defined the principle ($ἀρχή$) of every thing to be water. But Anaximander first made use of $ἀρχή$, and Thales thus did not possess this determination of thought at all; he recognized $ἀρχή$ as commencement in time, but not as the fundamental principle. Thales did not once introduce the determination of cause into his philosophy, and first cause is a further determination still. There are whole nations which have not this conception at all; indeed it involves a great step forward in development. And seeing that difference in culture on the whole depends on difference in the thought determinations which are manifested, this must be so still more with respect to philosophies.

Now, as in the logical system of thought each of its forms has its own place in which alone it suffices, and this form becomes, by means of ever-progressing development, reduced to a subordinate element, each philosophy is, in the third place, a particular stage in the development of the whole process and has its definite place where it finds its true value and significance. Its special character is really to be conceived of in accordance with this determination, and it is to be considered with respect to this position in order that full justice may be done to it. On this account nothing more must be demanded or expected from it than what it actually gives, and the satisfaction is not to be sought for in it, which can only be found in a fuller development of knowledge. We must not expect to find the questions of our consciousness and the interest of the present world responded to by the ancients; such questions presuppose a certain development in thought. Therefore every philosophy belongs to its own time and is restricted by its own limitations just because it is the manifestation of a particular stage in development. The individual is the offspring of his people, of his world, whose constitution and attributes are alone manifested in his form. He may spread himself out as he will, he cannot escape out of his time any more than out of his skin, for he belongs to the one universal mind which is his substance and his own existence. How should he escape from this? It is the same universal mind that is embraced by thinking philosophy; that philosophy is mind's thought of itself and therefore its determinate and substantial content. Every philosophy is the philosophy of its own day, a link in the whole chain of spiritual development, and thus it can only find satisfaction for the interests belonging to its own particular time.

On this account an earlier philosophy does not give satisfaction to the mind in which a deeper conception reigns. What mind seeks for in philosophy is this conception which already constitutes its inward determination and the root of its existence conceived of as object to thought; mind demands a knowledge of itself. But in the earlier philosophy the Idea is not yet present in this determinate character. Hence the philosophy of Plato and Aristotle, and indeed all philosophies, ever live and are present in their principles, but philosophy no longer has the particular form and aspect possessed by that of Plato and of Aristotle. We cannot rest content with them, and they cannot be revived; hence there can be no Platonists, Aristotelians, Stoics, or Epicureans today. To reawaken them would be to try to bring back to an earlier stage the mind of a deeper culture and self-penetration. But this cannot be the case; it would be an impossibility and as great a folly as were a man to wish to expend his energies in attaining the standpoint of the youth, the youth in endeavouring to be the boy or child again; whereas the man, the youth, and the child, are all one and the same individual. The period of revival in the sciences, the new epoch in learning which took place in the fifteenth and sixteenth centuries, began not only with the revived study of the old philosophies but also with their reanimation. Marsilius Ficinus was a Platonist; an Academy of Platonic philosophy was established and installed with professors by Cosmos de Medici, and Ficinus was placed at the head of it. There were pure Aristotelians like Pomponius: Gassendi later on maintained the Epicurean philosophy, for his philosophy dealt with physics after the manner of the Epicureans; Lipsius wished to be a Stoic, and so on. The sense of opposition was so great, ancient philosophy and Christianity—from or in which no special philosophy had developed—were so diverse, that no philosophy peculiar to itself could develop in Christianity. What was or could be had as philosophy, either in conformity with or in opposition to Christianity, was a certain ancient philosophy which was thus taken up anew. But mummies when brought amongst living beings cannot remain there. Mind had for long possessed a more substantial life, a more profound notion of itself, and hence its thought had higher needs than such as could be satisfied by these philosophies. A revival such as this is then to be regarded only as the transitory period in which we learn to know the forms which are implied and which have gone before, and as the renewal of former struggles through the steps necessary in development. Such reconstructions and repetitions in a distant time of principles which have become foreign to mind are in history transitory only, and formed in a language which is dead. Such things are translations only and not originals, and mind does not find satisfaction excepting in knowledge of its own origination.

When modern times are in the same way called upon to revert to the standpoint of an ancient philosophy (as is recommended specially in regard to the philosophy of Plato) in order to make this a means of escaping from complications and difficulties of succeeding times, this reversion does not come naturally as in the first case. This discreet counsel has the same origin as the request to cultivated members of society to turn back to the customs and ideas of the savages of the North American forests, or as the recommendation to adopt the religion of Melchisedec, which Fichte[9] has maintained to be the purest and simplest possible, and therefore the one at which we must eventually arrive. On the one hand, in this retrogression the desire for an origin and for a fixed point of departure is unmistakable, but such must be sought for in thought and Idea alone and not in an authoritatively given form. On the other hand, reversion of the developed, enriched mind to a simplicity such as this—which means to an abstraction, an abstract condition or thought—is to be regarded only as the escape of impotence which cannot enjoy the rich material of development which it sees before it, and which demands to be controlled and comprehended in its

9. *Grundzüge des gegenwärtigen Zeitalters,* pp. 211, 212; c.f. *Anweisung zum Seligen Leben,* pp. 178-348.

very depths by thought. Rather it seeks a refuge in fleeing from the difficulty and in mere sterility.

From what has been said it is quite comprehensible how so many of those who, whether induced by some special attraction such as this, or simply by the fame of a Plato or ancient philosophy in general, direct their way thereto in order to draw their own philosophy from these sources, do not find themselves satisfied by the study, and unjustifiably quit such altogether. Satisfaction is found in them to a certain extent only. We must know in ancient philosophy or in the philosophy of any given period, what we are going to look for. Or at least we must know that in such a philosophy there is before us a definite stage in the development of thought, and in it those forms and necessities of mind which lie within the limits of that stage alone are brought into existence. There slumber in the mind of modern times ideas more profound which require for their awakening other surroundings and another present than the abstract, dim, grey thought of olden times. In Plato, for instance, questions regarding the nature of freedom, the origin of evil and of wickedness, providence, etc. do not find their philosophic answer. On such subjects we certainly may in part take the ordinary serious views of the present time, and in part philosophically set their consideration altogether aside, or else consider evil and freedom as something negative only. But neither the one plan nor the other gives freedom to mind if such subjects have once been explicitly for it, and if the opposition in self-consciousness has given it the power of absorbing its interests therein. The case is similar with regard to questions regarding the faculty of knowledge, the opposition between subjectivity and objectivity which had not yet come up in Plato's age. The independence of the "I" within itself and its explicit existence was foreign to him. Man had not yet gone back within himself, had not yet set himself forth as explicit. The subject was indeed the individual as free, but as yet he knew himself only as in unity with his being. The Athenian knew himself to be free, just as the Roman citizen would, as *ingenuus*. But the fact that man is in and for himself free, in his essence and as man, free born, was known neither by Plato, Aristotle, Cicero, nor the Roman legislators, even though it is this conception alone which forms the source of law.

In Christianity the individual, personal mind for the first time becomes of real, infinite and absolute value; God wills that all men shall be saved. It was in the Christian religion that the doctrine was advanced that all men are equal before God, because Christ has set them free with the freedom of Christianity. These principles make freedom independent of any such things as birth, standing, or culture. The progress made through them is enormous, but they still come short of this, that to be free constitutes the very notion of man. The sense of this existent principle has been an active force for centuries and centuries, and an impelling power which has brought about the most tremendous revolutions; but the conception and the knowledge of the natural freedom of man is a knowledge of himself which is not old.

THE RELATION OF PHILOSOPHY TO OTHER FIELDS OF KNOWLEDGE

The history of philosophy has to represent this science in that form of time and individualities from which its outward form has resulted. Such a representation has, however, to shut out from itself the external history of the time, and to take into account only the general character of the people and time, and likewise their circumstances as a whole. But as a matter of fact, the history of philosophy does present this character, and that indeed in the highest possible degree; its connection with it is of the closest kind, and the particular appearance presented by a philosophy belonging to one special period is only a particular aspect or element in the character. Because of this inward correspondence we have partly to consider more closely the particular relation borne by a philosophy to its historical surroundings, and partly, but pre-eminently, what is proper to itself, from which alone, after separating everything related however closely, we can fix our standpoint. This connection, which is not merely external but essential, has thus two sides, which we must consider. The first is the distinctly historical side, the second is the connection with other matters—the connection of philosophy with religion, for instance, by which we at once obtain a closer conception of philosophy itself.

The Historical Side of this Connection

It is usually said that political affairs and such matters as religion are to be taken into consideration because they have exercised a great influence on the philosophy of the time, and similarly it exerts an influence upon them. But when people are content with such a category as "great influence" they place the two in an external relationship, and start from the point of view that both sides are for themselves independent. Here, however, we must think of this relationship in another category, and not according to the influence or effect of one upon the other. The true category is the unity of all these different forms, so that it is one mind which manifests itself in and impresses itself upon these different elements.

Outward and Historical Conditions Imposed upon Philosophy

It must be remarked in the first place, that a certain stage is requisite in the intellectual culture of a people in order that they may have a philosophy at all. Aristotle says, "Man first begins to philosophize when the necessities of life are supplied" (*Metaphysics*, I. 2); because since philosophy is a free and not self-seeking activity, cravings of want must have disappeared, a strength, elevation, and inward fortitude of mind must have appeared, passions must be subdued and consciousness so far advanced, before what is universal can be thought of. Philosophy may thus be called a kind of luxury, in so far as luxury signifies those enjoyments and pursuits which do not belong to external necessity as such. Philosophy in this respect seems more capable of being dispensed with than anything else; but that depends on what is called indispensable. From the point of view of mind, philosophy may even be said to be that which is most essential.

The Commencement in History of an Intellectual Necessity for Philosophy

However much philosophy, as the thought and conception of the spirit of a particular time, is *a priori,* it is at the same time just as really a result, since the thought produced and, indeed, the life and action are produced to produce themselves. This activity contains the essential element of a negation, because to produce is also to destroy. Philosophy in producing itself has the natural as its starting point in order to abrogate it again. Philosophy thus makes its appearance at a time when the spirit of a people has worked its way out of the indifference and stolidity of the first life of nature, as it has also done from the standpoint of the emotional, so that the individual aim has blotted itself out. But as mind passes on from its natural form, it also proceeds from its social code of morals and the robustness of life to reflection and conception. The result of this is that it lays hold of and shakes this real, substantial kind of existence, this social morality and faith, and thus the period of destruction commences. Further progress is then made through the gathering up of thought within itself. It may be said that philosophy first commences when a people for the most part has left its concrete life, when separation and change of class have begun, and the people approach their fall; when a gulf has arisen between inward strivings and external reality, and the old forms of religion, etc. are no longer satisfying; when mind manifests indifference to its living existence or rests unsatisfied therein, and moral life becomes dissolved. Then it is that mind takes refuge in the clear space of thought to create for itself a kingdom of thought in opposition to the world of actuality.

Philosophy is then the reconciliation following upon the destruction of that real world which thought has begun. When philosophy with its abstractions paints grey in grey, the freshness and life of youth has gone, the reconciliation is not a reconciliation in the actual, but in the ideal world. Thus the Greek philosophers held themselves far removed from the business of the state and were called by the people idlers, because they withdrew themselves within the world of thought.

This holds good throughout all the history of philosophy. It was so with Ionic philosophy in the decline of the Ionic states in Asia Minor. Socrates and Plato had no more pleasure in the life of the state in Athens, which was in the course of its decline; Plato tried to bring about something better with Dionysius. Thus in Athens, with the ruin of the Athenian people, the period was reached when philosophy appeared. In Rome, philosophy first expanded in the decline of the Republic and of Roman life proper, under the despotism of the Roman Emperors: a time of misfortune for the world and of decay in political life, when earlier religious systems tottered and everything was in the process of struggle and disintegration. With the decline of the Roman Empire, which was so great, rich, and glorious, and yet inwardly dead, the height and indeed the zenith of ancient philosophy is associated with the Neo-Platonists at Alexandria. It was also in the fifteenth and sixteenth centuries, when the Teutonic life of the Middle Ages acquired another form, that philosophy first became taught, though it was later on that it attained to independence. Before that, political life still existed in unity with religion, or if the state fought against the church, the church still kept the foremost place, but now the gulf between church and state came into existence. Philosophy thus comes in at a certain epoch only in the development of the whole.

Philosophy as the Thought of Its Time

But men do not at certain epochs merely philosophize in general, for there is a definite philosophy which arises among a people, and the definite character of the standpoint of thought is the same character which permeates all the other historical sides of the spirit of the people, which is most intimately related to them, and which constitutes their foundation. The particular form of a philosophy is thus contemporaneous with a particular constitution of the people amongst whom it makes its appearance, with their institutions and forms of government, their social morality, their societal life and the capabilities, customs and enjoyments of the same. It is contemporaneous with their attempts and achievements in art and science, with their religions, warfares, and external relationships, likewise with the decadence of the states in which this particular principle and form had maintained its supremacy, and with the origination and progress of new states in which a higher principle finds its manifestation and development. Mind in each case has elaborated and expanded in the whole domain of its manifold nature the principle of the particular stage of self-consciousness to which it has attained. Thus the mind of a people in its richness is an organization, and, like a cathedral, is divided into numerous vaults, passages, pillars, and vestibules, all of which have proceeded out of one whole and are directed to one end. Philosophy is one form of these many aspects. And which is it? It is the fullest blossom, the notion of mind in its entire form, the consciousness and spiritual essence of all things, the spirit of the time as spirit present in itself. The multifarious whole is reflected in it as in the single focus, in the notion which knows itself.

The philosophy which is essential with Christianity could not be found in Rome, for all the various forms of the whole are only the expression of one and the same determinate character. Hence political history, forms of government, art, and religion are not related to philosophy as its causes, nor, on the other hand, is philosophy the ground of their exist-

ence—one and all have the same common root, the spirit of
the time. It is one determinate nature, one determinate
character which permeates all sides and manifests itself in
politics and in all else as in different elements; it is a state of
affairs which hangs together in all its parts, and the various
parts of which contain nothing which is really inconsistent,
however diverse and accidental they may appear to be, and
however much they may seem to contradict one another.
This particular stage is the product of the one preceding. But
to show how the spirit of a particular time moulds its whole
actuality and destiny in accordance with its principle, to
show this whole edifice in its conception is far from us—for
that would be the subject matter of all philosophic world
history. Those forms alone concern us which express the
principle of the mind in the spiritual element related to
philosophy.

This is the position of philosophy amongst its varying
forms, from which it follows that it is entirely identical with
its time. But if philosophy does not stand above its time in
content, it does so in form, because, as the thought and
knowledge of that which is the substantial spirit of its time, it
makes that spirit its object. Insofar as philosophy is in the
spirit of its time, the latter is its determined content in the
world, although as knowledge, philosophy is above it, since it
places it in the relation of object. But this is in form alone,
for philosophy really has no other content. This knowledge
itself undoubtedly is the actuality of mind, the self-knowledge of mind which previously was not present: thus the
formal difference is also a real and actual difference. Through
knowledge, mind makes manifest a distinction between
knowledge and that which is; this knowledge is thus what
produces a new form of development. The new forms at first
are only special modes of knowledge, and it is thus that a
new philosophy is produced: yet since it already is a wider
kind of spirit, it is the inward birthplace of the spirit which
will later arrive at actual form. We shall deal further with this
in the concrete below, and we shall then see that what Greek

philosophy was, entered, in the Christian world, into actuality.

Separation of Philosophy from Other Allied Fields of Knowledge

The history of the other sciences, of culture, and above all the history of art and religion are, partly because of the elements contained in them and partly their particular subject matters, related to the history of philosophy. It is because of this relatedness that the treatment of the history of philosophy has been so confused. If it is to concern itself with the history of culture generally and also with scientific culture and also with popular myths and the dogmas contained in them, and further with the religious reflections which are already thoughts of a speculative kind, and which make their appearance in them, then no bounds are left to philosophy at all. This is so partly on account of the amount of material itself and the labour required in working it up and preparing it and partly because it is in immediate connection with so much else. But the separation must not be made arbitrarily or as by chance, but must be derived from fundamental determinations. If we merely hold to the name of philosophy, all this matter will pertain to its history.

I shall speak of this material from three points of view, for three related aspects are to be distinguished and separated from philosophy. The first of these is that which is generally considered to be the domain of science, and in which are found the beginnings of understanding thought. The second region is that of mythology and religion; the relation of philosophy to them seems often to be that of an enemy both in the time of the Greeks and of the Christians. The third is that of philosophizing and the metaphysics of the understanding. While we distinguish what is related to philosophy, we must also take note of the elements in this related matter which belong to the notion of philosophy, but which appear to us to be partially separated from it: and thus we may become acquainted with the notion of philosophy.

Relation of Philosophy to Scientific Knowledge

Knowledge and thought certainly form the element of whatever has to do with particular sciences as they form the element of philosophy. But their subjects are mainly finite subjects and appearance. A collection of facts known about this content is by its nature excluded from philosophy: neither this content nor such a form concerns philosophy. But even though the sciences are systematic and contain universal principles and laws from which they proceed, they are still related to a limited number of objects. The ultimate principles are assumed as are the objects themselves; that is, the outward experience or the feelings of the heart, natural or educated sense of right and duty, constitute the source from which they are created. Logic and the determinations and principles of thought in general are presuppositions in scientific method.

The forms of thought or the points of view and principles which hold good in the sciences and constitute the ultimate support of all their matter, are not peculiar to them, but are common to the condition and culture of the time and of the people. This culture consists mainly in the general ideas and aims, in the whole extent of the particular intellectual powers dominating consciousness and life. Our consciousness has these ordinary ideas and allows them to be considered ultimate determinations; it makes use of them as guiding and connecting links but does not know them and does not even make them the objects of its consideration. To give an abstract example, each act of consciousness has and requires the whole abstract thought determination of Being. "The sun is in the heavens, the bunch of grapes is ripe," and so on into infinitude. Again, in higher culture, such relations as those of cause and effect are involved, as also those of force and its manifestation. All its knowledge and ideas are permeated and governed by a metaphysic such as this; it is the net in which all the concrete matter which occupies mankind in action and in impulses is grasped. But this web and its knots in our ordinary consciousness are sunk into a manifold material, for it contains the objects and interests which we know and which we have before us. These common threads are not examined and made explicitly the objects of our reflection.

We Germans seldom now count general scientific knowledge as philosophy. And yet traces of this are found, as for instance, in the fact that the philosophic faculty contains all the sciences which have not as their immediate aim the church and state. In connection with this, the significance of the name of philosophy, which is even now an important matter of discussion in England, comes in question. Natural sciences are in England called philosophy. A Philosophic Journal in England, edited by Thompson, treats of chemistry, agriculture, manuring, husbandry, technology, like Hermbstadt's Journal, and gives inventions connected therewith. The English call physical instruments, such as the barometer and thermometer, philosophical instruments. Theories, too, and especially morality and the moral sciences, which are derived from the feelings of the human heart or from experience, are called philosophy, and finally this is also so with the theories and principles of political economy. And thus at least in England, is the name of philosophy respected. Some time ago a banquet took place at Liverpool in honor of the minister, Canning. In his speech of acknowledgment, he congratulated England in having philosophic principles of government there put into practice. There, at least, philosophy is no by-word.

In the first beginnings of culture, however, we are more often met by this admixture of philosophy and general knowledge. There comes a time to a nation when mind applies itself to universal objects, when, for example, in seeking to bring natural things under general modes of understanding, it tries to learn their causes. Then it is said that a people begins to philosophize, for this content has thought in common with philosophy. At such a time we find deliverances about all the common events of nature, as we also find intellectual maxims, moral sentences, general principles respecting morality, the will, duty, and the like,

and those who expressed them have been called wise men or
philosophers. Thus in the beginnings of Greek philosophy we
find the seven sages and the Ionic philosophers. From them a
number of ideas and discoveries are conveyed to us which
seem like philosophic propositions. Thus Thales, amongst
others, has explained that the eclipse of sun and moon is due
to the intervention of the moon or earth. This is called a
theorem. Pythagoras found out the principle of the harmony
of sounds. Others have had ideas about the stars: the heavens
were supposed to be composed of perforated metal, by which
we see throughout the empyrean region the eternal fire which
surrounds the world. Such propositions, as products of the
understanding, do not belong to the history of philosophy,
although they imply that the merely sensuous gaze has been
left behind, as also the representation of those objects by the
imagination only. Earth and heaven thus become unpeopled
with gods, because the understanding distinguishes things in
their outward and natural qualities from mind.

In a later time the epoch of the revival in the sciences is as
noteworthy in this respect. General principles regarding the
state, etc., were given expression to, and in them a philosophic side cannot be mistaken. Here the philosophic systems
of Hobbes and Descartes belong. The writings of the latter
contain philosophic principles, but his philosophy of nature
is quite empirical. Hugo Grotius composed an international
law in which what was historically held by the people as law,
the *consensus gentium,* was a main element. Though earlier,
medicine was a collection of isolated facts and a theosophic
combination mixed up with astrology, etc., (it is not so long
ago since cures were effected by sacred relics), a mode of
regarding nature came into vogue according to which men
went forth to discover the laws and forces of nature. The *a
priori* reasoning regarding natural things, according to the
metaphysics of the Scholastic philosophy or to religion, has
now been given up. The philosophy of Newton contains
nothing but natural science, that is, the knowledge of the
laws, forces, and general constitution of nature, derived from

observation and from experience. However much this may seem to be contrary to the principle of philosophy, it has in common with it the fact that the bases of both are universal, and still further that *I* have made this experience, that it rests on my consciousness and obtains its significance through me.

This form is in its general aspect antagonistic to the positive, and has come forward as particularly opposed to religion and to that which is positive in it. If, in the Middle Ages, the Church had its dogmas as universal truths, man, on the contrary, has now obtained from the testimony of his "own thought," feeling, and ideas a mistrust of these. It is merely to be remarked of this that "my own thought" is in itself a pleonasm, because each individual must think for himself, and no one can do so for another. Similarly this principle has turned against the recognised constitutions and has sought different principles instead, by them to correct the former. Universal principles of the state have now been laid down, while earlier, because religion was positive, the ground of obedience of subjects to princes and of all authority were also so. Kings, as the anointed of the Lord, in the sense that Jewish kings were so, derived their power from God, and had to give account to him alone, because all authority is given by God. Thus theology and jurisprudence were on the whole fixed and positive sciences, wherever this positive character might have been derived. Against this external authority reflection has been brought to bear, and thus, especially in England, the source of public and civil law became no longer mere authority derived from God like the Mosaic Law. For the authority of kings other justification was sought, such as the end implied in the state, the good of the people. This forms quite another source of truth, and it is opposed to that which is revealed, given and positive. This substitution of another ground than that of authority has been called philosophizing.

The knowledge was then a knowledge of what is finite—the world of the content of knowledge. Because this content proceeded through the personal insight of human reason,

man has become independent in his actions. This independence of the mind is the true moment of philosophy, although
the notion of philosophy through this formal determination,
which limits it to finite objects, has not yet been exhausted.
This independent thought is respected, has been called
human wisdom or worldly wisdom, for it has had what is
earthly as its object, and it took its origin in the world. This
was the meaning of philosophy, and men did rightly to call it
worldly wisdom. Friedrich von Schlegel revived this by-name
for philosophy, and desired to indicate by it that what
concerns higher spheres, such as religion, must be kept apart;
and he had many followers. Philosophy, indeed, occupies
itself with finite things, but, according to Spinoza, as resting
in the divine Idea: it has thus the same end as religion. To the
finite sciences which are now separated also from philosophy,
the churches objected that they led men away from God,
since they have as objects only what is finite. This defect in
them, conceived of from the point of view of content, leads
us to the second field allied to philosophy—that is to religion.

Relation of Philosophy to Religion

As the first field of knowledge was related to philosophy
principally by means of formal and independent knowledge,
religion, though in its content quite different from this first
kind or sphere of knowledge, is through it related to philosophy. Its object is not the earthly and worldly, but the infinite. In the case of art and still more in that of religion,
philosophy has in common a content composed entirely of
universal objects. They constitute the mode in which the
highest Idea is existent for the unphilosophical feeling, the
perceiving and imagining consciousness. Inasmuch as in the
progress of culture in time the manifestation of religion
precedes the appearance of philosophy, this circumstance
must really be taken account of. And the conditions requisite
for beginning the history of philosophy have to depend on
this, because it has to be shown in how far what pertains to

religion is to be excluded from it, and that a commencement must not be made with religion.

In religions, races of men have undoubtedly expressed their idea of the nature of the world, the substance of nature and of intellect and the relation of man thereto. Absolute being is here the object of their consciousness; and as such is for them pre-eminently the "Other," a "beyond," nearer or further off, more or less friendly or frightful and alarming. In the act and forms of worship this opposition is removed by man, and he raises himself to the consciousness of unity with his being, to the feeling of, or dependence on the Grace of God, in that God has reconciled mankind to himself. If in idea, as with the Greeks, for instance, this being is one which is implicitly and actually friendly to man, then worship is but the enjoyment of this unity. This being is now reason, which is existent in and for itself, the universal and concrete substance, the mind whose primal cause is objective to itself in consciousness; it thus is a representation of this last in which not only reason in general, but the universal infinite reason is. We must, therefore, comprehend religion, as philosophy, before everything else, which means to know and apprehend it in reason. For it is the work of self-revealing reason and is the highest form of reason. Such ideas as that priests have framed a people's religion in fraud and self-interest are consequently absurd; to regard religion as an arbitarary matter or a deception is as foolish as it is perverted. Priests have often profaned religion—the possibility of which is a consequence of the external relations and temporal existence of religion. It can thus, in this external connection, be laid hold of here and there, but because it is religion, it is really that which stands firm against finite ends and their complications and constitutes a region exalted high above them. This region of mind is really the holy place of truth itself, the holy place in which are dissolved the remaining illusions of the sensuous world, of finite ideas and ends, and of the sphere of opinion and caprice.

Inasmuch as it really is the content of religions, this

rational matter might now seem to be capable of being abstracted and expressed as a number of historical theorems. Philosophy stands on the same basis as religion and has the same object—the universal reason existing in and for itself. Mind desires to make this object its own, as is done with religion in the act and form of worship. But the form, as it is present in religion, is different from what is found to be contained in philosophy, and on this account a history of philosophy is different from a history of religion. Worship is only the operation of reflection; philosophy attempts to bring about the reconciliation by means of thinking knowledge, because mind desires to take up its being into itself. Philosophy is related in the form of thinking consciousness to its object; with religion it is different. But the distinction between the two should not be conceived of so abstractly as to make it seem that thought is only in philosophy and not in religion. The latter has likewise ideas and universal thoughts. Because both are so nearly related, it is an old tradition in the history of philosophy to deduce philosophy from Persian, Indian, or similar philosophy, a custom which is still partly retained in all histories of philosophy. For this reason, too, it is a legend universally believed that Pythagoras, for instance, received his philosophy from India and Egypt. The fame of the wisdom of these people, which wisdom is understood also to contain philosophy, is an old one. The Oriental ideas and religious worship which prevailed throughout the West up to the time of the Roman Empire likewise bear the name of Oriental philosophy. The Christian religion and philosophy are thought of in the Christian world as more definitely divided; in oriental antiquity on the other hand, religion and philosophy are conceived of as one in that the content has remained in the form in which it is philosophy. Considering the prevalence of these ideas and in order to have a definite limit to the relations between a history of philosophy and religious ideas, it is desirable to note some further considerations as to the form which separates religious ideas from philosophical theorems.

Religion has not only universal thought as inward content *implicite* contained in its myths, ideas, and imaginations and in its exact and positive histories, so that we require first of all to dig this content out of such myths in the form of theorems, but it often has its content *explicite* in the form of thought. In the Persian and Indian religions very deep, sublime, and speculative thoughts are even expressed. Indeed, in religion we even meet philosophies directly expressed, as in the philosophy of the Church Fathers. The scholastic philosophy really was theology; there is found in it a union or, if you will, a mixture of theology and philosophy which may very well puzzle us. The question which confronts us on the one side is how philosophy differs from theology, as the science of religion, or from religion as consciousness. And then, in how far have we in the history of philosophy to take account of what pertains to religion? For the reply to this last question three aspects have again to be dealt with; first of all the mythical and historical aspect of religion and its relation to philosophy; in the second place the theorems and speculative thoughts directly expressed in religion; and in the third place we must speak of philosophy within theology.

DIFFERENCE BETWEEN PHILOSOPHY AND RELIGION

The consideration of the mythical aspect of religion or the historical and positive side generally is interesting, because from it the difference in respect of form will show in what this content is antagonistic to philosophy. Indeed, taken in its connections, its difference passes into apparent inconsistency. This opposition not only is found in our contemplation but forms a very definite element in history. It is required by philosophy that it should justify its beginning and its manner of knowledge, and philosophy has thus placed itself in opposition to religion. On the other hand philosophy is combated and condemmed by religion and by the churches. The Greek popular religion, indeed, proscribed several philosophers; but the opposition is even more apparent in the Christian Church. The question is thus not only whether regard is to be paid to religion in the history of philosophy, for it has been the case that philosophy has paid attention to religion, and the latter to the former. Since neither of the two has allowed the other to rest undisturbed, we are not permitted to do so either. Of their relations, therefore, we must speak definitely, openly, and honestly— *aborder la question,* as the French say. We must not hesitate, as if such a discussion were too delicate, nor try to help ourselves out by beating about the bush; nor must we seek to find evasions or shifts, so that in the end no one can tell what we mean. We must not seem to wish to leave religion alone. This is nothing else than to appear to wish to conceal the fact that philosophy has directed its efforts against religion. Religion, that is, the theologians, are indeed the cause of this; they ignore philosophy, but only in order that they may not be contradicted in their arbitrary reasoning.

It may appear as if religion demanded that man should abstain from thinking of universal matters and philosophy because they are merely worldly wisdom and represent human operations. Human reason is here opposed to the divine. Men are, indeed, well accustomed to a distinction between divine teaching and laws and human power and inventions, such that under the latter everything is comprehended which in its manifestation proceeds from the consciousness, the intelligence or the will of mankind; which makes all this opposed to the knowledge of God and to things rendered divine by divine revelation. But the depreciation of what is human expressed by this opposition is then driven further still. While it implies the further view that man is certainly called upon to admire the wisdom of God in nature, and that the grain, the mountains, the cedars of Lebanon in all their glory, the song of the birds in the bough, the superior skill and the domestic instincts of animals are all magnified as being the work of God, it also implies that the wisdom, goodness and justice of God is, indeed, pointed out in human affairs, but not so much in the disposition or laws of man or in actions performed voluntarily and in the ordinary progress of the world as in human destiny—that is, in that which is external and even arbitrary in relation to knowledge and free will. Thus what is external and accidental is regarded as emphatically the work of God, and what has its root in will and conscience, as the work of man. The harmony between outward relations, circumstances, and events and the general aims of man is certainly something of a higher kind, but this is the case only for the reason that this harmony is considered with respect to ends which are human and not natural—such as those present in the life of a sparrow which finds its food. But if the summit of everything is found in this, that God rules over nature, what then is free will? Does he not rule over what is spiritual, or rather since he himself is spiritual, *in* what is spiritual? And is not the ruler over or in the spiritual region higher than a ruler over or in nature? But is that admiration of God as revealed in natural things as such, in trees and animals as opposed to what is human, far removed from the religion of the ancient Egyptians, which derived its knowledge of what is divine from the ibis, or from cats and dogs? Or does it differ from the deplorable condition of the ancient and the modern Indians, who held and still hold cows and apes in reverence, and are scrupulously concerned for the maintenance and nourishment of these animals, while they allow men to suffer hunger; who would commit a crime by removing the pangs of starvation through their slaughter or even by partaking of their food?

It seems to be expressed by such a view that human action as regards nature is ungodly; that the operations of nature are divine operations, but what man produces is ungodly. But the productions of human reason might, at least, be esteemed as much as nature. In so doing, however, we cede less to reason than is permitted to us. If the life and the action of animals be divine, human action must stand much higher, and must be worthy to be called divine in an infinitely higher sense. The pre-eminence of human thought must forthwith be avowed. Christ says on this subject (Matt. vi. 26-30), "Behold the fowls of the air", (in which we may also include the ibis and the *kokilas*), "are ye not much better than they? Wherefore, if God so clothe the grass of the field, which today is, and tomorrow is cast into the oven, shall He not much more clothe you?" The superiority of man, of the image of God, to animals and plants is indeed implicitly and explicitly established, but in asking wherein the divine element is to be sought and seen—in making use of such expressions—none of the superior but only the inferior nature is indicated. Similarly, in regard to the knowledge of God, it is remarkable that Christ places the knowledge of and faith in him not in any admiration of the creatures of nature nor in marvelling at any so-called dominion over them, nor in signs and wonders, but in the witness of the spirit. Spirit is infinitely high above nature, in it the divine nature manifests itself more than in nature.

But the form in which the universal content, which is in and for itself, first belongs to philosophy is the form of thought, the form of the universal itself. In religion, however, this content is for immediate and outward perception, and further for idea and feeling through art. The import is for the sensuous nature; it is the testimony of the mind which comprehends that content. To make this clearer, the difference must be recollected between that which we are and have, and how we know the same—that is, in what manner we know it and have it as our object. This distinction is an infinitely important matter, and it alone is concerned in the culture of peoples and of individuals. We are men and have reason; what is human or, above all, what is rational echoes within us, both in our feelings, mind, and heart and in our subjective nature generally. It is in this corresponding echo and in the corresponding motion effected that a particular content becomes our own and is like our own. The manifold nature of the determinations which it contains is concentrated and wrapt up within this inward nature—an obscure motion of mind in itself and in universal substantiality. The content is thus directly identical with the simple abstract certainty of ourselves and with self-consciousness. But mind, because it is mind, is as truly consciousness. What is confined within itself in its simplicity must be objective to itself and must come to be known. The whole difference lies in the manner and method of this objectivity, and hence in the manner and method of consciousness.

This method and manner extends from the simple expression of the dulness of mere feeling to the most objective form, to that which is in and for itself objective, to thought. The most simple, most formal objectivity is the expression of a name for that feeling and for the state of mind according with it, as seen in these words, worship, prayer, etc. Such expressions as "Let us pray" and "Let us worship" are simply the recalling of that feeling. But "Let us think about God" brings with it something more; it expresses the absolutely embracing content of that substantial feeling, and the object, which differs from mere feeling as subjective self-conscious activity; or which is content distinguished from this activity as form. This object, however, comprehending in itself the whole substantial content, is itself still undeveloped and entirely undetermined. To develop that content, to comprehend, express, and bring to consciousness its relations, is the commencement, creation, and manifestation of religion. The form in which this developed content first possesses objectivity is that of immediate perception, of sensuous idea or of a more defined idea deduced from natural, physical, or mental manifestations and relationships.

Art brings about this consciousness, in that it gives permanence and cohesion to the fleeting visible appearance through which objectivity passes in sensation. The shapeless, sacred stone, the mere place, or whatever it is to which the desire for objectivity first attaches itself, receives from art, form, feature, determinate character, and content which can be known and which is now present for consciousness. Art has thus become the instructress of the people. This was the case with Homer and Hesiod for instance, who, according to Herodotus (II. 53), "made the Greeks their theogony," because they elevated and consolidated ideas and traditions corresponding to the spirit of the people, wherever and in whatever confusion they might be found, into definite images and ideas. This is not the art which merely gives expression in its own way to the content, already perfectly expressed, of a religion which in thought, idea, and words have already attained complete development; that is to say, which puts its matter into stone, canvas, or words as is done by modern art, which, in dealing either with religious or with historical objects, takes as its groundwork ideas and thoughts which are already there. The consciousness of this religion is rather the product of thinking imagination, or of thought which comprehends through the organ of imagination alone and finds expression in its forms.

If the infinite thought, the absolute mind, has revealed and does reveal itself in true religion, that in which it reveals itself is the heart, the representing consciousness and the understanding of what is finite. Religion is not merely directed to every sort of culture: "To the poor is the Gospel preached." But it must as being religion, expressly directed towards heart and mind, enter into the sphere of subjectivity and consequently into the region of finite methods of representation. In the perceiving and, with reference to perceptions, reflecting consciousness, man possesses for the speculative relations belonging to the absolute, only finite relations, whether taken in an exact or in a symbolical sense, to serve him to comprehend and express those qualities and relationships of the infinite.

In religion as the earliest and the immediate revelations of God, the form of representation and of reflecting finite thought cannot be the only form in which he gives existence to himself in consciousness, but it must also appear in this form, for such alone is comprehensible to religious consciousness. To make this clearer, something must be said as to what is the meaning of comprehension. On the one hand, as has been remarked above, there is in it the substantial basis of content, which, coming to mind as its absolute being, affects it in its innermost, finds an answering chord, and thereby obtains from it confirmation. This is the first absolute condition necessary to comprehension; what is not implicitly there cannot come within it or be for it—that is, a content which is infinite and eternal. For the substantial as infinite, is just that which has no limitations in that to which it is related, for else it would be limited and not the true substantial. And mind is that alone which is not implicit, which is finite and external; for what is finite and external is no longer what is implicit but what is for another, what has entered into a relation. But, on the other hand, because the true and eternal must be for mind, become known, that is, enter into finite consciousness, the mind for which it is, in the first instance, is finite and the manner of its consciousness consists in the ideas and forms of finite things and relations. These forms are familiar and well known to consciousness, the general mode of finitude, which mode it has appropriated to itself, having constituted it the universal medium of its representation, into which everything that comes to consciousness must be resolved in order that it may have and know itself therein.

The assertion of religion is that the manifestation of truth which is revealed to us through it is one which is given to man from outside, and on this account it is also asserted that man has humbly to assent to it, because human reason cannot attain to it by itself. The assertion of positive religion is that its truths exist without having their source known, so that the content as given, is one which is above and beyond reason. By means of some prophet or other divine instrument, the truth is made known. Just as Ceres and Triptolemus, who introduced agriculture and matrimony, were honoured by the Greeks for so doing, likewise men have rendered thanks to Moses and to Mahomed. Through whatever individual the truth may have been given, the external matter is historical, and this is indifferent to the absolute content. The person is not the import of the doctrine. But the Christian religion has this characteristic: that the Person of Christ in his character of the Son of God himself partakes of the nature of God. If Christ be for Christians only a teacher like Pythagoras, Socrates, or Columbus, there would be here no universal divine content, no revelation or knowledge imparted about the nature of God, and it is regarding this alone that we desire to obtain knowledge.

Whatever stage it may itself have reached, the truth must undoubtedly in the first place come to men from without as a present object, sensuously represented, just as Moses saw God in the fiery bush, and as the Greeks brought the God into conscious being by means of sculpture or other representations. But there is the further fact that neither in religion nor in philosophy does this external form remain, nor can it so remain. A form of the imagination or a historical form, such as Christ, must for the spirit be spiritual; and thus it ceases to be an external matter, seeing that the form of externality is dead. We must know God "in spirit and in truth." He is the absolute and actual spirit. The relation borne by the human spirit to this spirit involves the following considerations.

When man determines to adopt a religion he asks himself, "What is the ground of my faith?" The Christian religion replies—"The spirit's witness to its content." Christ reproved the Pharisees for wishing to see miracles; the spirit alone comprehends spirit, the miracle is only a presentiment of that spirit; and if the miracle be the suspension of natural laws, spirit itself is the real miracle in the operations of nature. Spirit in itself is merely this comprehension of itself. There is only one spirit, the universal divine spirit. Not that it is merely everywhere; it is not to be comprehended as what is common to everything, as an external totality, to be found in many or in all individuals, which are essentially individuals. But it must be understood as that which permeates through everything, as the unity of itself and of a semblance of its "Other," as of the subjective and particular. As universal, it is object to itself, and thus determined as a particular, it is this individual. But as universal it reaches over this its "Other," so that its "Other" and itself are comprised in one. The true universality seems, popularly expressed, to be two—what is common to the universal itself and to the particular. A duality is formed in the understanding of itself, and the spirit is the unity of what is understood and the understanding person. The divine spirit which is comprehended is objective; the subjective spirit comprehends. But spirit is not passive, or else the passivity can be momentary only; there is one spiritual substantial unity. The subjective spirit is the active, but the objective spirit is itself this activity; the active subjective spirit is that which comprehends the divine, and in its comprehension of it is itself the divine spirit. The relation of spirit to self alone is the absolute determination; the divine spirit lives in its own community and presence. This comprehension has been called faith, but it is not a historical faith. We Lutherans—I am a Lutheran and will remain the same—have only this original faith. This unity is not the substance of Spinoza, but the apprehending substance in self-consciousness which makes itself eternal and relates to universality. The talk about the limitations of human thought is futile; to know God is the only end of religion. The testimony of the spirit to the content of religion is itself religion; it is a testimony that both bears witness and at the same time is that witness. The spirit itself bears witness and first in the witness; it is only in that it witnesses, attests itself, shows and manifests itself.

It has further to be said, that this testimony, this inward stirring and self-consciousness, reveals itself, while in the enshrouded consciousness of devotion it does not arrive at the proper consciousness of an object. This permeating and permeated spirit now enters into idea; God goes forth into the "Other" and makes himself objective. All that pertains to revelation and its reception, which comes before us in mythology, here appears; everything which is historical and which belongs to what is positive has here its proper place. To speak more definitely, we now have the Christ who came into the world nearly two thousand years ago. But he says, "I am with you even unto the ends of the earth; where two or three are gathered together in my name, there will I be in the midst." I shall not be seen of you in the flesh, but "the spirit of truth will guide you into all truth." The external is not the true relation; it will disappear.

The two stages have here been given, the first of which is the stage of devotion, of worship, such as that reached in partaking of the Communion. That is the perception of the divine spirit in the community in which the present, indwelling, living Christ as self-consciousness has attained to actuality. The second stage is that of developed consciousness, when the content becomes the object; here this present, indwelling Christ retreats two thousand years to a small corner of Palestine, and is an individual historically manifested far away at Nazareth or Jerusalem. It is the same thing in the Greek religion, where the God present in devotion changes into prosaic statues and marble; or in painting, where this externality is likewise arrived at, when the God becomes mere canvas or wood. The Supper is, according to the Lutheran conception, of faith alone; it is a divine satisfaction, and is not adored as if it were the Host. Thus a sacred image is no more to us than is a stone or thing. The second point of view must indeed be that with which consciousness begins; it must start from the external comprehension of this form; it must passively accept report and take it up into memory. But if it remain there, that is the unspiritual point of view. To remain fixed in this second standpoint in this dead faraway historic distance, is to reject the spirit. The sins of him who lies against the Holy Ghost cannot be forgiven. That lie is the refusal to be a universal, to be holy, that is to make Christ become divided, separated, to make him only another person as this particular person in Judea; or else to say that he now exists, but only far away in Heaven, or in some other place, and not in present actual form amongst his people. The man who speaks of the *merely* finite, of *merely* human reason, and of the limits to mere reason, lies against the spirit, for the spirit as infinite and universal, as self-comprehension, comprehends itself not in a "merely" nor in limits, nor in the finite as such. It has nothing to do with this, for it comprehends itself within itself alone, in its infinitude.

If it be said of philosophy that it makes reality the subject of its knowledge, the principal point is that the reality should not be one outside of that of which it is the reality. For example, if from the real content of a book, I abstract the binding, paper, ink, language, the many thousand letters that are contained in it, the simple universal content as reality is not outside of the book. Similarly law is not outside of the individual, but it constitutes the true being of the individual. The reality of my mind is thus in my mind itself and not outside of it; it is my real being, my own substance, without which I am without existence. This reality is, so to speak, the combustible material which may be kindled and lit up by the universal reality as such as objective. And only so far as this phosphorus is in men, is comprehension, the kindling and lighting up, possible. Feeling, anticipation, knowledge of God, are only thus in men; without such, the divine mind would not be the in and for itself universal. Reality is itself a real content and not that which is destitute of content and undetermined. Yet, as the book has other content besides, there is in the individual mind also a great amount of other matter which belongs only to the manifestation of this reality, and the individual, surrounded with what is external, must be separated from this existence. Since reality is itself spirit and not an abstraction, "God is not a God for the dead but for the living," and indeed for living spirits.

> The great Creator was alone
> And experienced desire,
> Therefore He created Spirits,
> Holy mirrors of His holiness.
> The noblest Being He found no equal;
> From out the bowl of all the spiritual world,
> There sparkled up to Him infinitude.

Religion is also the point of view from which this existence is known. But as regards the different forms of knowledge existing in religion and philosophy, philosophy appears to be opposed to the conception in religion that the universal mind first shows itself as external, in the objective mode of consciousness. Worship, commencing with the external, then turns against and abrogates it as has just been said, and thus philosophy is justified through the acts and forms of worship, and only does what they do. Philosophy has to deal with two different objects; first as in the religion present in worship, with the substantial content, the spiritual soul, and secondly with bringing this before consciousness as object, but in the form of thought. Philosophy thinks and conceives of that which religion represents as the object of consciousness, whether it is as the work of the imagination or as existent facts in history. The form of the knowledge of the object is, in religious consciousness, such as pertains to the ordinary idea, and is thus more or less sensuous in nature. In philosophy we do not say that God begot a son, which is a relation derived from natural life. The concept, or the substance of such a relation, is nevertheless still recognised in philosophy. Since philosophy thinks its object, it has the advantage of uniting the two stages of religious consciousness—which in religion are different moments—into one unity in philosophic thought.

It is these two forms which are different from one another and which, as opposed, may therefore seem to be mutually conflicting. And it is natural and it necessarily seems to be the case that on first definitely coming to view they are, so to speak, conscious of their diversity, and hence at first appear as inimical to one another. The first stage in the order of manifestation is definite existence, or a determinate being-for-self as opposed to the other. The later form is that thought embraces itself in the concrete, immerses itself in itself, and mind as such, comes in it to consciousness. In the earlier stage, mind is abstract, and in this constraint it knows itself to be different and in opposition to the other. When it embraces itself in the concrete, it is no more simply confined in determinate existence, only knowing or possessing itself in that diversity, but it is the universal which, inasmuch as it determines itself, contains its "other" within itself. As concrete intelligence, mind thus comprehends the substantial in the form which seemed to differ from it, of which it had only grasped the outward manifestation and had turned away from it; it recognises itself in its inward content, and so it for the first time grasps its object, and deals justice to its opposite.

Generally speaking, the course of this antithesis in history is that thought first of all comes forth within religion, as not free and in separate manifestations. Secondly, it strengthens itself, feels itself to be resting upon itself, holds and conducts itself inimically towards the other form, and does not recognise itself therein. In the third place, it concludes by acknowledging itself as in this other.

Philosophy has to begin with carrying on its work entirely on its own account, isolating thought from all popular beliefs, and taking for itself quite a different field of operation, a field for which the world of ordinary ideas lies quite apart, so that the two exist peacefully side by side, or, to put it better, so that no reflection on their opposition is arrived at. Just as little did the thought of reconciling them occur, since in the popular beliefs the same content appeared as in any external form other than the notion—the thought, that is, of explaining and justifying popular belief, in order thus to be able again to express the conceptions of free thought in the form of popular religion.

Thus we see philosophy first restrained and confined within the circle of the Greek heathen world; then resting upon itself, it goes forth against popular religion and takes up a hostile attitude to it, until it grasps that religion in its innermost being and recognises itself therein. Thus the more ancient Greek philosophers generally respected the popular religion, or at least they did not oppose it, or reflect upon it. Those coming later, including even Xenophanes, handled popular ideas most severely, and thus many so-called atheists made their appearance. But as the spheres of popular conception and abstract thought stood peacefully side by side, we also find Greek philosophers of even a later period in development, in whose case speculative thought and the act of worship, as also the pious invocation of and sacrifice to the gods, coexist in good faith, and not in mere hypocrisy. Socrates was accused of teaching other gods than those belonging to the popular religion; his δαιμόνιον was indeed opposed to the principles of Greek morals and religion. But at the same time he followed quite honestly the usages of his religion, and we know besides that his last request was to ask his friends to offer a cock to Aesculapius—a desire quite inconsistent with his conclusions regarding the existence of God and above all regarding morality. Plato declaimed against the poets and their gods. It was in a much later time that the Neo-Platonists first recognised in the popular mythology rejected earlier by the philosophers, the universal content. They transposed and translated it into what is significant for thought, and thus used mythology itself as a symbolical imagery for giving expression to their formulas.

Similarly do we see in the Christian religion thought which is not independent first placing itself in conjunction with the form belonging to this religion and acting within it—that is to say, taking the form as its groundwork, and proceeding from the absolute assumption of the Christian doctrine. We see later on the opposition between so-called faith and so-called reason; when the wings of thought have become strengthened, the young eaglet flies away for himself to the sun of truth; but like a bird of prey he turns upon religion and combats it. Latest of all philosophy permits full justice to be done to the content of religion through the speculative notion, which is through thought itself. For this end the notion must have grasped itself in the concrete and penetrated to concrete spirituality. This must be the standpoint of the philosophy of the present time; it has begun within Christianity and can have no other content than the world spirit.

When that spirit comprehends itself in philosophy, it also comprehends itself in that form which formerly was inimical to philosophy.

Thus religion has a content in common with philosophy the forms alone being different; and the only essential point is that the form of the notion should be so far perfected as to be able to grasp the content of religion. The truth is just that which has been called the mysteries of religion. These constitute the speculative element in religion such as were called by the Neo-Platonists μνεῖν, μνεῖσθαι (being initiated), or being occupied with speculative notions. By mysteries is meant, superficially speaking, the secret, what remains such and does not arrive at being known. But in the Eleusinian mysteries there was nothing unknown; all Athenians were initiated into them, Socrates alone shut himself out. Openly to make them known to strangers was the one thing forbidden, as indeed it was made a crime in the case of certain people. Such matters, however, as being holy, were not to be spoken of. Herodotus often expressly says (e.g. ii. 45-47) that he would speak of the Egyptian divinities and mysteries in as far as it was pious so to do: he knew more, but it would be impious to speak of them. In the Christian religion dogmas are called mysteries. They are that which man knows about the nature of God. Neither is there anything mysterious in this; it is known by all those who are partakers in that religion, and these are thus distinguished from the followers of other religions. Hence mystery here signifies nothing unknown, since all Christians are in the secret. Mysteries are in their nature speculative, mysterious certainly to the understanding, but not to reason; they are rational, just in the sense of being speculative. The understanding does not comprehend the speculative which simply is the concrete because it holds to the differences in their separation; their contradiction is indeed contained in the mystery, which, however, is likewise the resolution of the same.

Philosophy, on the contrary, is opposed to the so-called rationalism of the new theology, which forever keeps reason on its lips but is barren understanding only; no reason is recognisable in it except the moment of independent thought which really is abstract thought and that alone. When the understanding which does not comprehend the truths of religion calls itself the illuminating reason and plays the lord and master, it goes astray. Rationalism is opposed to philosophy in content and form, for it has made the content empty as it has made the heavens, and has reduced all that is to finite relations. In its form it is a rationalizing process which is not free and which has no conceiving power. The supernatural in religion is opposed to rationalism, and if indeed the former is related in respect of the real content to philosophy, yet it differs from it in form, for it has become unspiritual and wooden, looking for its justification to mere external authority. The scholastics were not supernaturalists in this sense; they knew the dogmas of the church in thought and in conception. If religion, in the inflexibility of its abstract authority as opposed to thought, declares of it that "the gates of hell shall not triumph over it," the gates of reason are stronger than the gates of hell, not to overcome the Church but to reconcile itself to the Church. Philosophy, as the conceiving thought of this content, has as regards the idea of religion, the advantage of comprehending both sides— it comprehends religion and also comprehends both rationalism and supernaturalism and itself likewise. But this is not the case on the other side. Religion from the standpoint of representational idea comprehends only what stands on the same level as itself, and not philosophy, the notion, the universal thought determinations. Often no injustice is done to a philosophy when its opposition to religion has been made matter of reproach. But often, too, a wrong has been inflicted where this is done from the religious point of view.

The form of religion is necessary to mind as it is in and for itself. It is the form of truth as it is for all men, and for every mode of consciousness. This universal mode is first of all for men in the form of sensuous consciousness, and then, secondly, in the intermingling of the form of the universal with sensuous manifestation or reflection. The representing consciousness, the mythical, positive, and historical form, is that pertaining to the understanding. What is received in evidence of mind becomes object to consciousness only when it appears in the form of the understanding—that is to say, consciousness must first be already acquainted with these forms from life and from experience. Now, because thinking consciousness is not the outward universal form for all mankind, the consciousness of the true, the spiritual and the rational, must have the form of religion, and this is the universal justification of this form.

We have here laid down the distinction between philosophy and religion, but taking into account what it is we wish to deal with in the history of philosophy, there is something still which must be remarked upon, and which partly follows from what has been already said. There is the question still confronting us as to what attitude we must take in reference to this matter in the history of philosophy.

The Religious Element To Be Excluded From The Content Of The History Of Philosophy

Mythology first meets us, and it seems as if it might be drawn within the history of philosophy. It is indeed a product of the imagination, but not of caprice, although that also has its place here. But the main part of mythology is the work of the imaginative reason, which makes reality its object, but yet has no other means of so doing than that of sensuous representation, so that the gods make their appearance in human guise. Mythology can now be studied for art, etc. But the thinking mind must seek out the substantial content, the thought and the theory implicitly contained therein, as reason is sought in nature. This mode of treating mythology was that of the Neo-Platonists; in recent times it has for the most part become the work of my friend Creuzer in symbolism. This method of treatment is combated and condemned by others. Man, it is said, must set to work historically alone, and it is not historical when a theory unthought of by the ancients is read into a myth or brought out of it. In one light, this is quite correct, for it points to a method adopted by Creuzer and also by the Alexandrians, who acted in a similar way. In conscious thought the ancients had not such theories before them, nor did anyone maintain that they had. Yet to say that such content was not implicitly present is an absurd contention. As the products of reason, though not of thinking reason, the religions of the people, as also the mythologies, however simple and even foolish they may appear, indubitably contain, as genuine works of art, thoughts, universal determinations, and truth. For the instinct of reason is at their base. Bound up with this is the fact that since mythology in its expression takes sensuous forms, much that is contingent and external becomes intermingled. For the representation of the notion in sensuous forms always possesses a certain incongruity, seeing that what is founded on imagination cannot express the Idea in its real aspect. This sensuous form, produced as it is by a historical or natural method, must be determined on many sides, and this external determination must, more or less, be of such a nature as not to express the Idea. It may also be that many errors are contained in that explanation, particularly in regard to details. All the customs, actions, furnishings, vestments, and offerings taken together may undoubtedly contain something of the Idea in analogy, but the connection is far removed, and many contingent circumstances must find their entrance. But that there is a reason there must certainly be recognised, and it is essential so to comprehend and grasp mythology.

But mythology must remain excluded from our history of philosophy. The reason of this is found in the fact that in philosophy we have to do not with theorems generally, or with thoughts which only are *implicite* contained in some particular form or other, but with thoughts which are explicit, and only in so far as they are explicit and in so far as a content such as that belonging to religion has come to consciousness in the form of thought. And this is just what forms the immense distinction which we saw above, between capacity and actuality. The theorems which are *implicite* contained within religion do not concern us; they must be in the form of thoughts, since thought alone is the absolute form of the Idea.

In many mythologies, images are certainly used along with their significance, or else the images are closely attended by their interpretation. The ancient Persians worshipped the sun, or fire, as being the highest being. The first cause in the Persian religion is Zervane Akerene—unlimited time, eternity. This simple eternal existence possesses according to Diogenes Laertius (I. 8) "the two principles Ormuzd ('Ωρομάσδης) and Ahriman ('Αρειμάνιος), the rulers over good and evil." Plutarch in writing on Isis and Osiris (T. II. p. 369, ed. Xyl.) says,

> It is not one existence which holds and rules the whole, but good is mingled with evil; nature as a rule brings forth nothing pure and simple; it is not one dispenser, who, like a host, gives out and mixes up the drink from two different barrels. But through two opposed and inimical principles of which the one impels towards what is right, and the other in the opposite direction, if not the whole world, at least this earth is influenced in different ways. Zoroaster has thus emphatically set up the one principle (Ormuzd) as being the Light, and the other (Ahriman) as the Darkness. Between the two (μέσος δὲ ἀμφοῖν) is Mithra, hence called by the Persians the mediator (μεοίτης).

Mithra is then likewise substance, the universal existence, the sun raised to a totality. It is not the mediator between Ormuzd and Ahriman by establishing peace and leaving each to remain as it was; it does not partake of good and evil both, like an unblest middle thing, but it stands on the side of Ormuzd and strives with him against the evil.

Ahriman is sometimes called the first-born son of the Light, but Ormuzd alone remained within the light. At the creation of the visible world, Ormuzd places on the earth in his incomprehensible kingdom of light, the firm arches of the heavens which are above yet surrounded on every side with

the first original light. Midway to the earth is the high hill
Albordi, which reaches into the source of light. Ormuzd's
empire of light extended uninterruptedly over the firm vault
of the heavens and the hill Albordi, and over the earth too,
until the third age was reached. Then Ahriman, whose kingdom of night was formerly bound beneath the earth, broke in
upon Ormuzd's corporeal world and ruled in common with
him. Now the space between heaven and earth was divided
into light and night. As Ormuzd had formerly only a spiritual
kingdom of light, Ahriman had only one of night, but now
that they were intermingled he placed the terrestrial light
thus created in opposition to the terrestrial night. From this
time on, two corporeal worlds stand opposed, one pure and
good, and one impure and evil, and this opposition permeates
all nature. On Albordi, Ormuzd created Mithra as mediator
for the earth. The end of the creation of the bodily world is
none other than to reinstate existence, fallen from its creator,
to make it good again, and thus to make the evil disappear
for ever. The corporeal world is the battle ground between
good and evil; but the battle between light and darkness is
not in itself an absolute and irreconcilable opposition, but
one which can be conquered, and in it Ormuzd, the principle
of light, will be the conqueror.

I would remark of this that when we consider the elements
in these ideas which bear some further connection with
philosophy, the universal aspects of that duality with which
the notion is necessarily set forth can alone be interesting and
noteworthy to us. For in it the notion is just the immediate
opposite of itself, the unity of itself with itself in the
"other": a simple being in which absolute opposition appears
as the opposition of existence, and the negation of that
opposition. Because properly the light principle is the only
reality of both, and the principle of darkness is the null and
void—the principle of light identifies itself with Mithra, which
was before called the highest existence. The opposition has
laid aside the appearance of contingency, but the spiritual
principle is not separate from the physical, because good and
evil are both determined as light and darkness. We thus here

see thought breaking forth from actuality, and yet not such a separation as only takes place in religion, where the super-sensuous is itself again represented in a manner sensuous, notionless, and dispersed, for the whole of what is dispersed in sensuous form is gathered together in the one single opposition, and movement is thus simply represented. These determinations lie much nearer to thought; they are not mere images or symbols, but yet these myths do not concern philosophy. In them thought does not take the first place, for the myth form remains predominant. In all religions this oscillation between images and thought is found, and such an intermixture still lies outside philosophy.

This is also so in the Sanchuniathonic cosmogony of the Phoenicians. These fragements, which are found in Eusebius (Praepar. Evang. I. 10), are taken from the translation of the Sanchuniathon from Phoenician into Greek made by a grammarian named Philo from Biblus. Philo lived in the time of Vespasian and ascribes great antiquity to the Sanchunia-thon. It is there said

> The principles of things are found in Chaos, in which the elements exist undeveloped and confused, and in a spirit of air. The latter permeated the chaos, and with it engen-dered a slimy matter or mud (ἰλύν) which contained within it the living forces and the germs of animals. By mingling this mud with the component matter of chaos and the resulting fermentation, the elements separated themselves. The fire elements ascended into the heights and formed the stars. Through their influence in the air, clouds were formed and the earth was made fruitful. From the mingling of water and earth, through the mud converted into putrefying matter, animals took their origin as imperfect and senseless. These again begot other animals more perfect and endowed with senses. It was the crash of thunder in a thunder-storm that caused the first animals still sleeping in their husks to waken up to life.[10]

10. Sanchuniathonis Fragment, ed. Richard Cumberland (London, 1720), 8; German by J. P. Kassel. (Magdeburg, 1755), 8, pp. 1 4.

The fragments of Berosus of the Chaldeans were collected from Josephus, Syncellus, and Eusebius under the title *Berosi Chaldaica,* by Scaliger, as an appendix to his work *De emendatione temporum,* and they are found complete in the Greek Library of Fabricius (T. xiv, pp. 175-211). Berosus lived in the time of Alexander and is said to have been a priest of Bel and to have drawn upon the archives of the temple at Babylon. He says

> The original god is Bel and the goddess Omoroka (the sea), but beside them there were yet other gods. Bel divided Omoroka in two, in order to create from her parts heaven and earth. Hereupon he cut off his own head and the human race originated from the drops of his divine blood. After the creation of man, Bel banished the darkness, divided heaven and earth, and formed the world into its natural shape. Since certain parts of the earth seemed to him to be insufficiently populated, he compelled another god to lay hands upon himself, and from his blood more men and more kinds of animals were created. At first the men lived a wild and uncultivated life, until a monster [called by Berosus, Oannes] joined them into a state, taught them arts and sciences, and in a word brought humanity into existence. The monster set about this end with the rising of the sun out of the sea, and with its setting he again hid himself under the waves.

What belongs to mythology may in the second place make a pretence of being a kind of philosophy. It has produced philosophers who availed themselves of the mythical form in order to bring their theories and systems more prominently before the imagination, for they made thoughts the content of the myth. But the myth is not a mere cloak in the ancient myths; it is not merely that thoughts were there and were concealed. This may happen in our reflecting times; but the first poetry does not start from a separation of prose and poetry. If philosophers used myths, it was usually the case that they had the thoughts and then sought for images appropriate to them. Plato has many beautiful myths of this kind. Others likewise have spoken in myths, as for example, Jacobi, whose philosophy took the form of the Christian religion, through which he gave utterance to matter of a highly speculative nature. But this form is not suitable to philosophy. Thought which has itself as object must have raised itself to its own form, to the form of thought. Plato is often esteemed on account of his myths; he is supposed to have evinced by their means greater genius than other philosophers were capable of. It is contended here that the myths of Plato are superior to the abstract form of expression, and Plato's method of representation is certainly a wonderful one. On closer examination we find that it is partly the impossibility of expressing himself after the manner of pure thought that makes Plato put his meaning so, and also such methods of expression are only used by him in introducing a subject. When he comes to the matter in point, Plato expresses himself otherwise, as we see in the Parmenides, where simple thought determinations are used without imagery. Externally these myths may certainly serve when the heights of speculative thought are left behind, in order to present the matter in an easier form, but the real value of Plato does not rest in his myths. If thought once attains power sufficient to give existence to itself within itself and in its element, the myth becomes a superfluous adornment, by which philosophy is not advanced. Men often lay hold of nothing but these myths. Hence Aristotle has been misunderstood just because he intersperses similes here and there. The simile can never be entirely in accord with thought, for it always carries with it something more. The difficulty of representing thoughts as thoughts always seizes the expedient of expression in sensuous form. Thought, too, ought not to be concealed by means of the myth, for the object of the mythical is just to give expression to and to reveal thought. The symbol is undoubtedly insufficient for this expression. Thought concealed in symbols is not yet possessed, for thought is self-revealing, and hence the myth does not form a medium adequate for its conveyance.

Aristotle (Metaph. III. 4) says, "It is not worth while to treat seriously of those whose philosophy takes a mythical form." Such is not the form in which thought allows itself to be stated, but only is a subordinate mode.

Connected with this, there is a similar method of representing the universal content by means of numbers, lines, and geometric figures. These are images, but not concretely so, as in the case of myths. Thus it may be said that eternity is a circle, the snake that bites its own tail. This is only an image, but mind does not require such a symbol. There are peoples who value such methods of representation, but these forms do not go far. The most abstract determinations can indeed be thus expressed, but any further progress brings about confusion. Just as the freemasons have symbols which are esteemed for their depth of wisdom—depth as a well is deep when one cannot see the bottom—that which is hidden very easily seems to men deep, or as if depth were concealed beneath. But when it is hidden, it may possibly prove to be the case that there is nothing behind. This is so in free-masonry, in which everything is concealed to those outside and also to many people within, and where nothing remarkable is possessed in learning or in science, and least of all in philosophy. Thought is, on the contrary, simply its manifestation; clearness is its nature and itself. The act of manifestation is not a condition which may be or may not be, so that thought may remain as thought when it is not manifested, but its manifestation is itself, its being.

Numbers, as will be remarked in respect of the Pythagoreans, are unsuitable mediums for expressing thoughts; thus μονάς, δυάς τριάς are, with Pythagoras, unity, difference, and unity of the unity and of the difference. The two first of the three are certainly united by addition; this kind of union is, however, the worst form of unity. In religion the three make their appearance in a deeper sense as the trinity, and in philosophy as the notion, but enumeration forms a bad method of expression. There is the same objection to it as would exist to making the mensuration of space the medium for expressing the absolute.

People also quote the philosophy of the Chinese, of the Foi, in which it is said that thoughts are represented by numbers. Yet the Chinese have explained their symbols and hence have made their meaning evident. Universal simple abstractions have been present to all people who have arrived at any degree of culture.

We have still to remark in the third place that religion, as such, does not merely form its representations after the manner of art; and also that poetry likewise contains actual thoughts. In the case of the poets whose art has speech as medium, we find also deep universal thought regarding reality. These are more explicitly expressed in the Indian religion, but with the Indians everything is mixed up. Hence it is said that such peoples have also had a philosophy proper to themselves; but the universal thoughts of interest in Indian books limit themselves to what is most abstract, to the idea of rising up and passing away, and thus of making a perpetual round. The story of the Phoenix is well known as an example of this; it is one which took its origin in the East. We are able similarly to find thoughts about life and death and of the transition of being into passing away; from life comes death and from death comes life; even in being, in what is positive, the negation is already present. The negative side must indeed contain within it the positive, for all change, all the process of life is founded on this. But such reflections only occasionally come forth; they are not to be taken as being proper philosophic utterances. For philosophy is only present when thought, as such, is made the absolute ground and root of everything else, and in these modes of representation this is not so.

Philosophy does not reflect on any particular thing or object already existing as a first substratum. Its content is just thought, universal thought which must plainly come first of all; to put it otherwise, the absolute must in philosophy be in the form of thought. In the Greek religion we find the thought determination "eternal necessity"; which means an absolute and clearly universal relation. But such thought has other subjects besides; it only expresses a relation; necessity is not the true and all-embracing being. Thus neither must we take this form into our consideration. We might speak in that way of a philosophy of Euripides, Schiller, or Goethe. But all such reflection, or general modes of representing what is true, the ends of men, morality, and so on, are in part only incidentally set forth, and in part they have not reached the proper form of thought, which implies that what is so expressed must be ultimate, thus constituting the absolute.

Particular Theories Found in Religion

In conclusion, the philosophy which we find within religion does not concern us. We find deep, speculative thoughts regarding the nature of God not only in the Indian religions, but also in the Fathers and the scholastics. In the history of dogmatism there is a real interest in becoming acquainted with these thoughts, but they do not belong to the history of philosophy. Nevertheless more notice must be taken of the scholastics than of the Fathers, for they were certainly great philosophers to whom the culture of Christendom owes much. But their speculations belong in part to other philosophies such as to that of Plato, which must in so far be considered for themselves. Partly, too, they emanate from the speculative content of religion itself which already exists as independent truth in the doctrine of the Church, and belongs primarily to faith. Thus such modes of thought rest on a hypothesis and not on thought itself; they are not properly speaking themselves philosophy or thought, which rests on itself, but as ideas already firmly rooted, they act on its behalf either in refuting other ideas and conclusions or in philosophically vindicating against them their own religious teaching. Thought in this manner does not represent and know itself as the ultimate and absolute culmination of the content, or as the inwardly self-determining thought. Hence, too, when the Fathers, seeing that the content of the Christian religion can only be grasped after the speculative form, did, within the teaching of the church, produce thoughts of a highly speculative nature, the ultimate justification of these was not found in thought as such, but in the teaching of the Church. Philosophic teaching here finds itself within a strongly bound system and not as thought which emanates freely from itself. Thus with the scholastics, too, thought does not construct itself out of itself, but depends upon hypotheses; and although it ever rests more and more upon itself, it never does so in opposition to the doctrine of the Church. Both must and do agree, since thought has to prove from itself what the Church has already verified.

Philosophy Proper Distinguished from Popular Philosophy

Of the two fields of knowledge allied to philosophy we found that the one, that of the special sciences, could not be called a philosophy in that it, as independent seeing and thinking immersed in finite matter, and as the active principle in becoming acquainted with the finite, was not the content, but simply the formal and subjective moment. The second sphere, religion, is deficient in that it only had the content or the objective moment in common with philosophy. In it independent thought was not an essential moment, since the object had a pictorial or historical form. Philosophy demands the unity and intermingling of these two points of view; it unites the Sunday of life when man in humility renounces himself, and the working day when he stands up independently, is the master of himself, and considers his own interests.

A third point of view seems to unite both elements, and that is popular philosophy. It deals with universal objects and philosophizes about God and the world; and thought is likewise occupied in learning about these matters. Yet this philosophy must also be cast aside. The writings of Cicero may be put under this category; they contain a kind of philosophy that has its own place and in which excellent things are said. Cicero formed many experiences both in the affairs of life and mind, and from them and after observing what takes place in the world, he deduced the truth. He expresses himself with culture on the concerns most important to man, and hence his great popularity. Fanatics and mystics may from another point of view be reckoned as in this category. They give expression to a deep sense of devotion, and have had experiences in the higher regions. They are able to express the highest content, and the result is attractive. We thus find the brightest gleams of thought in the writings of a Pascal—as we do in his *Pensées*.

But. the drawback that attaches to this philosophy is that the ultimate appeal—even in modern times—is made to the fact that men are constituted such as they are by nature, and with this Cicero is very free. Here the moral instinct comes into question, only under the name of feeling. Religion now rests not on what is objective but on religious feeling, because the immediate consciousness of God by men is its ultimate ground. Cicero makes copious use of the *consensus gentium;* in more modern times this appeal has been more or less left alone, since the individual subject has to rest upon himself. Feeling is first of all laid hold of, then comes reasoning from what is given, but in these we can appeal to what is immediate only. Independent thought is certainly here advanced; the content too, is taken from the self. But we must just as necessarily exclude this mode of thinking from philosophy. For the source from which the content is derived is of the same description as in the other cases. Nature is the source in finite sciences, and in religion it is spirit; but here the source is in authority; the content is given and the act of worship removes but momentarily this externality. The source of popular philosophy is in the heart, impulses and capacities, our natural being, my impression of what is right and of God; the content is in a form which is of nature only. I certainly have everything in feeling, but the whole content is also in mythology, and yet in neither is it so in veritable form. The laws and doctrines of religion are that in which this content always comes to consciousness in a more definite way, while in feeling there still is intermingled the arbitrary will of that which is subjective.

Commencement of Philosophy and of Its History

Now that we have thus defined the notion of philosophy to be the thought which, as the universal content, is complete being, it will be shown in the history of philosophy how the determinations in this content make their appearance little by little. At first we only ask where philosophy and its history begin.

Freedom of Thought as a First Condition

The general answer is in accordance with what has been said. Philosophy begins where the universal is comprehended as the all-embracing existence, or where the existent is laid hold of in a universal form, and where thinking about thought first commences. Where, then, has this occurred? Where did it begin? That is a question of history. Thought must be for itself, must come into existence in its freedom, liberate itself from nature, and come out of its immersion in mere sense perception. It must, as free, enter within itself and thus arrive at the consciousness of freedom. Philosophy is properly to be commenced where the absolute is no more in the form of ordinary conception, and free thought not merely thinks the absolute but grasps its Idea; that is to say, where thought grasps as thought the being (which may be thought itself), which it recognises as the essence of things, the absolute totality and the immanent essence of everything. This may be said, even though that essence were an external being, it is still comprehended as thought. The simple essence which is not sensuous and which the Jews thought of as God (for all religion is thinking), is thus not a subject to be treated of by philosophy, but just such a proposition as that "The essence or principle of things is water, fire, or thought."

Thought, this universal determination which sets forth itself, is an abstract determinateness. It is the beginning of philosophy, but this beginning is at the same time in history, the concrete form taken by a people, the principle of which constitutes what we have stated above. If we say that the consciousness of freedom is connected with the appearance of philosophy, this principle must be a fundamental one with those with whom philosophy begins; a people having this consciousness of freedom founds its existence on that principle, seeing that the laws and the whole circumstances of the people are based only on the notion that mind forms of itself and in the categories which it has. Connected with this on the practical side is the fact that actual freedom develops political freedom, and this only begins where the individual knows himself as an independent individual to be universal and real, where his significance is infinite, or where the subject has attained the consciousness of personality and thus desires to be esteemed for himself alone. Free, philosophic thought has this direct connection with practical freedom: that as the former supplies thought about the absolute, universal, and real object, the latter, because it thinks itself, gives itself the character of universality. Thinking means the bringing of something into the form of universality; hence thought first treats of the universal, or determines what is objective and individual in the natural things which are present in sensuous consciousness, as the universal, as an objective thought. Its second attribute is that in recognising and knowing this objective and infinite universal, I, at the same time, remain confronting it from the standpoint of objectivity.

On account of this general connection between political freedom and the freedom of thought, philosophy only appears in history where and in as far as free institutions are formed. Since mind requires to separate itself from its natural will and engrossment in matter if it wishes to enter upon philosophy, it cannot do so in the form with which the world spirit commences and which precedes that separation. This stage of the unity of mind with nature, which as immediate is not the true and perfected state, is mainly found in the Oriental conception of existence, therefore philosophy first begins in the Grecian world.

Separation of the East and Its Philosophy

Some explanations have to be given regarding this first form. Since mind in it, as consciousness and will, is but desire, self-consciousness still stands upon its first stage in which the sphere of its idea and will is finite. As intelligence is thus finite too, its ends are not yet a universal for themselves. But if a people makes for what is moral, if laws and justice are possessed, the character of universality underlies its will. This presupposes a new power in mind with which it commences to be free, for the universal will as the relation of thought to thought or as the universal, contains a thought which is at home with itself. If a people desire to be free, they will subordinate their desires to universal laws, while formerly that which was desired was only a particular. Now finitude of the will characterizes the Orientals, because with them the will has not yet grasped itself as universal, for thought is not yet free for itself. Hence there can but be the relation of lord and slave, and in this despotic sphere fear constitutes the ruling category. Because the will is not yet free from what is finite, it can therein be comprehended and the finite can be shown forth as negative. This feeling of negation, that something cannot last, is just fear as distinguished from freedom which does not consist in being finite but in being for itself, and this cannot be laid hold of.

Religion necessarily has this character, since the fear of the Lord is the essential element beyond which we cannot get "The fear of the Lord is the beginning of wisdom" is indeed correct; man must begin with this in order to know the finite ends in their negative character. But man must also have overcome fear through the relinquishment of finite ends, and the satisfaction which that religion affords is confined to what is finite, seeing that the chief means of reconciliation are natural forms which are impersonated and held in reverence.

The Oriental consciousness raises itself, indeed, above the natural content to what is infinite; but it only knows itself as accidental in reference to the power which makes the individual fear. This subordination may take two forms and must indeed from one extreme pass to the other. The finite, which is for consciousness, may have the form of finitude as finite, or it may become the infinite, which is, however, an abstraction. The man who lives in fear and he who rules over men through fear both stand upon the same platform; the difference between them is only in the greater power of will which can go forth to sacrifice all that is finite for some particular end. The despot brings about what his caprice directs, including certainly what is good, not as law, but as arbitrary will: the passive will, like that of slavery, is converted into the active energy of will, which will, however, is arbitrary still. In religion we even find self-immersion in the deepest sensuality represented as the service of God, and then there follows in the East a flight to the emptiest abstraction as to what is infinite, as also the exaltation attained through the renunciation of everything, and this is specially so amongst the Indians, who torture themselves and enter into the most profound abstraction. The Indians look straight before them for ten years at a time, are fed by those around, and are destitute of other spiritual content than that of knowing what is abstract, which content therefore is entirely finite. This, then, is not the soil of freedom.

In the East, mind indeed begins to dawn, but it is still true of it that the subject is not presented as a person, but appears in the objectively substantial, which is represented as partly supersensuous and partly, and even more, material, as negative and perishing. The highest point attainable by the individual, the everlasting bliss, is made an immersion into substance, a vanishing away of consciousness, and thus of all distinction between substance and individuality—hence an annihilation. A spiritually dead relation thus comes into existence, since the highest point there to be reached is insensibility. So far, however, man has not attained that bliss, but finds himself to be a single existent individual, distinguished from the universal substance. He is thus outside the unity, has no significance, and as being what is accidental and without rights, is finite only; he finds himself limited through nature—in caste, for instance. The will is not here the substantial will; it is the arbitrary will given up to what is outwardly and inwardly contingent, for substance alone is the affirmative.

With it greatness, nobility, or sublimity of character are certainly not excluded, but they are only present as the naturally determined or the arbitrary will, and not in the objective forms of morality and law to which all owe respect, which hold good for all, and in which for that same reason all are recognised. The Oriental subject thus has the advantage of independence, since there is nothing fixed. However undetermined is the substance of the Easterns, as undetermined, free, and independent may their character be. What for us is justice and social morality is also in their state, but in a substantial, natural, patriarchal way, and not in subjective freedom. Conscience does not exist, nor does individual morality. Everything is simply in a state of nature, which allows the noblest to exist as it does the worst.

The conclusion to be derived from this is that no philosophic knowledge can be found here. To philosophy belongs the knowledge of substance, the absolute universal, that whether I think it and develop it or not, confronts me still as for itself objective; and whether this is to me substantial or not, still just in that I think it, it is mine, that in which I possess my distinctive character or am affirmative: thus my thoughts are not mere subjective determinations or opinions, but, as being my thoughts, are also thoughts of what is objective, or are substantial thoughts.

The Eastern form must therefore be excluded from the history of philosophy, but still, upon the whole, I will take some notice of it. I have touched on this elsewhere,[11] for some time ago we for the first time reached a position to judge of it. Earlier a great parade was made about the Indian wisdom without any real knowledge of what it was; now this is for the first time known, and naturally it is found to be in conformity with the universal character of wisdom.

Beginnings of Philosophy in Greece

Philosophy proper commences in the West. It is in the West that this freedom of self-consciousness first comes forth; natural consciousness disappears, and mind therewith descends into itself. In the brightness of the East the individual merely disappears; the light first becomes in the West the flash of thought which strikes within itself, and from thence creates its world out of itself. The blessedness of the West is thus so determined that in it the subject as such endures and continues in the substantial. The individual mind grasps its being as universal, but universality is just this relation to itself. This being at home with self, this personality and infinitude of the "I" constitutes the being of mind; it is thus and can be none else. For a people to know themselves as free, and to be only as universal, is for them to be; it is the principle of their whole life as regards morality and all else. To take an example, we only know our real being insofar as personal freedom is its first condition, and hence we never can be slaves. Were the mere arbitrary will of the prince a law, and should he wish slavery to be introduced, we would have the knowledge that this could not be. To sleep, to live, to have a certain office, is not our real being, and certainly to be no slave is such, for that has come to mean the being in nature. Thus in the West we are upon the soil of genuine philosophy.

Because in desire I am subject to another, and my being is in a particularity, I am, as I exist, unlike myself; for I am "I,"

---

11. That is to say in the lectures preceding these, delivered in the Winter session 1825-1826.

the universal complete, but hemmed in by passion. This last is self-will or formal freedom, which has desire as content. Amongst the Greeks we first find the freedom which is the end of true will, the equitable and right, in which I am free and universal, and others, too, are free, are also "I" and like me; where a relationship between free and free is thus established with its actual laws, determinations of the universal will, and justly constituted states. Hence it is here that philosophy began.

In Greece we first see real freedom flourish, but still in a restricted form and with a limitation, since slavery was still existent, and the states were conditioned by slavery. In the following abstractions we may first of all superficially describe the freedom of the East, of Greece, and of the Teutonic world. In the East only one individual is free, the despot; in Greece the few are free; in the Teutonic world the proposition is true that all are free, that is, man is free as man. But since the one in Eastern countries cannot be free because that would necessitate the others also being free for him, impulse, self-will and formal freedom can be found there alone. Since in Greece the particular proposition "the few are free" prevails, the Athenians and Spartans are free but not the Messenians or Helots. We shall have to see what the principle of this "few" may be, for this implies some modifications of the Greek point of view, which we want to consider in the history of philosophy. To take these distinctions into account means simply that we should proceed to divide up and classify the subject matter in the history of philosophy.

DIVISION, SOURCES AND METHOD ADOPTED IN TREATING OF THE HISTORY OF PHILOSOPHY

Division of the History of Philosophy

Since we set to work systematically this division or classification must present itself as necessary. Speaking generally, we have properly only two epochs to distinguish in the history of philosophy, as in ancient and modern art—these are the Greek and the Teutonic. The Teutonic philosophy is the philosophy within Christendom in so far as it belongs to the Teutonic nations; the Christian-European people, inasmuch as they belong to the world of science, possess collectively Teutonic culture; for Italy, Spain, France, England, and the rest have through the Teutonic nations received a new form. The influence of Greece also reaches into the Roman world, and hence we have to speak of philosophy in the territory of the Roman world; but the Romans produced no proper philosophy any more than any proper poets. They have only received from and imitated others, although they have often done this ingeniously. Even their religion is derived from the Greek, and the special character that it has makes no approach to philosophy and art, but is unphilosophical and unartistic.

A further description of these two outstanding opposites must be given. The Greek world developed thought as far as to the Idea; the Christian Teutonic world, on the contrary, has comprehended thought as spirit; Idea and spirit are thus the distinguishing features. More particularly the facts are as follows. Since the universal (God), still undetermined and immediate, as being or objective thought, zealously allowing nothing to exist beside itself, is the substantial basis of all philosophy, it never alters but rather descends ever deeper into itself and by this development of determinations manifests and brings itself to consciousness. We may thus designate the particular character of the development in the first period of philosophy by saying that this development is a simple process of determinations, figurations, abstract qualities, issuing from the one principle that potentially already contains the whole.

The second stage in this universal principle is the gathering up of the determinations manifested thus, into ideal, concrete unity, in the mode of subjectivity. The first determinations as immediate, were still abstractions, but now the absolute, as the endlessly self-determining universal, must furthermore be comprehended as active thought, and not as the universal in this determinate character. Hence it is manifested as the totality of determinations and as concrete individuality. Thus, with the νοῦς of Anaxagoras, and still more with Socrates, there commences a subjective totality in which thought grasps itself and thinking activity is the fundamental principle.

The third stage, then, is that this totality, which is at first abstract, in that it becomes realized through the active, determining, distinguishing thought, sets itself forth even in the separated determinations, which, as ideal, belong to it. Since these determinations are contained unseparated in the unity, and thus each in it is also the other, these opposed moments are raised into totalities. The quite general forms of opposition are the universal and the particular, or, in another form, thought as such and external reality, feeling, or perception. The notion is the identity of universal and particular. Each of these is thus set forth as concrete in itself, the universal is in itself at once the unity of universality and particularity, and the same holds good of particularity. Unity is thus posited in both forms. The whole concrete universal is now mind; and the whole concrete particular, nature. The abstract moments can be made complete through this unity alone. Thus it has come to pass that the differences themselves are each raised up to a system of totality, which confront one another as the philosophy of Stoicism and of Epicureanism.

In Stoicism pure thought develops into a totality; if we make the other side from mind—natural being or feeling—into a totality, Epicureanism is the result. Each determination is formed into a totality of thought, and, in accordance with the simple mode which characterizes this sphere, these principles seem to be for themselves and independent, like two antagonistic systems of philosophy. Implicitly both are identical, but they themselves take up their position as conflicting, and the Idea is also, as it is apprehended, in a one-sided determinateness.

The higher stage is the union of these differences. This may occur in annihilation, in scepticism; but the higher point of view is the affirmative, the Idea in relation to the notion. If the notion is, then, the universal—that which determines itself further within itself, but yet remains there in its unity and in the ideality and transparency of its determinations which do not become independent—the further step is, on the other hand, the reality of the notion in which the differences are themselves brought to totalities. Thus the fourth stage is the union of the Idea, in which all these differences, as totalities, are yet at the same time blended into one concrete unity of notion. This comprehension at first takes place without constraint, since the ideal is itself only apprehended in the element of universality.

The Greek world got as far as this Idea, since they formed an ideal intellectual world; and this was done by the Alexandrian philosophy, in which the Greek philosophy perfected itself and reached its end. If we wish to represent this process figuratively, A. Thought, is (a) speaking generally abstract, as in universal or absolute space, by which empty space is often understood; (b) then the most simple space determinations appear, in which we commence with the point in order that we may arrive at the line and angle; (c) what comes third is their union into the triangle, that which is indeed concrete, but which is still retained in this abstract element of surface, and thus is only the first and still formal totality and limitation which corresponds to the νοῦς. B. The next point is that since we allow each of the enclosing lines of the triangle to be again surface, each forms itself into the totality of the triangle and into the whole figure to which it belongs; that is the realisation of the whole in the sides as we see it in Scepticism or Stoicism. C. The last stage of all is, that these surfaces or sides of the triangle join themselves into a body or a totality: the body is for the first time the perfect spacial determination, and that is a reduplication of the triangle. But in as far as the triangle which forms the basis is outside of the body, this simile does not hold good.

Grecian Philosophy in the Neo-Platonists finds its end in a perfect kingdom of thought and of bliss, and in a potentially existent world of the ideal, which is yet unreal because the whole only exists in the element of universality. This world still lacks individuality as such, which is an essential moment in the notion. Actuality demands that in the identity of both sides of the Idea, the independent totality shall be also posited as negative. Through this self-existent negation, which is absolute subjectivity, the Idea is first raised into mind. Mind is the subjectivity of self-knowledge; but it is only mind inasmuch as it knows what is object to itself, and that is itself, as a totality, and is for itself a totality. That is to say, the two triangles which are above and below in the prism must not be two in the sense of being doubled, but they must be one intermingled unity. Or, in the case of body, the difference arises between the centre and the peripheral parts. This opposition of real corporeality and centre as the simple existence, now makes its appearance, and the totality is the union of the centre and the substantial—not, however, the simple union, but a union such that the subjective knows itself as subjective in relation to the objective and substantial. Hence the Idea is this totality, and the Idea which knows itself is essentially different from the subjective; the latter manifests itself independently, but in such a manner that as such it is considered to be for itself substantial. The subjective Idea is at first only formal, but it is the real possibility of the substantial and of the potentially universal; its end is to realise itself and to identify itself with substance. Through this subjectivity and negative unity, and through this absolute negativity, the ideal becomes no longer our object merely, but object to itself. This principle has taken effect in the world of Christianity. Thus in the modern point of view the subject is for itself free, man is free as man, and from this comes the idea that because he is mind he has from his very nature the eternal quality of being substantial. God becomes known as mind which appears to itself as double, yet removes the difference that it may in it be for and at home with itself. The business of the world, taking it as a whole, is to become reconciled with mind, recognising itself therein, and this business is assigned to the Teutonic world.

The first beginning of this undertaking is found in religion which is the contemplation of and faith in this principle as in an actual existence before a knowledge of the principle has been arrived at. In the Christian religion this principle is found more as feeling and idea; in it man as man is destined to everlasting bliss and is an object of divine grace, compassion and interest, which is as much as saying that man has an absolute and infinite value. We find it further in that dogma revealed through Christ to men, of the unity of the divine and human nature, according to which the subjective and the objective Idea—man and God—are one. This, in another form, is found in the old story of the Fall, in which the serpent did not delude man, for God said, "Behold, Adam has become as one of us, to know good and evil." We have to deal with this unity of subjective principle and of substance; it constitutes the process of mind that this individual one or independent existence of subject should put aside its immediate character and bring itself forth as identical with the substantial. Such an aim is pronounced to be the highest end attainable by man. We see from this that religious ideas and speculation are not so far asunder as was at first believed. I cite these ideas in order that we may not be ashamed of them, seeing that we still belong to them, and so that if we do get beyond them, we may not be ashamed of our progenitors of the early Christian times, who held these ideas in such high esteem.

The first principle of that philosophy which has taken its place in Christendom is thus found in the existence of two totalities. This is a reduplication of substance which now, however, is characterized by the fact that the two totalities are no longer external to one another, but are clearly both required through their relation to one another. If formerly

Stoicism and Epicureanism, whose negativity was Scepticism, came forth as independent, and if finally the implicitly existent universality of both was established, these moments are now known as separate totalities, and yet in their opposition they have to be thought of as one. We have here the true speculative Idea, the notion in its determinations, each of which is brought into a totality and clearly relates to the other. We thus have really two Ideas, the subjective Idea as knowledge, and then the substantial and concrete Idea; and the development and perfection of this principle and its coming to the consciousness of thought, is the subject treated by modern philosophy. Thus the determinations in it are more concrete than with the ancients. This opposition in which the two sides culminate, grasped in its widest significance, is the opposition between thought and being, individuality and substance, so that in the subject himself his freedom stands once more within the bounds of necessity; it is the opposition between subject and object, and between nature and mind, in so far as this last as finite stands in opposition to nature.

The Greek philosophy is free from restraint because it does not yet have regard to the opposition between being and thought, but proceeds from the unconscious presupposition that thought is also being. Certainly certain stages in the Greek philosophy are encountered which seem to stand on the same level as the Christian philosophies. Thus when we see, for instance, in the philosophy of the Sophists, the new Academics, and the Sceptics, that they maintain the doctrine that the truth is not capable of being known, they might appear to accord with the later subjective philosophies in asserting that all thought determinations were only subjective in character, and that hence from these no conclusions could be arrived at as regards what is objective. But there is really a difference. In the case of ancient philosophies, which said that we know only the phenomenal, everything is confined to that. It is as regards practical life that the new Academy and the Sceptics also admitted the possibility of conducting oneself rightly, morally and rationally, when one adopts the phenomenal as one's rule and guide in life. But though it is the phenomenal that lies at the foundation of things, it is not asserted that there is likewise a knowledge of the true and existent, as in the case of the merely subjective idealists of a more modern day. These last still keep in the background a potentiality, a beyond which cannot be known through thought or through conception. This other knowledge is an immediate knowledge—a faith in, a view of, and a yearning after the beyond such as was evinced by Jacobi. The ancients have no such yearning: on the contrary, they have perfect satisfaction and rest in the certitude that only that which appears is for knowledge. Thus it is necessary in this respect to keep strictly to the point of view from which we start, else through the similarity of the results, we come to see in that old philosophy all the determinate character of modern subjectivity. Since in the simplicity of ancient philosophy the phenomenal was itself the only sphere, doubts as to objective thought were not present to it.

The opposition defined, the two sides of which are in modern times really related to one another as totalities, also has the form of an opposition between reason and faith, between individual perception and the objective truth which must be taken without reason of one's own, and even with a complete disregard for such reason. This is faith as understood by the church, or faith in the modern sense, i.e. a rejection of reason in favour of an inward revelation, called a direct certainty or perception, or an implicit and intuitive feeling. The opposition between this knowledge, which has first of all to develop itself, and that knowledge which has already developed itself inwardly, arouses a peculiar interest. In both cases the unity of thought or subjectivity and of truth or objectivity is manifested. Only in the first form it is said that the natural man knows the truth since he intuitively believes it, while in the second form the unity of knowledge and truth is shown, but in such a way that the subject raises itself above the immediate form of sensuous consciousness and reaches the truth first of all through thought.

The final end is to think the absolute as mind, as the universal, that which, when the infinite bounty of the notion in its reality freely emits its determinations from itself, wholly impresses itself upon and imparts itself to them, so that they may be indifferently outside of or in conflict with one another, but so that these totalities are one only, not alone implicitly (which would simply be our reflection) but explicitly identical, the determinations of their difference being thus explicitly merely ideal. Hence if the starting point of the history of philosophy can be expressed by saying that God is comprehended as the immediate and not yet developed universality, and that its end—the grasping of the absolute as mind through the two and a half thousand years' work of the thus far inert world spirit—is the end of our time, it makes it easy for us from one determination to go on through the manifestation of its needs, to others. Yet in the course of history this was difficult.

We thus have altogether two philosophies—the Greek and the Teutonic. As regards the latter we must distinguish the time when philosophy made its formal appearance as philosophy and the period of formation and of preparation for modern times. We may first begin Teutonic philosophy where it appears in proper form as philosophy. Between the first period and those more recent, comes, as an intermediate period, that fermentation of a new philosophy which on the one side keeps within the substantial and real existence and does not arrive at form, while on the other side, it perfects thought, as the bare form of a presupposed truth, until it again knows itself as the free ground and source of truth. Hence the history of philosophy falls into three periods— that of the Greek philosophy, the philosophy of the Middle Ages, and the modern philosophy. Of these the first is, speaking generally, regulated by thought, the second falls into the opposition between essence and formal reflection, but the third has the notion as its ground. This must not be taken to mean that the first contains thought alone; it also has notions and Ideas, just as the latter begins from abstract thoughts which yet constitute a dualism.

First Period.—This commences at the time of Thales, about 600 B.C., and goes on to the coming to maturity of the Neo-Platonic philosophy with Plotinus in the third century; from thence to its further progress and development with Proclus in the fifth century until the time when all philosophy was extinguished. The Neo-Platonic philosophy then made its entrance into Christianity later on, and many philosophies within Christianity have this philosophy as their only basis. This is a space of time extending to about 1000 years, the end of which coincides with the migration of the nations and the decline of the Roman Empire.

Second Period. The second period is that of the Middle Ages. The Scholastics are included in it, and Arabians and Jews are also historically to be noticed, but this philosophy mainly falls within the Christian Church. This period is of something over 1000 years' duration.

Third Period. The philosophy of modern times made its first independent appearance after the Thirty Years' War, with Bacon, Jacob Böhme, and Descartes; it begins with the distinction contained in *cogito ergo sum.* This period is one of a couple of centuries and the philosophy is consequently still somewhat modern.

Sources of the History of Philosophy

We have to seek for sources of another kind in this than in political history. There historians are the fountainheads, which again have as sources the deeds and sayings of individuals; and the historians who are not original have, to be sure, performed their work at secondhand. But historians always have the deeds already present in history—that is to say, here brought into the form of ordinary conception. For the word history has two meanings: it signifies on the one hand the deeds and events themselves, and on the other, it denotes them in so far as they are formed through conception for conception. In the history of philosophy there are, on the contrary, not any sources which can be derived from historians, but the deeds themselves lie before us, and these—the philosophic works themselves—are the true sources. If we wish to study the history of philosophy in earnest, we must go to such springs as these. Yet these works form too wide a field to permit of our keeping to them alone in this history. In the case of many philosophers it is absolutely necessary to confine oneself to the original authors, but in many periods, in which we cannot obtain original sources, seeing that they have not been preserved to us (as, for instance, in that of the older Greek philosophy), we must certainly confine our attention simply to historians and other writers. There are other periods, too, where it is desirable that others should have read the works of the philosophers and that we should receive extracts therefrom. Several schoolmen have left behind them works of sixteen, twenty-four and twenty-six folios, and hence we must in their case confine ourselves to the researches of others. Many philosophic works are also rare and hence difficult to obtain. Many philosophers are for the most part important from an historic or literary point of view only, and hence we may limit ourselves to the compilations in which they are dealt with. The most noteworthy works on the history of philosophy are, however, the following, regarding which I refer for particulars to the summary of Tennemann's *History of Philosophy,* by A. Wendt, since I do not wish to give any complete list.

1. One of the first histories of philosophy, which is only interesting as an attempt, is the *History of Philosophy,* by Thomas Stanley (London, 1655, folio ed. III., 1701, 4). This history is no longer much used and only contains the old philosophic schools in the form of sects and as if no new ones had existed. That is to say, it keeps to the belief commonly held at that time that there only were ancient philosophies and that the period of philosophy came to an end with Christianity, as if philosophy were something belonging to heathendom and the truth only could be found in Christianity. In it a distinction was drawn between truth as it is created from

natural reason in the ancient philosophies and the revealed truth of the Christian religion, in which there was consequently no longer any philosophy. In the time of the revival of learning there certainly were no proper philosophies, and above all in Stanley's time systems of philosophy proper were too young for the older generations to have the amount of respect for them necessary to allow of their being esteemed as realities.

2. *Jo. Jac. Bruckeri Historia critica philosophiae Lipsiae,* 1742-1744, four parts, or five volumes in four, for the fourth part has two volumes. The second edition, unaltered, but with the addition of a supplement, 1766-1767, four parts in six quartos, the last of which forms the supplement. This is an immense compilation which is not drawn from the original sources, but is mixed with reflections after the manner of the times. As we have seen from an example above, the accounts given are in the highest degree inaccurate. Brucker's manner of procedure is entirely unhistorical, and yet nowhere ought we to proceed in a more historical manner than in the history of philosophy. This work is thus simply so much useless ballast. An epitome of the same is *Jo. Jac. Bruckeri Institutiones historiae philosophicae, usui academicae juventutis adornatae. Lipsiae,* 1747, 8; second edition, Leipzig, 1756; third edition prepared by Born, Leipzig, 1790,8.

3. Dietrich Tiedmann's *Geist der Speculativen Philosophie,* Marburg, 1791-1797,6 vols., 8. He treats of political history diffusely, but without any life, and the language is stiff and affected. The whole work is a melancholy example of how a learned professor can occupy his whole life with the study of speculative philosophy and yet have no idea at all of speculation. His *argumenta* to the Plato of Zweibrucker are of the same description. In every history he makes abstracts from the philosophers so long as they keep to mere ratiocination, but when the speculative is arrived at, he becomes irate, declaring it all to be composed of empty subtleties, and stops short with the words "we know better." His merit is that he

has supplied valuable extracts from rare books belonging to the Middle Ages and from cabalistic and mystical works of that time.

4. Joh. Gottlief Buhle: *Lehrbuch der Geschichte der Philosophie und einer kritischen Literatur derselben.* Göttingen 1796-1804, eight parts, 8. Ancient philosophy is treated with disproportionate brevity; the further Buhle went on, the more detailed he became. He has many good extracts of rare works, as for instance those of Giordano Bruno, which are in the Göttingen Library.

5. Wilh. Gottl. Tennemann's *Geschichte der Philosophie,* Leipzig, 1798-1819, eleven parts, 8. The eighth part, the scholastic philosophy, occupies two volumes. The philosophies are fully described, and the more modern times are better done than the ancient. The philosophies of recent times are easier to describe, since it is only necessary to make an abstract or to translate directly, for the thoughts contained in them lie nearer to ours. It is otherwise with the ancient philosophers, because they stand in another stage of the notion, and on this account they are likewise more difficult to grasp. That is to say, what is old is easily replaced by something else more familiar to us, and where Tennemann comes across such, he is almost useless. In Aristotle, for instance, the misinterpretation is so great that Tennemann foists upon him what is directly opposite to his beliefs, and thus from the adoption of the opposite to what Tennemann asserts to be Aristotle's opinion, a better idea of Aristotelian philosophy is arrived at. Tennemann is then candid enough to place the reference to Aristotle underneath the text, so that the original and the interpretation often contradict one another. Tennemann thinks that it is really the case that the historian should have no philosophy, and he glories in that. Yet he really has a system and he is a Critical philosopher. He praises philosophers, their work, and their genius, and yet the end of the lay is that all of them will be pronounced to be wanting in that they have one defect, which is not to be Kantian philosophers and not yet to have

sought the source of knowledge. From this the result is that the truth could not be known.

Of compendiums, three have to be noticed. 1. Friedrich Ast's *Grundriss einer Geschichte der Philosophie.* (Landshut 1807,8; second edition, 1825) is written from a better point of view; the philosophy is that of Schelling for the most part, but it is somewhat confused. Ast by some formal method has distinguished ideal philosophy from real. 2. Professor Wendt's Göttingen summary of Tennemann (fifth edition, Leipzig, 1828,8). It is astonishing to see what is represented as being philosophy, without any consideration as to whether it has any meaning or not. Such so-called new philosophies grow like mushrooms out of the ground. There is nothing easier than to comprehend in harmony with a principle; but it must not be thought that hence something new and profound has been accomplished. 3. Rixner's *Handbuch der Geschichte der Philosophie,* 3 vols., Sulzbach, 1822-1823, 8 (second amended edition, 1829) is most to be commended, and yet I will not assert that it answers all the requirements of a history of philosophy. There are many points which leave much to desire, but the appendices to each volume in which the principal original authorities are quoted, are particularly excellent for their purpose. Selected extracts, more specially from the ancient philosophers, are needed, and these would not be lengthy, since there are not very many passages to be given from the philosophers before Plato.

Method of Treatment Adopted in This History of Philosophy

As regards external history I shall only touch upon that which is the concern of universal history, the spirit or the principle of the times, and likewise I will refer to conditions of life in reference to the outstanding philosophers. Of philosophies, however, only those are to be mentioned the principles of which have caused some stir, and through which science has made an advance. Hence I shall put aside many names which would be taken up in a learned treatise, but which are of little value in respect to philosophy. The history of the dissemination of a doctrine, its fate, those who have merely taught a particular doctrine, I pass over, such as the deduction of the whole world from one particular principle.

The demand that in philosophy an historian should have no system, should put into the philosophy nothing of his own, nor assail it with his ideas, seems a plausible one. The history of philosophy should show just this impartiality, and it seems advisable to give only summaries of the philosophers. He who understands nothing of the matter, and has no system, but merely historic knowledge, will certainly be impartial. But political history has to be carefully distinguished from the history of philosophy. That is to say, though in the former, one is not indeed at liberty to limit oneself to representing the events chronologically only, one can yet keep to what is entirely objective, as is done in the Homeric epic. Thus Herodotus and Thucydides, as free men, let the objective world do freely and independently as it would; they have added nothing of their own, neither have they taken and judged before their tribunal the actions which they represented.

Yet even in political history there is also a particular end kept in view. In Livy the main points are the Roman rule, its enlargement, and the perfecting of the constitution; we see Rome arise, defend itself, and exercise its mastery. It is thus that the self-developing reason in the history of philosophy makes of itself an end, and this end is not foreign or imported, but is the matter itself, which lies at the basis as universal, and with which the individual forms of themselves correspond. Thus when the history of philosophy has to tell of deeds in history, we first ask what a deed in philosophy is and whether any particular thing is philosophic or not. In external history everything is in action—certainly there is in it what is important and that which is unimportant—but action is the idea immediately placed before us. This is not the case in philosophy, and on this account the history of philosophy cannot be treated at all without the introduction of the historian's judgments.

Index

75 76 77 78 79 80   12 11 10 9 8 7 6 5

harper ☀ torchbooks

American Studies: General

HENRY STEELE COMMAGER, Ed.: The Struggle for Racial Equality TB/1300
CARL N. DEGLER: Out of Our Past: *The Forces that Shaped Modern America* CN/2
CARL N. DEGLER, Ed.: Pivotal Interpretations of American History
Vol. I TB/1240; Vol. II TB/1241
A. S. EISENSTADT, Ed.: The Craft of American History: *Selected Essays*
Vol. I TB/1255; Vol. II TB/1256
ROBERT L. HEILBRONER: The Limits of American Capitalism TB/1305
JOHN HIGHAM, Ed.: The Reconstruction of American History TB/1068
ROBERT H. JACKSON: The Supreme Court in the American System of Government TB/1106
JOHN F. KENNEDY: A Nation of Immigrants. *Illus. Revised and Enlarged. Introduction by Robert F. Kennedy* TB/1118
RICHARD B. MORRIS: Fair Trial: *Fourteen Who Stood Accused, from Anne Hutchinson to Alger Hiss* TB/1335
GUNNAR MYRDAL: An American Dilemma: *The Negro Problem and Modern Democracy. Introduction by the Author.*
Vol. I TB/1443; Vol. II TB/1444
GILBERT OSOFSKY, Ed.: The Burden of Race: *A Documentary History of Negro-White Relations in America* TB/1405
ARNOLD ROSE: The Negro in America: *The Condensed Version of Gunnar Myrdal's An American Dilemma. Second Edition* TB/3048
JOHN E. SMITH: Themes in American Philosophy: *Purpose, Experience and Community* TB/1466
WILLIAM R. TAYLOR: Cavalier and Yankee: *The Old South and American National Character* TB/1474

American Studies: Colonial

BERNARD BAILYN: The New England Merchants in the Seventeenth Century TB/1149
ROBERT E. BROWN: Middle-Class Democracy and Revolution in Massachusetts, 1691–1780. *New Introduction by Author* TB/1413
JOSEPH CHARLES: The Origins of the American Party System TB/1049
WESLEY FRANK CRAVEN: The Colonies in Transition: 1660-1712† TB/3084

CHARLES GIBSON: Spain in America † TB/3077
CHARLES GIBSON, Ed.: The Spanish Tradition in America + HR/1351
LAWRENCE HENRY GIPSON: The Coming of the Revolution: 1763-1775. † *Illus.* TB/3007
PERRY MILLER: Errand Into the Wilderness TB/1139
PERRY MILLER & T. H. JOHNSON, Eds.: The Puritans: *A Sourcebook of Their Writings*
Vol. I TB/1093; Vol. II TB/1094
EDMUND S. MORGAN: The Puritan Family: *Religion and Domestic Relations in Seventeenth Century New England* TB/1227
WALLACE NOTESTEIN: The English People on the Eve of Colonization: 1603-1630. † *Illus.* TB/3006
LOUIS B. WRIGHT: The Cultural Life of the American Colonies: 1607-1763. † *Illus.* TB/3005

American Studies: The Revolution to 1860

JOHN R. ALDEN: The American Revolution: 1775-1783. † *Illus.* TB/3011
RAY A. BILLINGTON: The Far Western Frontier: 1830-1860. † *Illus.* TB/3012
GEORGE DANGERFIELD: The Awakening of American Nationalism, 1815-1828. † *Illus.* TB/3061
CLEMENT EATON: The Growth of Southern Civilization, 1790-1860. † *Illus.* TB/3040
LOUIS FILLER: The Crusade against Slavery: 1830-1860. † *Illus.* TB/3029
WILLIM W. FREEHLING: Prelude to Civil War: *The Nullification Controversy in South Carolina, 1816-1836* TB/1359
THOMAS JEFFERSON: Notes on the State of Virginia. ‡ *Edited by Thomas P. Abernethy* TB/3052
JOHN C. MILLER: The Federalist Era: 1789-1801. † *Illus.* TB/3027
RICHARD B. MORRIS: The American Revolution Reconsidered TB/1363
GILBERT OSOFSKY, Ed.: Puttin' On Ole Massa: *The Slave Narratives of Henry Bibb, William Wells Brown, and Solomon Northup* ‡ TB/1432
FRANCIS S. PHILBRICK: The Rise of the West, 1754-1830. † *Illus.* TB/3067
MARSHALL SMELSER: The Democratic Republic, 1801-1815 † TB/1406

† The New American Nation Series, edited by Henry Steele Commager and Richard B. Morris.
‡ American Perspectives series, edited by Bernard Wishy and William E. Leuchtenburg.
å History of Europe series, edited by J. H. Plumb.
§ The Library of Religion and Culture, edited by Benjamin Nelson.
‖ Researches in the Social, Cultural, and Behavioral Sciences, edited by Benjamin Nelson.
≍ Harper Modern Science Series, edited by James A. Newman.
° Not for sale in Canada.
+ Documentary History of the United States series, edited by Richard B. Morris.
# Documentary History of Western Civilization series, edited by Eugene C. Black and Leonard W. Levy.
ʌ The Economic History of the United States series, edited by Henry David et al.
¶ European Perspectives series, edited by Eugene C. Black.
** Contemporary Essays series, edited by Leonard W. Levy.
* The Stratum Series, edited by John Hale.

LOUIS B. WRIGHT: Culture on the Moving Frontier TB/1053

American Studies: The Civil War to 1900

T. C. COCHRAN & WILLIAM MILLER: The Age of Enterprise: *A Social History of Industrial America* TB/1054
W. A. DUNNING: Reconstruction, Political and Economic: 1865-1877 TB/1073
HAROLD U. FAULKNER: Politics, Reform and Expansion: 1890-1900. † *Illus.* TB/3020
GEORGE M. FREDRICKSON: The Inner Civil War: *Northern Intellectuals and the Crisis of the Union* TB/1358
JOHN A. GARRATY: The New Commonwealth, 1877-1890 † TB/1410
HELEN HUNT JACKSON: A Century of Dishonor: *The Early Crusade for Indian Reform.* † *Edited by Andrew F. Rolle* TB/3063
WILLIAM G. MCLOUGHLIN, Ed.: The American Evangelicals, 1800-1900: An Anthology ‡ TB/1382
JAMES S. PIKE: The Prostrate State: *South Carolina under Negro Government.* ‡ *Intro. by Robert F. Durden* TB/3085
VERNON LANE WHARTON: The Negro in Mississippi, 1865-1890 TB/1178

American Studies: The Twentieth Century

RAY STANNARD BAKER: Following the Color Line: *American Negro Citizenship in Progressive Era.* ‡ *Edited by Dewey W. Grantham, Jr. Illus.* TB/3053
RANDOLPH S. BOURNE: War and the Intellectuals: *Collected Essays, 1915-1919.* ‡ *Edited by Carl Resek* TB/3043
A. RUSSELL BUCHANAN: The United States and World War I. † *Illus.*
Vol. I TB/3044; Vol. II TB/3045
THOMAS C. COCHRAN: The American Business System: *A Historical Perspective, 1900-1955* TB/1080
FOSTER RHEA DULLES: America's Rise to World Power: 1898-1954. † *Illus.* TB/3021
HAROLD U. FAULKNER: The Decline of Laissez Faire, 1897-1917 TB/1397
JOHN D. HICKS: Republican Ascendancy: 1921-1933. † *Illus.* TB/3041
WILLIAM E. LEUCHTENBURG: Franklin D. Roosevelt and the New Deal: 1932-1940. † *Illus.* TB/3025
WILLIAM E. LEUCHTENBURG, Ed.: The New Deal: *A Documentary History* + HR/1354
ARTHUR S. LINK: Woodrow Wilson and the Progressive Era: 1910-1917. † *Illus.* TB/3023
BROADUS MITCHELL: Depression Decade: *From New Era through New Deal, 1929-1941* ∆ TB/1439
GEORGE E. MOWRY: The Era of Theodore Roosevelt and the Birth of Modern America: 1900-1912. † *Illus.* TB/3022
WILLIAM PRESTON, JR.: Aliens and Dissenters: TWELVE SOUTHERNERS: I'll Take My Stand: *The South and the Agrarian Tradition. Intro. by Louis D. Rubin, Jr.; Biographical Essays by Virginia Rock* TB/1072

Art, Art History, Aesthetics

ERWIN PANOFSKY: Renaissance and Renascences in Western Art. *Illus.* TB/1447
ERWIN PANOFSKY: Studies in Iconology: *Humanistic Themes in the Art of the Renaissance. 180 illus.* TB/1077
HEINRICH ZIMMER: Myths and Symbols in Indian Art and Civilization. *70 illus.* TB/2005

Asian Studies

WOLFGANG FRANKE: China and the West: *The Cultural Encounter, 13th to 20th Centuries. Trans. by R. A. Wilson* TB/1326
L. CARRINGTON GOODRICH: A Short History of the Chinese People. *Illus.* TB/3015

Economics & Economic History

C. E. BLACK: The Dynamics of Modernization: *A Study in Comparative History* TB/1321
GILBERT BURCK & EDITORS OF Fortune: The Computer Age: *And its Potential for Management* TB/1179
ROBERT L. HEILBRONER: The Future as History: *The Historic Currents of Our Time and the Direction in Which They Are Taking America* TB/1386
ROBERT L. HEILBRONER: The Great Ascent: *The Struggle for Economic Development in Our Time* TB/3030
FRANK H. KNIGHT: The Economic Organization TB/1214
DAVID S. LANDES: Bankers and Pashas: *International Finance and Economic Imperialism in Egypt. New Preface by the Author* TB/1412
ROBERT LATOUCHE: The Birth of Western Economy: *Economic Aspects of the Dark Ages* TB/1290
W. ARTHUR LEWIS: The Principles of Economic Planning. *New Introduction by the Author*° TB/1436
WILLIAM MILLER, Ed.: Men in Business: *Essays on the Historical Role of the Entrepreneur* TB/1081
HERBERT A. SIMON: The Shape of Automation: *For Men and Management* TB/1245

Historiography and History of Ideas

J. BRONOWSKI & BRUCE MAZLISH: The Western Intellectual Tradition: *From Leonardo to Hegel* TB/3001
WILHELM DILTHEY: Pattern and Meaning in History: *Thoughts on History and Society.*° *Edited with an Intro. by H. P. Rickman* TB/1075
J. H. HEXTER: More's Utopia: *The Biography of an Idea. Epilogue by the Author* TB/1195
H. STUART HUGHES: History as Art and as Science: *Twin Vistas on the Past* TB/1207
ARTHUR O. LOVEJOY: The Great Chain of Being: *A Study of the History of an Idea* TB/1009
RICHARD H. POPKIN: The History of Scepticism from Erasmus to Descartes. *Revised Edition* TB/1391
BRUNO SNELL: The Discovery of the Mind: *The Greek Origins of European Thought* TB/1018

History: General

HANS KOHN: The Age of Nationalism: *The First Era of Global History* TB/1380
BERNARD LEWIS: The Arabs in History TB/1029
BERNARD LEWIS: The Middle East and the West ° TB/1274

History: Ancient

A. ANDREWS: The Greek Tyrants TB/1103
THEODOR H. GASTER: Thespis: *Ritual Myth and Drama in the Ancient Near East* TB/1281

A. H. M. JONES, Ed.: A History of Rome through the Fifth Century # *Vol. I: The Republic* HR/1364
Vol. II The Empire: HR/1460
· SAMUEL NOAH KRAMER: Sumerian Mythology TB/1055
NAPHTALI LEWIS & MEYER REINHOLD, Eds.: Roman Civilization *Vol. I: The Republic* TB/1231
Vol. II: The Empire TB/1232

History: Medieval

NORMAN COHN: The Pursuit of the Millennium: *Revolutionary Messianism in Medieval and Reformation Europe* TB/1037
F. L. GANSHOF: Feudalism TB/1058
F. L. GANSHOF: The Middle Ages: *A History of International Relations. Translated by Rémy Hall* TB/1411
HENRY CHARLES LEA: The Inquisition of the Middle Ages. || *Introduction by Walter Ullmann* TB/1456

History: Renaissance & Reformation

JACOB BURCKHARDT: The Civilization of the Renaissance in Italy. *Introduction by Benjamin Nelson and Charles Trinkaus. Illus.* Vol. I TB/40; Vol. II TB/41
JOHN CALVIN & JACOPO SADOLETO: A Reformation Debate. *Edited by John C. Olin* TB/1239
J. H. ELLIOTT: Europe Divided, 1559-1598 *a* ° TB/1414
G. R. ELTON: Reformation Europe, 1517-1559 ° *α* TB/1270
HANS J. HILLERBRAND, Ed., The Protestant Reformation # HR/1342
JOHAN HUIZINGA: Erasmus and the Age of Reformation. *Illus.* TB/19
JOEL HURSTFIELD: The Elizabethan Nation TB/1312
JOEL HURSTFIELD, Ed.: The Reformation Crisis TB/1267
PAUL OSKAR KRISTELLER: Renaissance Thought: *The Classic, Scholastic, and Humanist Strains* TB/1048
DAVID LITTLE: Religion, Order and Law: *A Study in Pre-Revolutionary England.* § *Preface by R. Bellah* TB/1418
PAOLO ROSSI: Philosophy, Technology, and the Arts, in the Early Modern Era 1400-1700. || *Edited by Benjamin Nelson. Translated by Salvator Attanasio* TB/1458
H. R. TREVOR-ROPER: The European Witch-craze of the Sixteenth and Seventeenth Centuries and Other Essays ° TB/1416

History: Modern European

ALAN BULLOCK: Hitler, A Study in Tyranny. ° *Revised Edition. Illus.* TB/1123
JOHANN GOTTLIEB FICHTE: Addresses to the German Nation. *Ed. with Intro. by George A. Kelly* ¶ TB/1366
ALBERT GOODWIN: The French Revolution TB/1064
STANLEY HOFFMANN et al.: In Search of France: *The Economy, Society and Political System In the Twentieth Century* TB/1219
H. STUART HUGHES: The Obstructed Path: *French Social Thought in the Years of Desperation* TB/1451
JOHAN HUIZINGA: Dutch Civilisation in the 17th Century and Other Essays TB/1453

JOHN MCMANNERS: European History, 1789-1914: *Men, Machines and Freedom* TB/1419
HUGH SETON-WATSON: Eastern Europe Between the Wars, 1918-1941 TB/1330
ALBERT SOREL: Europe Under the Old Regime. *Translated by Francis H. Herrick* TB/1121
A. J. P. TAYLOR: From Napoleon to Lenin: *Historical Essays* ° TB/1268
A. J. P. TAYLOR: The Habsburg Monarchy, 1809-1918: *A History of the Austrian Empire and Austria-Hungary* ° TB/1187
J. M. THOMPSON: European History, 1494-1789 TB/1431
H. R. TREVOR-ROPER: Historical Essays TB/1269

Literature & Literary Criticism

W. J. BATE: From Classic to Romantic: *Premises of Taste in Eighteenth Century England* TB/1036
VAN WYCK BROOKS: Van Wyck Brooks: The Early Years: *A Selection from his Works, 1908-1921 Ed. with Intro. by Claire Sprague* TB/3082
RICHMOND LATTIMORE, Translator: The Odyssey of Homer TB/1389
ROBERT PREYER, Ed.: Victorian Literature ** TB/1302

Philosophy

HENRI BERGSON: Time and Free Will: *An Essay on the Immediate Data of Consciousness* ° TB/1021
H. J. BLACKHAM: Six Existentialist Thinkers: *Kierkegaard, Nietzsche, Jaspers, Marcel, Heidegger, Sartre* ° TB/1002
J. M. BOCHENSKI: The Methods of Contemporary Thought. *Trans. by Peter Caws* TB/1377
ERNST CASSIRER: Rousseau, Kant and Goethe. *Intro. by Peter Gay* TB/1092
MICHAEL GELVEN: A Commentary on Heidegger's "Being and Time" TB/1464
J. GLENN GRAY: Hegel and Greek Thought TB/1409
W. K. C. GUTHRIE: The Greek Philosophers: *From Thales to Aristotle* ° TB/1008
G. W. F. HEGEL: Phenomenology of Mind. ° || *Introduction by George Lichtheim* TB/1303
MARTIN HEIDEGGER: Discourse on Thinking. *Translated with a Preface by John M. Anderson and E. Hans Freund. Introduction by John M. Anderson* TB/1459
F. H. HEINEMANN: Existentialism and the Modern Predicament TB/28
WERER HEISENBERG: Physics and Philosophy: *The Revolution in Modern Science. Intro. by F. S. C. Northrop* TB/549
EDMUND HUSSERL: Phenomenology and the Crisis of Philosophy. § *Translated with an Introduction by Quentin Lauer* TB/1170
IMMANUEL KANT: Groundwork of the Metaphysic of Morals. *Translated and Analyzed by H. J. Paton* TB/1159
WALTER KAUFMANN, Ed.: Religion From Tolstoy to Camus: *Basic Writings on Religious Truth and Morals* TB/123
QUENTIN LAUER: Phenomenology: *Its Genesis and Prospect. Preface by Aron Gurwitsch* TB/1169
MICHAEL POLANYI: Personal Knowledge: *Towards a Post-Critical Philosophy* TB/1158
WILLARD VAN ORMAN QUINE: Elementary Logic *Revised Edition* TB/577
WILHELM WINDELBAND: A History of Philosophy *Vol. I: Greek, Roman, Medieval* TB/38

3